A Whole New Ball Game

A Whole New Ball Game

Confronting the Myths and Realities of New Zealand Rugby

Paul Thomas

Hodder Moa Beckett

National Library of New Zealand Cataloguing-in-Publication Data

Thomas, Paul, 1951–
A whole new ball game : confronting the myths and realities of
New Zealand rugby / Paul Thomas. 1st ed.
ISBN 1-86958-966-1
1. Rugby Union football—New Zealand. I. Title.
796.3330993—dc 21

Original text © Paul Thomas 2003
The moral rights of the author have been asserted

Design and format © Hodder Moa Beckett Publishers Limited 2003

Published in 2003 by Hodder Moa Beckett Publishers Limited
[a member of the Hodder Headline Group]
4 Whetu Place, Mairangi Bay, Auckland

Text design and production by BookNZ
Cover image by Getty Images
Cover design by Nick Turzynski
Produced by Hodder Moa Beckett
Printed by Printlink, Wellington

All rights reserved. No part of this publication may be reproduced or transmitted in any form or by any means, electronic or mechanical, including photocopying, recording, or any information storage and retrieval system, without permission in writing from the publisher.

To my father for all those afternoons at the park

and to the memory of Gordon Hunter

Contents

	Acknowledgements 8
1.	A good idea at the time? 9
2.	That was then . . . and this is now 26
3.	The not-so-good old days 45
4.	End of the world, part one 62
5.	End of the world, part two 85
6.	Society is to blame 111
7.	Shaking the money tree 137
8.	If it is broke 150
9.	Worthy of their hire? 165
10.	The shock of the new 181
11.	Matters of opinion 199
12.	Survival of the fittest 214
	About the author 236

Acknowledgements

My sincere thanks to all those to whom I spoke in the course of researching this book for their time, openness and thoughtful contributions. Thanks, too, to the authors from whose works I've quoted: James Belich, *Paradise Reforged* (Penguin), Phil Gifford, *Loyal* (Hodder Moa Beckett), Bob Howitt (editor), *1973 DB Rugby Annual* (Moa), Josh Kronfeld and Brian Turner, *On The Loose* (Longacre Press), David Kirk, *Black & Blue* (Hodder Moa Beckett), Chris Laidlaw, *Mud In Your Eye* (Reed), Christopher Lane (editor), *A Century Of Wisden* (John Wisden), Michael Laws, *Gladiator* (Darius Press), Terry McLean, *Kings of Rugby* (A.H. & A.W. Reed) and *They Missed The Bus* (Reed), Austin Mitchell, *The Half Gallon, Quarter Acre Pavlova Paradise* (Whitcombe & Tombs), Andrew Mulligan, *All Blacks Tour 1963–4* (Whitcombe & Tombs), John Reason (editor), *The Lions Speak* (Rugby Books), Joseph Romanos, *The Judas Game* (Darius Press), Brian Turner, *Meads* (Hodder Moa Beckett), Jeff Wilson and Ron Palenski, *Seasons Of Gold* (Hodder Moa Beckett), Spiro Zavos, *Winters Of Revenge* (Viking) and *After The Final Whistle* (Fourth Estate).

I am grateful to Warren Adler and Kevin Chapman at Hodder Moa Beckett for their enthusiasm and support, to Dave Smith for giving me access to his private library and to Susan Freeman-Greene whose interest in this project went far beyond the call of duty.

1

A good idea at the time?

New Zealand rugby in the first flush of professionalism is a little like a lottery winner coming to the painful realisation that being an instant millionaire isn't all it's cracked up to be.

Our lucky winner had it all worked out: he'd pay off the mortgage, shift Mum and Dad out of that tacky old bungalow on the wrong side of town into a nice little unit, all mod cons, trade in the Japanese import for the biggest, baddest four-wheel drive on the market and take a long holiday — first-class, five-star, no expense spared. And there'd still be plenty more where that came from.

Well, talk about best-laid plans . . . Mum misses her old neighbours and claims the unit makes her claustrophobic. Dad's new bowls club is full of dickheads, so he says, *and* it serves the wrong brand of beer. They both go on about the number of Asians at the supermarket. The wife's spending money like there's no tomorrow and the in-laws have had their hands out since day one. To top it all off, every time he takes the tank into town, it gets coined.

Everyone told him his worries were over. Yeah, right. Sometimes he thinks, if I had my time over again . . .

When amateurism was mercifully put to sleep, few in the New Zealand rugby community spared it a thought beyond good riddance. We were ready for the brave new world; we'd been professional in all but name and overt remuneration for years. We'd scorned the enforcement of amateurism — barring Graham Mourie from coaching for pocketing the proceeds from his autobiography, for instance — as fingers-in-the-dyke stuff by old farts who didn't even have the nous to realise that their time was up. Young New Zealanders had fanned out across the globe, sporting mercenaries who'd go wherever there was money to be made playing footy. In the looming shape of Andy Haden, we'd unleashed a troublemaker of near-genius proportions on unsuspecting administrators the world over. He duly proceeded to white-ant the system by flouting its rules and getting away with it.

We'd pushed for a World Cup, unmoved by the warnings from British administrators who were invariably 'gin-swilling', a handy code for their remoteness from real rugby folk who stuck to beer, thanks very much. The gin-swillers fretted that a World Cup would lead inexorably to professionalism by increasing the playing load beyond what was reasonable to expect of amateurs and by generating revenue that the players were bound to demand a share of.

The gin-swillers warned that money would change everything. Professionalism, they argued, took a sport out of the community, away from its roots. At the top level it became an industry driven on and off the field by people whose primary motivation was commercial. Even though we had no professional sport to speak of and therefore no first-hand experience of it or real awareness of the wider implications, we took no notice. We believed that nothing much would change apart from the players being rewarded for their sacrifice, endeavour and excellence, which in turn would put an end to the talent-stripping raids from rugby league. Who in their right mind could argue with that? Professionalism would simply further entrench rugby's unassailable position as our national sport, the game for all New Zealanders.

Seven years on, that blithe confidence is in short supply. Indeed sometimes it seems as if rugby is having to call on its strategic reserves of optimism. Even among those who work in 'the industry' and see the wider picture, one is more likely to encounter exasperation at the negative sentiment or wary defensiveness or a dogged insistence that things are on the right track rather than jauntiness. Out in the clubs and provinces there is precious little sense of rugby thriving in a bright new era. On the contrary, the mood seems to be one of sullen, simmering dissatisfaction, a dissatisfaction that precludes enjoyment of success because it springs from, among other things, a gnawing suspicion that another calamity is just around the corner. This reflex pessimism echoes the observation of the much-sacked soccer manager Tommy Docherty: 'As one door shuts, another slams in your face.'

Even Haden, the ex-guerrilla, is uneasy: 'I naïvely thought professionalism would be egalitarian. The wings might be the glamour boys and score the tries but if the tighthead prop can't lock up his side of the scrum, the wing's opportunities are going to be reduced. A lot of things have to be done right inside him for the wing to get the ball with the space and time to beat a man and I thought the player payments would reflect the fact that rugby is the ultimate team game. One guy can't win the game for you by scoring a blazing century or skittling the opposition batsmen.

'Fans pay the wages but the players are no longer ordinary blokes — just like them except for the fact that they happen to be good at footy. They're some of the highest-paid people in the land. That link has been broken and when they fail or behave badly, the public is far less tolerant than they used to be. Now the attitude is, "These pricks are paid X hundred grand a year and they come up with a performance like that." In the old days if a player got pissed and slept it off on the side of the road, it'd be "Well, boys will be boys" and turn a blind eye. Now they go and buy a camera.'

You know it's getting serious when the political left, which has traditionally viewed rugby as the game of choice of the forces of darkness, joins the chorus. In his editorial in the summer 2002–03 issue of *New Zealand Political Review*, commentator Chris Trotter laments the fact that 'the professionalisation of the All Blacks has fatally undercut the egalitarian ideals which fuelled New Zealand's abiding rugby legends. The game, once a celebration of mateship and a common national identity, has fallen victim to the same processes of commodification which have hollowed out so much of the rest of New Zealand's conceptions of itself. Rugby is becoming just one of the multitude of sporting delights on Rupert Murdoch's global media menu.'

It's a truism that the public will tolerate anything as long as the All Blacks win and win they did in the first two years of professionalism. Under new coach John Hart, a figure regarded with suspicion in most parts of the country lying south of the Bombay Hills, and with fear and loathing in his two immediate predecessors' necks of the woods, the All Blacks became indisputably the best team in the world. South Africa were official world champions, having defeated the All Blacks in the knife-edge 1995 World Cup final, a victory clouded — for New Zealanders anyway — by the food poisoning that struck down a number of All Blacks on the eve of the game. However, the Springboks' legitimacy was stripped away the following year when the All Blacks defeated them four times in five meetings, in the process winning the first Tri-Nations championship and accomplishing New Zealand rugby's historic mission — a series win in South Africa. Another Tri-Nations clean sweep followed in 1997, with the winning streak over Australia extended to seven matches. Having subjugated the south, the All Blacks romped through Ireland, Wales and England undefeated to complete what is arguably the most impressive run of any team in the history of international rugby. After winning 10 out of 12 under Laurie Mains in 1995, the All Blacks in 1996/97 played 22 tests for 20 wins, a loss and a draw, the sole loss — to South Africa in Johannesburg — coming in a dead rubber match.

The 1962–69 era was certainly more impressive in terms of duration, but what of the opposition? Twenty of those 34 matches in 1995–97 were against first-division opposition: Australia, England, France and South Africa; 14 of those 20 were away from home. In the 1960s neither Australia nor England were the powers they have since become, and a golden era of Welsh rugby had barely dawned. The 1966 Lions were a divided and dysfunctional team who fell well short of their brilliant predecessors, the class of '59. Most significantly, there was just one series against the great foe South Africa — at home in 1965.

Another strong contender is the 1987–90 period, during which the All Blacks won 23 and drew one of 25 tests and stormed to victory at the inaugural World Cup. Hugely impressive as the record is, this team didn't confront the Springboks at all. The Wallabies may have supplanted the Springboks as our major adversary but that's a recent development: it wasn't until 1996 that the All Blacks got on the right side of the win-loss ledger in games against the Springboks. And we could put forward cold, hard arithmetic to support New Zealand's claim to being the greatest rugby nation on earth. But if the public is benignly tolerant when the All Blacks are winning, it is unforgiving when they lose. And lose they did in 1998 — five games on the trot. The public still hasn't recovered its sense of well-being — or its sense of humour.

This malaise might have lifted if another great team had quickly emerged from the rubble, but great teams — like great players — are rarer than the media would have us believe, and the public chooses to believe. While the one step forward, one step back rebuilding process stretched the patience of a public drip-fed the myth of unchallenged All Black dominance, the unexpected defeat by France at the semi-final stage of the 1999 World Cup and the loss of sub-host status for the 2003 World Cup dealt hammer-blows to its confidence in the New Zealand game and those running it. The fact that Australia was the beneficiary on both occasions has heightened the queasy suspicion that our infuriatingly successful neighbours are about to add rugby to the long list of sports at which they are better than us.

Both these events are now routinely referred to as 'disasters'. Just as true disasters involving significant loss of life must be inquired into and picked over in order to identify the immediate and wider causes, they too had to be dissected and explained. In both instances, analysis took a back seat to blame. Those in charge were found guilty and vilified but the acrimony couldn't be contained. It spread like ink through blotting paper, staining everything in its path and, ultimately, the game itself.

There's a perception that something is rotten in the state of New Zealand rugby. And, as the marketing gurus keep telling us, perception is reality.

Following the provincial unions' scorched-earth purge of the New Zealand Rugby Union (NZRU) board over the loss of the World Cup sub-hosting rights, public opinion virtually propelled former All Black captain Jock Hobbs to the chairmanship. With his flanker's build and his lawyer's domed forehead, Hobbs certainly looks the part. Now a financier, he still chooses his words as carefully as a barrister tip-toeing around a short-fused judge. In his view, there was no spontaneous combustion; they'd been hot under the collar out in the heartland since the 1999 World Cup campaign, as much because of the hype and swagger — the All Blacks front row painted on an Air New Zealand 747 — and self-indulgence — chilling out in the south of France — as the actual on-field collapse.

'The upheaval on the board was a response to the loss of the World Cup hosting rights but I suspect there were other factors involved and the loss was the catalyst. There was a feeling that money, the professional element of the game, had a focus and emphasis at the expense of a closer consideration of the issues and difficulties faced by the base of the game. My underlying feeling is that there was a perception that the base of the game wasn't getting the focus and consideration many felt it deserved. People felt frustrated by that. John Hart, because of who he was and how he came across, fed that perception. The painting on the plane was a symbol of that, as was the sojourn in the south of France. A lot of people were put off by that and I was among them.

'Was that feeling justified? It's difficult for me because I don't have an appreciation and understanding of what was being done and considered, but there were certain attitudes and messages that fed that perception. And, as we know, perception is reality.'

One might almost think that Hobbs had spent the previous seven years in a state of suspended animation with a sign around his neck saying 'Reactivate in case of emergency.' This is his second coming, the second time he's burst out of the telephone booth to save the day. Shortly after he was elected to the old 17-man NZRU council in 1995, Hobbs and another former All Black captain Brian Lochore were entrusted with the task of persuading New Zealand's top 150-odd players not to take the highly attractive bait being dangled by the entrepreneurial, if somewhat hazy, World Rugby Corporation (WRC) and Rupert Murdoch's massively funded rugby league concept, Super League. They succeeded and Hobbs' reward was to be denied a place on the new nine-man board following the NZRU's reform of its governance structures.

One theory put forward for his rejection was that the provincial unions were appalled by the amount of money that was thrown at the players to buy their loyalty. If so, they didn't appreciate how high the stakes were or that Hobbs and Lochore were having to recruit in a once-in-a-lifetime sellers' market. Hobbs argues that things started to get out of hand well after he'd been patted on the back and shown the door: 'I think under the circumstances, given that we didn't have the luxury of time, the transition was managed reasonably well both in terms of the transactions which underpinned the move to professional rugby and the structures that needed to be put in place. I think the concerns began to grow later when the payments got bigger and the messages and attitudes being expressed created the perception that the professional elements of the game were going corporate.'

That perception of a game gone wrong, changed for the worse and detached from its core constituency — the sort of people who sustained it for a century while the legend grew and the glorious tradition was established — has many strands which together form a persuasive case: club rugby is out on its feet, schoolboy rugby is down-sizing, white boys are being bullied out of the game by their overgrown Polynesian peers, experienced players are deserting in droves to collect hard currency superannuation packages in Europe and Japan, and we have to pay for the privilege of seeing our national sport live on television.

All these cracks in the edifice converge, forming a fault-line that runs right to the dark heart of the matter: the All Blacks aren't what they used to be. We haven't won the World Cup since 1987; the Wallabies have won two of the last three. The All Blacks no longer have the fear factor: they don't intimidate, they don't trample over everyone in their path. We haven't held the Bledisloe Cup since 1997; the Wallabies have won eight of the last 11 trans-Tasman encounters. The All Blacks can't hold their nerve and nail tight games at the death because we no longer breed hard-nosed, mentally tough players who know how to win and will do whatever it takes.

When the All Blacks toured Ireland and Wales in 1989, a reporter from the BBC interviewed New Zealand's most celebrated rugby league coach, Graham Lowe, then plying his trade at Wigan. 'He asked me who'd win. I said, "Your team's full of lawyers and stockbrokers, the All Blacks are full of farmers and guys who make a living hitting cows on the head with sledgehammers or fixing cars — or stealing them. Who do you think's going to win?"'

The perception of decline holds that the game has become disconnected from the social context, the ethos and the landscape from which it sprang. It has sold out, thrown in its lot with the commercial world. In a word — and this is a word one hears all the time — rugby has gone corporate.

When a rugby person uses the word 'corporate', they're unlikely to be dishing out a compliment, but what does it mean? More pertinently, what do they *think* it means?

In his biography *Gladiator*, written by Michael Laws, former wild man and All Black Norm Hewitt reflects on a seminar on the perils of professionalism organised by Hart in early 1996: 'Despite Hart's ostensibly altruistic aims, Norm felt uncomfortable with the new coach and with the sudden trappings of corporate rugby. "At that time professionalism was just a word. And a bucketload of money."

'[Hart was] speaking a language that emphasised off-the-field professionalism as much as on-field endeavour. The All Blacks were no longer just elite rugby players. Overnight they had become corporate stars and role models.'

So what exactly were these discomforting 'trappings of corporate rugby'? Having to attend a seminar put on for the players' benefit and absorb some sobering statistics from American football — that 50 per cent of the players were broke when their careers finished, that 80 per cent of their marriages failed, that their average life expectancy was 54 years? Being told that more would be expected of them on and off the field now that they were being paid 'bucketloads of money'?

Broadcaster Murray Deaker has been a fierce critic of corporate rugby: 'My understanding is that it refers to rugby doing things in a business-like way, but the term has become disparaging and associated within the minds of most New Zealanders with various elements of the Hart era — people who know nothing about the game, Auckland wankers, people watching games from corporate boxes, tickets not being available to rank and file club members.'

There's a chip-on-the-shoulder, slightly redneck tinge to this blacklist. 'Auckland wankers' speaks for itself. Whether the spectators in the stands or on the terraces know more about the game than the tossers in the corporate boxes is a moot point. In my experience, both settings have their share of know-alls and know-nothings. Given that there are corporate boxes at grounds from Whangarei to Invercargill, one can't help but wonder if there aren't a few ordinary working Kiwis — middle management types, say, or self-employed small businessmen — up there rubbing shoulders with the likes of Paul Holmes and Nicky Watson. Surely they can't all be software millionaires and pony-tailed advertising whiz-kids. And while we're on the subject, how many of the refurbishments that have recently transformed our rugby grounds would have taken place without the capital generated through the sale of corporate boxes?

Former All Black manager Andrew Martin doubts that people who use the term really know what they mean. 'I think a lot of it is people in clubrooms where the membership is diminishing talking about not being able to get tickets to matches because the corporates have taken them all. I have sympathy for people who see folk for whom rugby isn't central to their lives going along to test matches when they either can't get access to tickets or can't afford them, but we shouldn't lose sight of the fact that it's still a lot cheaper here than in Australia or England. And, frankly, who cares how many free tickets adidas gets when set against what they put into our game? One of our challenges is managing the finances of the game so that it is available to the average Kiwi, but we're not in an industry that can afford to run test matches at a loss.'

Caught in the cross-hairs is the turbulent figure of John Hart: 'People like Deaker keep saying we don't want this corporate thing in rugby. What do they mean? If they're talking about me, what I tried to do was organise things in a professional way, recognising that there was a group of stakeholders out there for whom we had to deliver — sponsors, the media and so on. The word is a bloody nonsense. People started to bandy it around because I came from a corporate background. That was the best thing I had going for me because it enabled me to understand professionalism.'

For people averse to change, 'Things aren't what they used to be' is an age-old mantra. Rugby, like all sports, has always had its share of those who, despite the evidence of their own eyes, insist that things were better in their day. As former All Black Chris Laidlaw wrote in his ground-breaking autobiography *Mud In Your Eye*, published in 1973, 'I am convinced that anyone over 50 firmly believes that the best days that the sport will ever see have been and gone.'

With the advent of professionalism and the influx of people — administrators, marketing executives, spectators, even players — who can give the impression that they don't give a damn for rugby's history and traditions or its stalwart supporters and unpaid volunteers, that nostalgia has taken on a resentful edge. New Zealand rugby has undergone rapid, startling change, much of it reflecting the seismic social and economic changes that have shaken up the nation in the last two decades. The game is no longer essentially the preserve of white adult males, some of whom, particularly those who can remember when that was the case, aren't happy about it. In sports industry jargon they feel 'disenfranchised'.

The disenfranchised have an icon who symbolises everything that was great about the game they grew up with and everything that is lacking in the game that seems to be abandoning them. Step forward Colin 'Pinetree' Meads.

Meads has always been larger than life, a figure of myth and red-blooded romance. Like the mythical frontiersmen of the American West, he came to personify his countrymen's masculine ideal: practical, devoid of airs and graces, stoic, resilient, resolute, fair-minded but uncompromising and always willing to take up a physical challenge. He cleared a 200-acre block of hill country scrub, he carried a sheep under each arm, he took on the Springboks with a broken arm, he was held in fear and awe by opponents the world over.

Andrew Mulligan, an Irish and British Lions halfback turned journalist, wrote this of Meads after the All Blacks 1962/63 tour of Britain, Ireland and France: 'What does the best forward in the world mean? Is it applicable to anyone? The answer to both is probably Colin Meads. He knew no fear. And no limit to the drive of the mind over his own matter.'

In a review of hard men he had known, the outstanding Wales and Lions number eight Mervyn Davies assembled a cast of bullies and bruisers before anointing Meads as the hardest of them all. Not that Meads had left his mark on him; the opposite in fact. Playing for the 1971 Lions against King Country-Wanganui, Davies speared his bony shoulder into Meads' rib cage as he stretched up for the ball. Meads, blindsided, wasn't prepared for what was a severe impact. He got back to his feet and gave Davies a stare that caused his bowels to flutter. Thereafter, the Welshman avoided the dark places where retribution could have been meted out.

So far, so good but when Meads, still wearing an expression of narrow-eyed menace, approached him at the after-match function, Davies feared he'd underestimated the man's implacability. With no apparent effort, Meads picked Davies up, bounced him in his arms as if he was an infant, set him back on his feet and acknowledged that he'd caught him a good one. It turned out that Meads had sustained a sprung rib cartilage as a result of Davies' shoulder charge. The Lions' manager, Dr Doug Smith, a medical man, told Davies afterwards that Meads' apparently playful gesture would certainly have caused him intense pain.

Meads was an All Black from 1957 to 1971 and still holds the record for the most appearances in the black jersey. He is the greatest All Black. And 'public opinion' effectively forced him to give up the game.

'Newspapers and critics at large crucified [Meads] in 1971–72 for "not retiring",' wrote Laidlaw. 'Listening to the callous cries for his withdrawal, I was infuriated at the attitude of so many who had elevated this sincerely simple man to such a position. Although in retrospect he should have been selected for the tour of Britain — it's a fair guess that if he had, there would not have been half the trouble there was — he succumbed to the noise of the critics, embarrassed by the controversy he had generated, and was forced to end his career himself. Meads must have felt like the suspect who is handed a revolver with one bullet in the chamber and left to seal his own fate.'

Meads' post-retirement involvement in rugby was varied and distinguished and occasionally questionable. His involvement with the Cavaliers while an All Black selector was naïve, to put a generous complexion on it, and foreshadowed his somewhat equivocal behaviour for an All Black manager and NZRU councillor during the WRC crisis. For all his apparent lack of guile, he ended up becoming quite a power behind the throne on the NZRU council.

But these episodes did him no lasting harm. In fact by bringing him down — momentarily — from his pedestal and revealing his tendency to follow the heart rather than the head, they have if anything topped up the reservoir of public affection and admiration. Meads would never claim to be rugby's voice of conscience — he has too much dirt under his fingernails for that — but his homespun wisdom spiced with sly, straight-faced humour is much in demand. Whether he wishes it or not, he is the patron saint of the disenfranchised, the disillusioned and those who would turn back the clock to a simpler, better time.

(The humour, incidentally, has always been there. When a young Andy Haden sought his advice on how to go about getting himself noticed in an All Black trial, Meads replied, 'Wear white head-gear. No one else will.')

The great man feels his followers' pain.

'The fact that Meads thinks the All Blacks are not physically or technically, or tactically for that matter, dominant in the way they were for a time when he was in his pomp irritates him even now,' writes Brian Turner in the second volume of Meads' biography, a runaway best-seller like the first, *Colin Meads All Black* by Alex Veysey which came out in 1974. 'It is almost as if, in his heart of hearts, Meads wants to believe, or at least help continue to assert, that there is something termed The Divine Right of All Blacks.'

The key words in this paragraph are 'for a time when he was in his pomp'. For while it is beyond argument that the All Blacks were the dominant force in world rugby for most of the 1960s, Meads was on the losing side in his last two series — against South Africa in 1970 and the Lions in 1971. The good old days weren't quite as good as they are often made out to be by those looking back through rose-tinted lenses or seeking to crank up the pressure on today's players and coaches by insisting that anything short of total success compromises the great legacy of Meads and the other giants of the past.

There is also a grim irony in the fact that the hero of those who believe, among other things, that money has spoilt the game has latterly been bedevilled by financial problems. Turner relates how Meads and his wife borrowed overseas through a local bank to extend their land holdings, then woke up one morning to find that they owed half a million dollars more than they thought they did. Not surprisingly, the forced sale of part of their farm and a 14-year battle with the bank left them 'dejected and, at times, angry and despairing. By their own admission they never recovered from it.'

Ironic too that the amount in question is roughly what the current superstars of New Zealand rugby earn each year. Would those who begrudge Jonah Lomu his pay cheque also begrudge Colin Meads? Then again, would Meads have given 15 years of unwavering commitment to the All Black cause if he'd been earning that sort of money?

The disenfranchised have their patron saint and their outlet — talkback radio — and in late 2002 their manifesto cum call to arms appeared: *The Judas Game* by veteran sports writer Joseph Romanos. This book doesn't beat around the bush: as if the title wasn't sufficiently inflammatory, the cover also bears two stark subtitles: 'All Blacks For Sale' and 'The betrayal of New Zealand rugby'.

To begin with, at least, the text delivers on the cover's promise. The very first line asserts that, 'Rugby union might be New Zealand's national game, but it is a game in crisis.' The second paragraph begins, 'There is every chance that within 30 years rugby will not be New Zealand's national sport.' Over the page Romanos slaps his cards down on the table: 'I believe the reason for rugby's imminent eclipse is simple: money.'

Soon some big — if antique — guns are deployed to support this full frontal assault. According to Fred Allen, 'The All Blacks aren't a sports team, they are a commodity that everyone is using in some way or other to get rich . . . The All Blacks are out there playing for money now. They say they are playing for pride but I don't see the same tremendous feeling that former All Blacks had when they pulled on the black jersey. The passion is missing. It's definitely the money. Who'd have believed it?'

And Bob Scott: 'I cried one time when we lost. Now the players run round after a game and shake each other's hands and smile. Why should they worry?'

Just as one starts to get the feeling that these old boys might be over-egging the pudding just a tad, Fred the Needle lets rip with this baffling diatribe: 'Rugby's our national game and we have to pay to watch the big games live. I sit here and ask myself what I went to war for — democracy and freedom of speech. Well, that's gone. Now if you want something, it isn't your right. You have to pay for it.'

While this statement resists penetration from whichever angle it's approached, it does serve to illustrate that, when confronted with wholesale and, at first blink, unfathomable change, older folk are liable to respond with anxiety, confusion, contrariness and perhaps a touch of jaundice.

Hobbs sympathises: 'As a generalisation, there will always be resistance to change and people aren't comfortable with change. Rugby changed into a professional sport and we don't have a tradition of professional sport. It's going to take time for people to understand fully that change and be comfortable with it, but it was incumbent on the powers that were to help people as much as possible through that change so that they didn't feel disenfranchised from the game and still felt that they understood it. There are a number of aspects to that but it was important to retain a balance and convey that because perception becomes reality.'

Regardless of what the marketing gurus tell us, however, perception is not reality. Reality is reality; perception is what people believe or assume or accept to be the case. It is the view we individually and collectively come to on the basis of the information we choose to avail ourselves of. If the information is flawed and/or incomplete and if in the processing of it preconceived notions or prejudices come into play, the perception that emerges may bear little relation to reality. It may, in fact, be an illusion.

A GOOD IDEA AT THE TIME?

'What we're up against is perception,' says David Rutherford, the former NZRU chief executive who dematerialised in the fallout from the loss of the World Cup sub-hosting rights. He cites an All Blacks training session at the Blackrock College club in Ireland in 2001 that was watched by more than 8000 schoolchildren. 'A New Zealand journalist came up to me to ask why we didn't do this back home. I told him, "We do, mate. We've done it at your club." There's a gap between what people think is happening and what is actually happening.'

2

That was then . . . and this is now

Every generation harks back to a mythical golden age of order and stability.

— MELANIE PHILLIPS, ENGLISH NEWSPAPER COLUMNIST

Those who cannot remember the past are condemned to repeat it.

— GEORGE SANTAYANA, SPANISH PHILOSOPHER

What if the All Blacks lose more? What if they not only can't land the World Cup and not only continue to lose often to Australia and South Africa, but also start to get beaten by England, France and other Northern Hemisphere teams?

— JOSEPH ROMANOS, *THE JUDAS GAME*

The year is 1973.

The All Blacks, captained by Ian Kirkpatrick and coached by Bob Duff, have just returned from a 32-match tour of North America, Britain, Ireland and France that will not go down as one of the finest chapters in the annals of New Zealand rugby.

In terms of living up to the great legacy of previous All Black teams in Europe, the tour was an unvarnished failure. Five matches were lost, including those against France and the Barbarians, the British Lions in sheep's clothing. The other losses were to Llanelli, North-West Counties and Midland Counties (West). Two matches were drawn, including the Irish test. Off the field, the tour was a public relations nightmare that tarnished the All Blacks' hitherto outstanding image in the UK. Bob Howitt, the editor of the *1973 DB Rugby Annual* — who, interestingly, considered that the tour was 'with reservations, a success' — wrote that the team, while well-organised on the field, 'tended to set their own rules off it, and left a trail of disappointed, disillusioned hosts throughout Britain'.

T.P. (Sir Terry) McLean, the great chronicler and conscience of the New Zealand game, was more austere. In his account of the tour *They Missed The Bus*, he wrote, '[The All Blacks] preferred not to appreciate that the obligations and responsibilities of international status in a sport which is as much a way of national life as rugby has been in New Zealand are both individual and collective. By brash acts or snarling words or gestures of dissent which conveyed that they did not appreciate the abilities of their leader, they scored momentary hits which, however satisfying, served to reduce both their team — and themselves.'

Beneath a photo of Alan Sutherland, Tane Norton and Alex Wyllie in their infamous gaucho hats, McLean commented, 'Many a lip, at home and abroad, curled at the thought that men could seem so little to cherish the distinction of their uniform.'

The defining event of the tour was the expulsion of the Otago prop Keith Murdoch. In the early hours of the Sunday morning following the Welsh test, the original game of two halves, Murdoch staged a sort of one-man riot in Cardiff's Angel Hotel that culminated in him biffing a security guard in the hotel kitchens. He was thrown off the tour and has led a strange, itinerant life in the Australian outback ever since. At home, public sympathy was on Murdoch's side. The general view of the affair was that it was pretty much par for the course for a prop forward whooping it up after a big win, the sort of hearty mayhem that generations of tourists had been getting up to — and away with — since 1905; all it warranted was a stiff ticking-off. But the manager, Ernie Todd, buckled under pressure from the upper-class twits of the Four Home Unions Tours Committee and banished Murdoch into the limbo in which he's wandered ever since.

The Murdoch who emerges from McLean's forensic account is a somewhat different animal to the victimised hard case of legend. He was trouble waiting to happen and one can only wonder what he would have done for an encore if the rumble at the Angel had been winked at. He had previous to burn. At after-match functions he was prone to getting into ugly arguments that sometimes ended in violence. In South Africa in 1970, he injured an ankle in a fight with friends of the Springbok Piet Visagie outside a dance hall, missing 10 matches as a result. During the 1971 Lions tour he cried off on the morning of no fewer than four games, three of which were tests. He threatened and roughed up members of the press. He had been put on notice by Todd very early on the tour.

In what McLean described as a 'pathetically revealing' admission, Murdoch told a member of the Western Counties team: 'I am not the same as you ordinary blokes. Nine tenths of the time I am OK. But the other tenth, I have got to blow. I can't take it, I have to stand up for myself and explode.' Dr Doug Smith, manager of the

1971 Lions, provided this sombre diagnosis: 'Medically speaking, I would say Murdoch is a disturbed person.'

McLean documented that Murdoch caroused loudly and tiresomely on the flight from Auckland to Honolulu, and from then on it was downhill all the way: drunkenness, vandalism, boorishness, physical assault . . . How many previous All Blacks had really got away with serial offending on this scale? This team's two immediate predecessors — Wilson Whineray's side of 1962/63 and Brian Lochore's of 1967 — conducted themselves well on and off the field and were enormously popular as a result. Therein, perhaps, lies Murdoch's plea in mitigation: it was his misfortune to be in a team that lacked the character of its predecessors. He needed to be in an environment with high standards but he wasn't and, with little to live up to, he reverted to type.

Thus far the 1970s hadn't been kind to the All Blacks. This ill-starred tour followed series defeats in South Africa in 1970 and to the British Lions at home in 1971. Players, administrators and fans alike were rudely disabused of their dreams of revenge and redemption when Labour Prime Minister Norman Kirk cancelled the scheduled Springbok tour. Faced with the prospect of a domestic season without an international component, the NZRU invited the Scots, who declined because a number of their leading players were unavailable, a consideration which doesn't seem to weigh so heavily on the Four Home Unions these days. The NZRU then hastily put together an internal tour, pitting the All Blacks against the New Zealand Juniors, the New Zealand Maoris and twice against an invitational President's XV. When England withdrew from its tour of Argentina because of kidnap threats, a four-match tour was arranged at short notice. It was a far cry from a full-scale Springbok tour but beggars couldn't be choosers.

What transpired was, well, inconceivable. In his season review, Bob Howitt wrote, 'It's inconceivable that the All Blacks could lose to the Juniors, to a bits-and-pieces invitation side and to a scantily prepared England side in the space of a month. Yet it has happened.'

For the record, the Juniors beat the All Blacks 14–10 at Carisbrook with one Graham Mourie scoring a try for the victors. J.J. Stewart, the All Blacks' third coach in 15 months, had 24 hours to prepare the team and had to play a prop at lock after Peter Whiting's late withdrawal. Howitt commented that it was 'embarrassing to see the Juniors dictating in the scrums. It was more embarrassing to see them win.'

On to Wellington and the President's XV featuring Sid Going, who'd been unavailable for the All Blacks, and a locking combination — Colin Meads and Brian Lochore — with a combined age of 70. The invitation team won 35–28, scoring six tries and taking five tightheads, three of which were obtained by shoving the All Blacks off the ball. After the third tighthead, Meads supposedly told his forwards to 'take it easy'.

The All Blacks hauled themselves off the floor to beat the Maoris 18–8 in a downpour at Rotorua and win the return match against the President's XV 22–10. Howitt, who thought that two wins out of four was, under the circumstances, 'a pass', felt sorry for the new All Blacks: 'Here they were in the All Black blazer with players who didn't care whether the tour went on or not, whether the team won or lost. A sign of the times? No, just sportsmen who've lost sight of where they are going, who is leading them and what it's all about.'

The All Blacks couldn't have been fizzing with confidence when they took on England at Eden Park, but given that England had lost all three of its lead-up games, that worked both ways. England won 16–10.

Afterwards, England's high-class wing David Duckham drew an interesting comparison between New Zealand and Wales: 'I always thought Wales was the nation of nations as far as rugby goes but in

Wales they go a bit sour if they lose. They can be very bad losers. I don't hold the same view about New Zealand. If their teams lose, it's not the end of the world.'

The overbearing confidence of the Welsh and their bitterness in defeat undoubtedly helped poison the atmosphere on the recent tour. Duckham's comment bolsters the suspicion that the public reaction to defeat in both countries is linked to expectations. In 1972 Welsh expectations were sky-high. Wales had won the 1969 and 1971 Five Nations championships without dropping a game and been undefeated in the truncated 1972 championship. With a Welsh coach, a Welsh captain and 13 Welshmen in the 30-strong touring party, the 1971 Lions were seen in Wales as being very much a Welsh project and their success as confirmation that Wales was setting the standard in international rugby. And, of course, the first time Kirkpatrick's All Blacks ventured onto Welsh soil, they met blood, thunder and defeat at the hands of Llanelli.

The All Blacks, however, were in the midst of a poor run by historical standards. I don't remember the internal tour well — I was a student at the time — but I have a hazy recollection that the general reaction to the Juniors defeat was fatalistic humour of the 'just when we thought things couldn't get any worse' variety. There was so little rugby on television that seeing a game meant, by and large, being there. Those who weren't there had to go on second-hand information — radio and newspaper coverage was rather more reportage and rather less opinion than is the case now — which perhaps made them less quick to take strong positions on individual and team performances. Moreover, there was no talkback to turn disappointment into disaffection and provide a nationwide soapbox for the raucous minority.

The saving grace of this *annus horribilis* was Marlborough wresting the Ranfurly Shield from a Canterbury team containing 11 All Blacks or All Blacks-to-be. Marlborough then held on to the shield for the rest of the season, seeing off challenges from Wairarapa-Bush, North Otago, Wanganui, Nelson Bays and Mid-Canterbury. This was the sort of fairy tale that created the mystique surrounding the log o' wood and which, we are continually told, couldn't happen today because of the consolidation of resources in the main centres. Maybe not, but it was hardly commonplace back then either. Marlborough was the first minor union to hold the shield since 1950, a situation highlighted in a Neville Lodge cartoon showing a Marlborough man, shield tucked under his arm, pressing the buzzer of the Ranfurly Club despite the sign on the door saying, 'Membership available to major unions only'. Aghast members watch the upstart through the window, with one saying, 'Gad! We're going to have to permit minors into the club.'

Marlborough accepted challenges from minor unions because those were the teams they played year in, year out. In 15 years of representative rugby, Marlborough's captain Ray Sutherland had never played against Wellington.

Some things haven't changed quite as much as the critics of the contemporary game would have us believe. Some things certainly have: Ray's brother Alan sheared 50 sheep on the morning of the Nelson Bays match. The big games drew large crowds, although most of the grounds had greater capacity than they do now. There were 48,000 at Eden Park to watch the All Blacks play the President's XV and 55,000 for the only test match of the season. On the other hand, 30,000 turned out at Athletic Park on a fine September day to watch Wellington beat England, which isn't much more than the average Hurricanes crowd at the new stadium.

On the face of it, player numbers are a good indicator of a sport's health. Accurate data for New Zealand rugby has been hard to come by until quite recently so one is forced to fall back on anecdotal evidence, the value of which can depend on who's relating the anecdote. In an investigation into the state of rugby that appeared in

The New Zealand Herald in May 2001, the writers cited anecdotal evidence that player numbers peaked at 400,000 in the 1970s. That figure seems extraordinarily high, effectively one in three males, able-bodied or otherwise. Mourie, who as a NZRU board member takes a close interest in participation trends here and overseas, believes that there were about 180,000 rugby players in his day, which seems more likely. According to the NZRU's annual report, there were 122,280 players registered with schools or clubs in 2002, which was up on 2001 by more than the target 2 per cent. Interestingly, the *Herald*'s anecdotal evidence also suggested that player numbers dropped below 100,000 in the early 1990s.

The annual report makes the point that the issue is retention rather than attraction. Rugby has little trouble attracting youngsters — 25 per cent of 10 year olds play the game — but a lot of them give it away at secondary school: between the ages of 13 and 20, there is a 44 per cent drop in playing numbers. This raises the question: how much of the historic decline is due to the fact that most secondary schools no longer put pressure on their male pupils to play rugby?

After the cancellation of the Springbok tour and Marlborough's capture of the shield, the biggest rugby event of 1973 was probably the publication of Chris Laidlaw's *Mud In Your Eye*, sub-titled *A worm's eye view of the changing world of rugby*.

Players' books weren't the annual events they are now; Alex Veysey's blockbuster *Colin Meads All Black*, which probably created the market, would appear in 1974. And Laidlaw — inventor of the spin pass, All Black at 19, dissident on the South African issue, Rhodes Scholar — wasn't your average rugby player. The book's starting point was the countless requests he'd had in Britain for the 'inside story on the phenomenon that was New Zealand rugby'. He set to work on that theme in 1969 but had to throw away half his material after the 1970 tour of South Africa, and the other half after the 1971 Lions tour. The All Blacks' abrupt fall to earth worked to

Laidlaw's advantage: in a time of triumph the public — and, for that matter, his publishers — might have baulked at the penetrating agnosticism he brought to bear on the national game.

Among the aspects he found fault with were the widespread compulsion to play rugby and the cult of conformity within the game, which had become a liability in an era of rebellion and social upheaval.

'Many headmasters insist that boys play rugby whether they want to or not. Headmasters mask their obsession with the trite claim that rugby is essential for teamwork and discipline. Any such claim is, of course, a nonsense: enforced activity, particularly when someone is no good at it, breeds the very reverse of team spirit or discipline. There often exists a compulsion to play rugby even to the exclusion of other, perhaps more suitable, sports. I have grown up with boys whose social and cultural life has been a misery because of their inability to succeed at rugby. I have watched potentially brilliant personalities lose much of their self-confidence because the sole measure of success in the school was rugby.' Laidlaw said that many boys' lives had been made a misery because of their inability to succeed at rugby, something that damaged their self-confidence.

He also thought that the 'sterile formality' of the approach to rugby in New Zealand and South Africa bred sterile formality in the players, and this was 'the very quality that youngsters today most abhor. The number of rugby defectors among the emerging generation is clearly mounting and the alarm bells, heavy and hitherto unused, are beginning to toll.'

Laidlaw believed that New Zealand coaching was stuck in a time warp — 'having witnessed the best of British coaches in action, I have little doubt that they are superior to New Zealanders' — and lamented the neglect of gifted non-conformists such as Grahame Thorne and Tony Davies, 'who should have become one of the greatest players of the decade, he had a great deal more talent than any other midfield back in New Zealand.'

The higher one went, the more relentless the pressure to conform: 'I soon realised after entering the All Black fold that any expression of my habits which by normal standards were mildly unconventional would be distinctly unwise. There existed a rigid code that demanded a sameness among all the players that on first experience was extremely depressing.'

Almost two decades later, the same pressure would force another halfback and Rhodes Scholar to turn his back on the All Blacks. Within 24 hours of holding the Webb Ellis trophy aloft, David Kirk sat down to write an article for a French newspaper explaining why he was opting out: 'While I loved the All Blacks, the culture of the team and the demands of tradition were too demanding. The need to conform and to accept a system of behaviour and values that are not your own, but those of the rugby culture, is known as "discipline". It is true that discipline is an essential element of success on the rugby field. It too often becomes a tyranny of the majority off the field. Those who refuse to conform are seen either as undisciplined or as selfish and egotistical.'

No sport, and particularly not one that aspires to be the national game, can quarantine itself from the society in which it functions and from which it draws its human resources and support. To do so is to choose irrelevance and, ultimately, extinction. While it was no accident that New Zealanders were drawn to rugby in the first place — 'Rugby suits us,' said Lochore after coaching the All Blacks to victory in the first World Cup, 'it suits our temperament, it suits our physique' — its swift consolidation as the national sport reflected its neat fit with the prevailing values. In 1973 New Zealand's prevailing values were still those of the white conservative male.

In 1972 Austin Mitchell had published *The Half-gallon Quarter-acre Pavlova Paradise*, an allegedly humorous anatomy of the New

Zealand way of life. Mitchell, an Englishman, came to New Zealand to teach history at Otago University but made a name for himself on television. He wrote the book on his return to the UK, where he became a long-serving Labour MP. From the vantage point of 2003, the enthusiastic reception the book received in this country seems like the cultural cringe at its most cringe-making: Kiwis were too flattered that this clever boots had written a book about them to notice that they were being patronised. But in among the condescension and wearying striving for cleverness, Mitchell provided some insight into the drab uniformity of the times.

On national identity, he noted: 'New Zealand owes much of its national character to the smallness of the population. A mass society is hierarchical and fragmented; a small one is uniform . . . A Briton would define someone by reference to some category, usually exact social position. The Kiwi does so by reference to his personal characteristics, usually his precise degree of "good or bad blokiness".'

On equality: 'With socialists, equality is a matter of principle, until they reach power, when it's a matter of amnesia. In New Zealand, it is a simple fact of group conformity. It is a negative, not a positive. Its basis is a widespread feeling that if we can't all have something, no one should.'

On the place of women: 'Most countries have oppressed minorities. New Zealand has an oppressed near majority, sometimes called the New Zealand Woman. [She] leaves school almost a year before the male and she's half as likely to go to university. New Zealanders are low on the world league for the proportion of women working. Only a third go out to work and then usually in lowly paid jobs.'

On the moral climate: 'Compared with Britain, this looks to be a cautiously antiseptic society. Prostitutes are as common as coelacanths and in most places taxi drivers will ask *you* where *they* can get a woman.'

As L.P. Hartley wrote in *The Go-Between*, 'The past is a different country: they do things differently there.'

In 1973 Britain joined the European Economic Community.

In his book *Paradise Reforged*, historian James Belich develops the thesis that New Zealand's virtually exclusive economic and political relationship with Britain, dating from 1882 when the refrigerated ship *Dunedin* put to sea with a cargo of frozen meat, amounted to what he calls 'recolonisation'. At a time when the new country should have been distancing itself from the colonising power and starting to make its own way in the world, New Zealand went scurrying back to mother.

'In conceptual geography, New Zealand became smaller, its parts knit more tightly. It shifted away from Australia and towards Britain. In history, robust and ruthless town — and camp-led — progress was written out, steady and virtuous farm-led progress was written in. New Zealand's view of its future became more modest. It shifted away from the American model and towards the Scottish model.'

In 1973, Mother Britain effectively kicked her clingy child out onto the street, ending what Belich calls 'the years of the Golden Weather'. The effect on New Zealand's economy was immediate and traumatic, shifting the decline of New Zealand's British market 'from gradual and relative to rapid and absolute. Coupled with the oil shock, New Zealand's terms of trade deteriorated by over 40 per cent in the mid 1970s — similar to the decline in the Great Depression. Britain's share of our exports halved.'

Almost overnight, New Zealand went from recolonisation to decolonisation and the stage was set for the convulsive economic changes of Rogernomics that would transform virtually every aspect of society.

Belich: 'If, by courtesy of some time machine, New Zealanders had been transposed from 1960 to 2000, or vice versa, they would have encountered a land transformed. In 1960, New Zealand was a tight society . . . It was homogeneous, conformist, masculist, egalitarian and mono-cultural, subject to heavy formal and informal regulation. There were no licensed restaurants, little weekend shopping, one supermarket, and a very limited range of goods and foods to buy in the shops and unlicensed restaurants that did exist. Most forms of gambling on anything other than horses, drinking in pubs after 6 pm and Sunday newspapers were banned by law. School milk was free but you had to drink it; compulsory military service had just been reintroduced; and a New Zealand folk motto was "What will the neighbours say?" There was no television, no radio stations other than those run by the state, and only four New Zealand feature films had been made in the previous 20 years. The cars on the street were very old and very British and the novel *Lolita* had just been banned.

'By 2000 New Zealand, for better and for worse, was one of the least regulated societies in the world. There were a dozen television channels, numerous private radio stations, and 120 New Zealand feature films had been made in the previous 20 years. There were innumerable licensed restaurants, bars and cafés, and pervasive supermarket shopping, on Sunday, Saturday and the rest of the week. There were also Sunday papers and Sunday sport. The cars were now modern and Japanese; and a New Zealand academic had recently completed the definitive biography of [Vladimir] Nabokov, whose work he would not have been able to legally read a generation before. The bars still closed at 6 o'clock but am not pm. In 1960, most Aucklanders could scarcely bring themselves to say "homosexual"; by 2000 they lined the streets in thousands to watch the Hero Parade redefine Queen Street.

'In 1960 a woman's place was predominantly in the home; in 2000 the heads of both major political parties, the Chief Justice, the Governor-General designate and the head of the largest corporation were all women. [In 1960] the claim that New Zealand was "98.5 per cent British" could still be heard. Today there is considerable ethnic diversity, especially in Auckland where almost 10 per cent of the population is Asian, 13 per cent Pacific Island and 12 per cent Maori.'

This is the reality. This is the community that rugby must live among, engage with and be relevant to. The accommodation is a work in progress. The South African issue was, in military terms, the last set-piece battle. When the forces of old New Zealand and old rugby retired from the field to rethink their tactics, the game was able to begin the process of remaking itself in an image that reflected the transformed society. Given the nature of that transformation, it is difficult, if not impossible, to see how rugby could have retained its relevance and therefore remained part of our national identity without going professional.

The 2002 NZRU annual report reminds us that the All Blacks won the Tri-Nations series, the Sevens team won the gold medal at the Manchester Commonwealth Games and retained the World Sevens Series title, the Black Ferns won the World Cup, the Under-19s won the World Championship and the Crusaders won the Super 12. Overall attendance and average crowds for Super 12 games were the highest on record while the National Provincial Championship (NPC) crowds were significantly higher than in 2001.

Discussion of the apparently negative trends in New Zealand rugby over the past 30 years — notably the drop-out rate at secondary school level, the decline of club rugby and the problems facing the smaller, rural provinces — cannot take place in isolation. The context must be the far-reaching social, economic, demographic and technological changes that have transformed the way young New Zealanders look, think and behave.

In 1973 the former All Black loose forward and captain John Graham became headmaster of Auckland Grammar School, our foremost — in terms of All Blacks produced — rugby school. Andrew Mulligan described him as, 'Pound for pound about the best forward I have ever seen. Hard, relentless, with the energy of a Chinese firecracker, only more consistent.' Living proof that it is possible to be both strong-minded and open-minded, Graham has accumulated a remarkable record of public service. Now 68, 'D.J.' — as he is widely known — is, among other things, Chancellor of the University of Auckland, deputy chairman of the Owens Group, vice-president of the NZRU, a member of the committee that reviews Super 12 coaches and a director of the Auckland Cricket Association Board.

'My sense as a school teacher is that there's been a massive shift away from team sport,' he says. 'The individual nature of society means that team games are no longer the dominant way of obtaining recreational or competitive sport. There are more demands on people now: people work longer hours and recreational time is better achieved through such individual pursuits as jogging and going to the gym. At the University blues dinner, the majority of the blues awarded are for individual sports. There used to be a lot of rugby players but you had to play team sport and there was a certain amount of pressure to play rugby. There was a time when boys basically played rugby and cricket; there might have been five or six sports available at secondary school, now there's 20 or 30.

'People are more individualistic these days or at least under pressure to appear so and a lot of potential athletes don't play any more. In my day no one ever talked about self-esteem and so on; you just did what was in front of you. People are far more aware of themselves than they were 20 or 30 years ago. My 15-year-old granddaughter is very adult in the way she thinks and talks.'

One consequence of this welter of change is that it is becoming harder to maintain a connection to the past. The nature of contemporary life and the range of entertainment choices mean that even sports-mad youngsters are unlikely to do much reading about the history of the game, the great matches and the great players. 'This is a here and now generation,' says former All Black manager Andrew Martin. 'They don't read books about the old players.'

Graham notes that for a lot of All Blacks, 'the 1949 tour is as distant as the Crusades' but sees this as a societal trend rather than a rugby one. During Graham's stint as manager of the New Zealand cricket team, the Australian left-arm fast bowler of the 1950s and 1960s, Alan Davidson, spent an hour at a net session with the Black Caps left-arm quickies Geoff Allott and Shayne O'Connor. Davidson took 186 test wickets at an average of 20.5, which, if my reading of Wisden is correct, is the best average among bowlers who have taken more than 150 test wickets. A genuinely great player, in other words. As Allott was having his back rubbed afterwards, he told Graham that it had been really worthwhile, he'd learned a lot and, by the way, who was that guy?

Why would teenagers today bother reading about the great players of the past when they could be watching the great players of the present live on television? Sport on television was in its infancy in 1973, both in terms of volume and technical quality. Those who stayed up to watch the live broadcast of the 1973 All Blacks-Barbarians match at Cardiff Arms Park were presented with a blank screen for most of the pulsating first half. With the advent of professional rugby, TV coverage has exploded. In 1995 there were 38 rugby matches shown on TVNZ of which only five — 13 per cent — were shown live. In 2000 there were 184 games on Sky TV and the free-to-air TV3, of which 124 were live. Only 18 per cent of the games shown on TV3 were not live.

Belich points out that 'nightlife on Main Street is one of the triumphs of restructuring although social "untightening" had begun earlier as symbolised by the demise of six o'clock closing in 1967'.

However, while the lawmakers loosened with one hand, they tightened with the other in the form of increasingly restrictive drink-driving laws accompanied by increasingly confrontational publicity campaigns portraying driving under the influence as the height of sociopathic behaviour.

Effective zero tolerance for drink-driving was an unwelcome development for sports clubs. While it would be difficult if not impossible to quantify the impact, it would seem a reasonable proposition that the drink-driving laws have played a significant part in the decline of sports clubs as centres of social activity. When I played club cricket in Auckland in the 1970s, we thought nothing of driving home from practice — across the Harbour Bridge in my case — with two or three quarts of DB Brown or Lion Red on board. And that was just practice for Saturday night.

'Drink-driving is another social change of huge significance as is the growth of the café, restaurant, entertainment world which simply didn't exist,' says Graham. 'This has made a huge difference to the way we behave. What impact has that had on the game? We spent hours at the club after games talking about rugby, debating the respective merits of players, remembering the history of the game.'

Drink-driving's partner in crime here is the feminisation of society. 'In my day,' says Graham, 'we never saw the women until it was time to go home. Today the players' partners aren't going to be sidelined; they want a joint social life.'

And, one would suggest, most of those partners' ideas of a night out would tend more towards a bar or restaurant or nightclub than the rugby club. Especially if they've got to spring for a taxi.

Some traditionalists will argue that rugby could and should have resisted this tide of change more stubbornly, but that sort of 'circle the wagons' mentality resembles the mind-set of ideologues in political parties who place a premium on doctrinal purity and denounce as a sell-out any attempt to tailor policy to public opinion.

The British Labour party spent some time in this ostrich-like posture during the Thatcher years, putting forward at one election a manifesto so wilfully at odds with the public mood that it became known as 'the longest suicide note in history'.

Whether by accident or design, rugby has gone with the flow quite successfully. Given how far into a corner rugby painted itself in 1981 and the depth of the resentment and anger towards the game in many sections of society, its widespread social acceptance today would seem to indicate that the game has made a sustained effort to engage with the community on a broad front.

'Rugby players weren't cool in the seventies and eighties,' says Graham, 'mainly due to the Springbok factor. These days, with their dreadlocks and the number 11 carved into their eyebrow and tattooed under their left tit and the attractive gear they wear, they are.'

On a flight out of Christchurch early in 2003, Graham found himself across the aisle from a 12-year-old Asian girl with a Crusaders flag. She was indeed a Crusaders fan even though she didn't live in Christchurch. She was most impressed to hear that he'd just been at a Crusaders training run: 'That was "cool".'

The nexus with white, male, conservative New Zealand — old New Zealand — wasn't sustainable. Times were a-changing and the game had no choice but to move with them and engage with the new forces and trends shaping New Zealand's future. Alvin Toffler coined the term 'culture shock' to describe the process of being overwhelmed by social, economic and technological change and the feelings of powerlessness and alienation as old certainties crumble and unsettling new realities are, seemingly, imposed in their place.

New Zealand rugby is still experiencing tremors of culture shock but, as Jock Hobbs acknowledges, we are past the point of no return: 'Inevitably there will be those who find it very difficult to understand that the changes have been primarily brought about by social and economic forces and the world we live in and will always hanker for the past. I'm not worried by the expectations. It's impossible to go back to how rugby was in every aspect in the sixties because a lot of those changes are outside rugby's control.

'I don't know how large that constituency is but you'll never be able to please some people because what they seek is unreasonable and unrealistic.' What is important, Hobbs feels, is 'that there's a vision for the game for the next 10 years that people can understand and embrace; that we work steadily towards that . . . But people also need to understand that there are changes to the game and the environment it's played in and certain business and commercial imperatives are part of the mix.'

In *The Judas Game*, Joseph Romanos recalls Brian Lochore being persuaded to come out of retirement to play a test against the 1971 Lions: 'So Lochore departed his Wairarapa farm on the Friday before the Saturday test. He left a note for his wife Pam on the kitchen table. It said, "Gone to play in the test match." No match fees to be discussed, no agents to be consulted. No Rugby Union spin doctors to give the story a positive slant. Lochore's pedigree was well known. If the All Black coach wanted him to play, and he said he would, then that was that. There was no need for him to confirm his availability in a series of Super 12 matches. Everything has changed. That third test was played at Athletic Park. The ground doesn't exist now.'

It's a nice story but it's not the whole story. Firstly, it's a sad commentary on New Zealand's depth that Lochore had to be pulled out of retirement and played out of position; secondly, the visitors from the Northern Hemisphere won that test 13–3; thirdly, their coach Carwyn James believed the selection of Lochore compromised the All Black tight-forward effort and was a key factor in the winning of the series.

But there was a happy ending. It's called the Westpac Trust Stadium.

3

The not-so-good old days

Just as professionalism does now, amateurism meant different things to different people.

To New Zealanders it meant playing for nothing. It meant that, no matter how seriously you took rugby, how hard you trained, how good you were and how far you went in the game, all you'd have to show for it was a scrapbook, a few stamps in your passport, some life-long friends and an obituary in the local paper when you passed away. Today we bemoan the player exodus to greener pastures overseas; in the old, amateur days, many players retired in their prime usually because they simply couldn't afford to keep playing. Allan Stewart, who at the age of 22 locked the All Black scrum with Colin Meads and in the view of experienced rugby writer Alex Veysey was 'certain to become one of New Zealand rugby's more memorable players', is one example. Stan Meads, regarded by his brother as the best lock he ever played with and according to Andrew Mulligan, 'in New Zealand circles often thought to be a harder-working forward than his distinguished sibling', is another.

While New Zealanders accepted the lack of remuneration as a fact of life, it was more an article of faith in England and other countries where the game was essentially a private school, middle-class activity — notably Scotland, Ireland and, oddly enough, Argentina. (Amateurism never really caught on in continental Europe; the French and Italians paid lip service to it but otherwise did things their way in the knowledge that, if challenged, they could always take cover behind the language barrier.) The purists across the Channel, however, held a burning belief that money was the root of all evil, a lethal virus from which the game had to be quarantined. In their view, the talent drain to rugby league wasn't a small price to pay, it was, in fact, a blessing: rugby was better off without people who weren't committed to the game's core values. Rugby league was their version of Devil's Island — an unspeakable place where undesirable elements went, never to return.

Their attitude — and the class assumptions underlying it — was summed up in this pronouncement attributed to an English bigwig of the 1960s: if players can't afford the privilege of playing rugby, they will have to do without it. Perhaps it's an apocryphal statement but if it wasn't said, it was certainly widely believed. By contrast, cricket in England was played by both the middle and working classes. Obviously the cloth-cap brigade couldn't afford to play county cricket six days a week for nothing but they were kept in their place by the distinction that was drawn between amateurs (gentlemen) and professionals (players). Up until the Second World War, this distinction extended to the scorecards published in newspapers: Mr W.R. Hammond was a gentleman, L. Hutton was not. Len Hutton, a masterful opening batsman from a Yorkshire mining village, played for long enough to become, in 1952, the first professional to captain England.

This class-based, ideological concept of amateurism held that one played for fun and it was therefore ungentlemanly if not downright unsporting to take it too seriously. When, in 1947, Denis Compton broke Jack Hobbs' record for centuries in an English season, an agitated admirer wrote to a cricket writer, 'I hardly expected [Compton] to score 18 hundreds in a season. I thought him too good a player for that sort of thing. Am I right in assuming that Denis played his usual cricket and the 18 hundreds just happened in the process?' The irony here is that Compton was a professional who happened to look and play like the devil-may-care gentleman sportsman from central casting.

In its favour this approach meant that eccentricity and otherworldliness were not necessarily barriers to high honours. A participant in the 1951 England-France game remembered the Twickenham dressing room toilets being full of smokers, which was presumably why one of the French wings had to relieve himself behind the goalposts at halftime. In *Kings Of Rugby*, his marvellous account of the 1959 British Lions tour of New Zealand, T.P. McLean related how Reginald Marques of Harlequins and England wouldn't be seen dead without his bowler hat and furled umbrella. In Sydney, some prankster appropriated the bowler and filled it with water, beer, oyster shells and dead marigolds. Unperturbed, Marques emptied out the refuse, persuaded the hotel to put the hat in the oven and 'drew it out some hours later, done to a turn'.

Playing Wairarapa-Bush, and with the raw-boned locals hot on attack, the Lions centre David Hewitt wandered over to his wing Tony O'Reilly. 'You know, Tony,' he said, 'I wish I had my camera with me. There are some lovely views around here. I think I'll come back afterwards to take some shots.'

McLean observed that 'the last such statement by an All Black centre under similar circumstances was made in 1822'.

An anachronism in a rampantly materialistic age, isolated, ridiculed and undermined from within by its own contradictions, amateurism began to fray at the edges. In an attempt to buy time or delay the inevitable, depending on whether they were optimists or realists, the pillars of the rugby establishment swallowed hard and made a deal with the devil: they allowed the game to go shamateur, by default. Shamateurism, as the term implies, was a deceit. The authorities turned a blind eye to under-the-table payments in the hope that by buying off the players with the proceeds from their clandestine transactions they could stall the push for professionalism while still, on the face of it, preserving amateurism.

When he was playing in Italy, John Kirwan said that, 'If I was getting paid, I'd be a bloody fool to admit it, wouldn't I?' This breezy cynicism perfectly captured the essence of the tacit understanding between players and administrators: if you don't tell, we won't ask. Take the money by all means but be discreet. Don't put us in a position where we can't ignore what's going on. Don't force us to do something about it.

Andy Haden, the original shamateur, tells a story that illustrates how it bound everyone involved in a conspiracy of hypocritical silence. For a period of about 20 weeks, he was being paid to play a supposedly amateur sport for two clubs in two different countries. During the week he was based in Rome, training with the Lazio club. On Thursday he'd fly to London and turn out for Harlequins on Saturday afternoon, then fly back to Rome to play for Lazio on Sunday.

'The Harlequins coach would ring me up and ask, "Can you make it?" I'd say, "Sure, send me the tickets," and my wife and I would have a few days in London. We'd fly over on mail flights — Air Sudan, Ethiopian Airways — and they'd reimburse me to the value of five or six tickets. A bit of money changed hands — not much. Before shooting out to Heathrow to get back to Rome, I'd have a beer in the clubrooms and Wing Commander Bob Weighell, the RFU's honorary secretary or whatever he was, one of England's delegates to the IRB and a Harlequins man, would make a beeline for me. He'd stand in front of me, remove his monocle, and study me for a few seconds. He always said the same thing: "I don't think you should come back next week, Haden." And I always replied, "Well, don't effin ask me." He was under pressure from the IRB because it was obvious what was going on with me turning up on Thursday and buggering off after the game. What was really

The greatest conversion since St Paul's? Andy Haden was a revolutionary in the amateur era but now has reservations about professional rugby.

Where are they now? John Hart (right) is in limbo and his successor Wayne Smith coaches English club Northampton.

NEWS MEDIA AUCKLAND

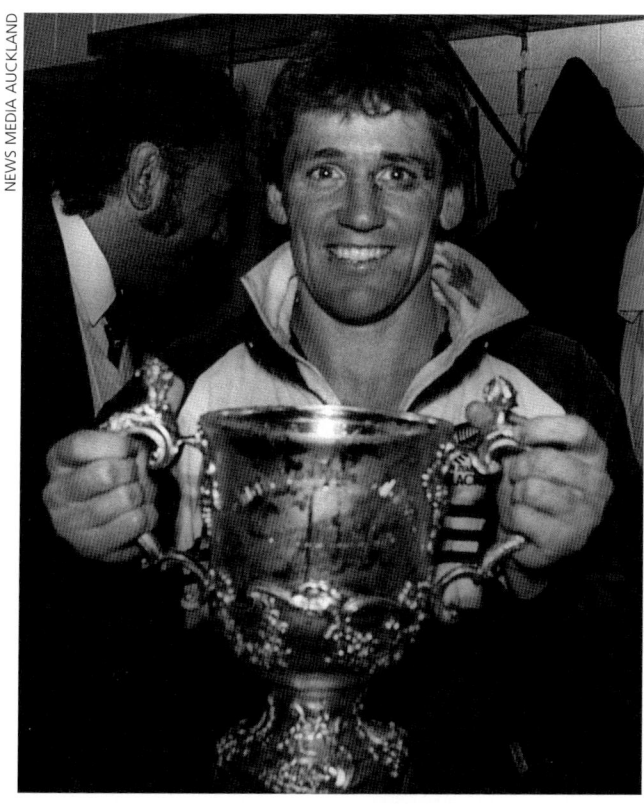

Left: *Every mother's dream, every Cavalier's nightmare. David Kirk with the William Webb Ellis trophy.*

Below: *You talking to me? Colin Meads goes eyeball-to-eyeball with the ref while John Graham (right) strikes an exasperated headmaster pose.*

NEWS MEDIA AUCKLAND

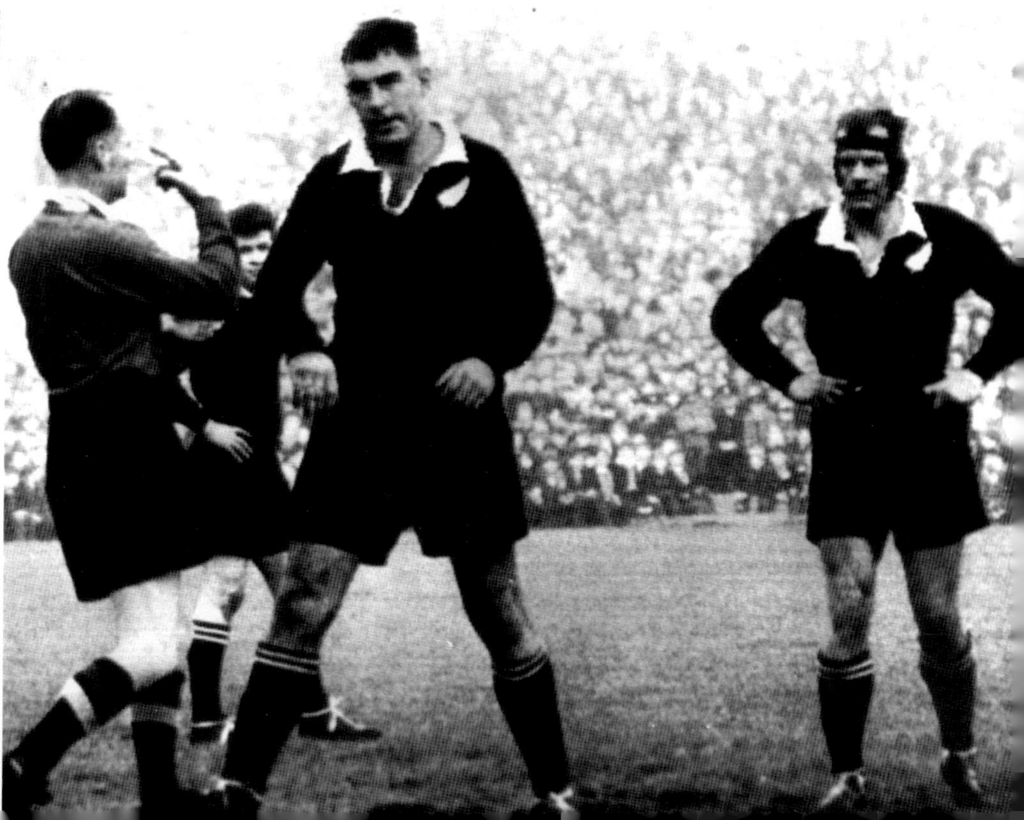

Above: *The face of heartland rugby — Marlborough's Ranfurly Shield-winning captain Ray Sutherland.*

Left: *Three amigos — Alan Sutherland (left), Tane Norton (centre) and Alex Wyllie in their infamous gaucho hats.*

Above: *Don 'The Boot' Clarke, the Jonah Lomu of his day in more ways than one.*

Left: *John 'D.J.' Graham, a man for all seasons.*

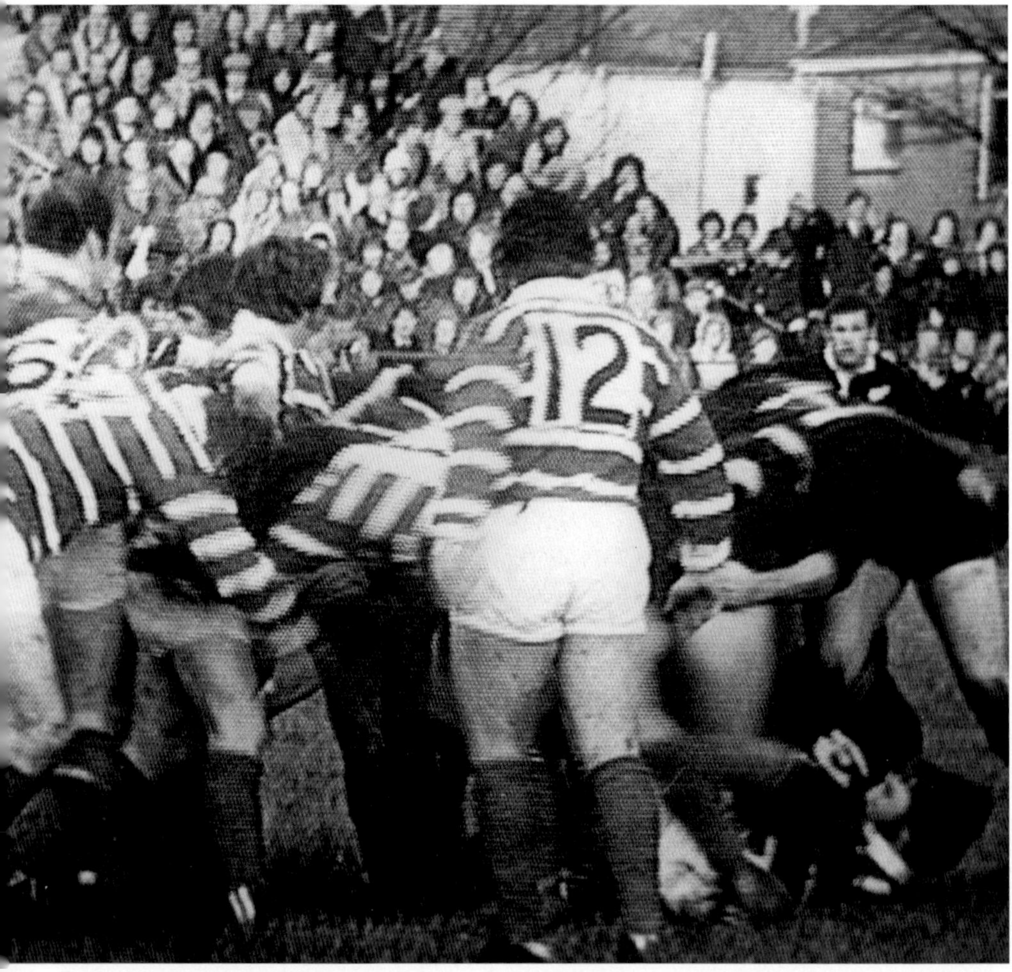

NEWS MEDIA AUCKLAND

NEWS MEDIA AUCKLAND

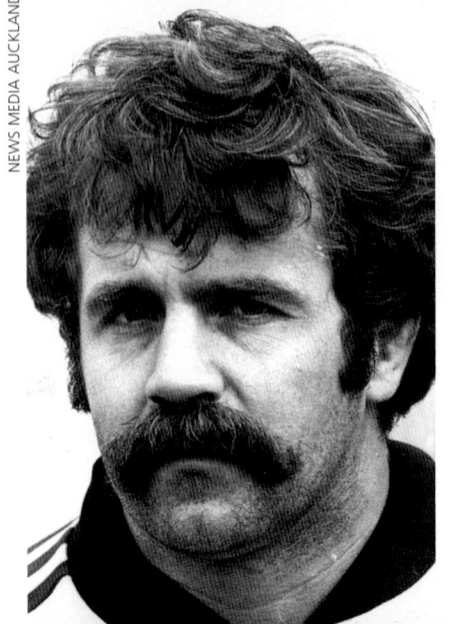

Above: *J.P.R. Williams (bottom right of picture) puts his head in harm's way for Bridgend against the 1978 All Blacks only for John Ashworth to confuse it with the ball. An easy mistake to make?*

Left: *Wallaby hit-man Steve Finnane.*

tormenting him was the fact that his precious Harlequins, one of the real toff clubs, was conniving in this under-the-table flouting of the amateur code. But it didn't just apply to me — everyone in the team was getting flicked some money and every club in London was paying players.'

Haden also recalls the International Rugby Board (IRB) centenary dinner, which followed a Northern Hemisphere versus Southern Hemisphere match at Twickenham in 1986. Sitting at a table near the front, he was unable to contain himself when Shiggy Kono, Japan's Mr Rugby, waxed lyrical on the amateur ethos while proposing a toast to amateurism.

'He began rambling about rugby in Japan where the game's development was based on large investments from commercial organisations that paid backhanders to Japan rugby to run the teams. Everyone knew these organisations recruited players from the universities on grossly inflated salaries but here he was going on about what a damn fine thing amateurism was. Shiggy saw me laughing and came over to me afterwards. I told him I thought he'd convinced most of the audience, but it was the biggest load of horseshit I'd ever heard. He flew into a rage and accused me of undermining Japanese rugby.'

Shamateurism depended on double-think so it's not surprising that when the All Black front row of Andy Dalton, Gary Knight and John Ashworth made money from their joint venture book, *The Geriatrics*, the NZRU could ban one, suspend another and let the third off scot-free.

Haden puts on an old-fart voice: 'That Ashworth's not really our cup of tea — let's ban him. Knight might have a year or two left in him — we'll give him a suspension. Dalton's a good chap, clean jawline, might make a good president of the NZRU one day and, besides, we need him to captain the side — we'll let him off.'

Shamateurism made serial deceivers of them all. Eventually,

Haden came to realise that the players had been drawn into a sticky web.

'I was one of those who pushed for professionalism because I was ashamed of the deceitful and demeaning system of under-the-table payments that had developed and which I thought was unworthy of the game,' he says. '[NZRU chairman] Eddie Tonks and [deputy chairman] Malcolm Dick were being put under a lot of pressure by the Brits to pull me into line. I told them the Brits were doing it themselves. They went off to the IRB and told them that and were told that I was bullshitting. When they came back and passed the message on, I went out and got 20 affidavits, 20 sworn statements from players in similar circumstances, including Kiwis playing in Italy, to back it up. The names were protected unless it was absolutely essential to reveal them in confidence. I gave them to Tonks and Dick to take to the IRB. When they told the IRB what they had, the other delegates said they didn't want to see the evidence. Next item please.

'They had 20 years warning that professionalism was coming — I'd been telling them for that long — but they were still taken unawares. We'd been pushing them to address professionalism and the fact that the game was dirty with under-the-table payments but in those days being a professional meant something nefarious. Amateurism, which is today considered irrelevant, was something to be treasured.'

Furtive and demeaning though it was, shamateurism worked after a fashion because there was something in it for both sides. The players pocketed some money — as NZRU deputy chief executive Steve Tew puts it, 'The guys who went to Italy and France are less grumpy about professionalism not being backdated.' What is more, the administrators were able to put off the evil day until 1995 when the citadel of amateurism collapsed like the walls of Jericho with a handful of hard-nosed Australian businessmen and their chequebooks in the roles of Gideon and his trumpet.

The Not-so-good Old Days

Some traditionalists are unimpressed by the extravagant movement — and points-scoring — in many matches nowadays. The game, they complain, has become 'airy-fairy'. There are two sub-texts to this charge: the first is that the game is now driven by marketing imperatives and is becoming more and more a branch of the entertainment industry rather than an earthy sporting contest. The second is that in the rush to make rugby more appealing to the casual, uncommitted audience, it is being sanitised and robbed of the very quality which has for a hundred years fired New Zealanders' passion for the game — the physical struggle of 'good, old-fashioned forward play'. Leaving aside the dubious validity of this contention, it represents nostalgia at its most selective because it skates over the fact that much old-fashioned rugby, particularly at international level, was grindingly dull.

When the New Zealand Maoris played the 1959 British Lions, the whistle was blown 227 times: there were 72 lineouts, 35 scrums and 42 penalties. Says John Graham, who played 53 games for the All Blacks between 1958 and 1964, 'Look at the scores — six–nil, six–five. We played the game in the forwards and the order went out to sew the ball up and close the game down.'

On their 34-match tour of Britain, Ireland and France in 1963–64, the All Blacks defeated Ireland 6–5, Wales 6–0, England 14–0, France 12–3 and drew with Scotland 0–0. They averaged one try per test. Only in the Barbarians match, the tour's finale, did this outstanding side let its hair down, scoring eight tries in a 36–3 win.

Mulligan regretted that they didn't approach every game in this spirit, commenting prophetically, 'Unfortunately the enjoyment never went to their heads, as in the Baa Baa match, but when it does one day, the All Blacks will be both invincible as well as aesthetic.'

It could be argued that that was how everybody played rugby in those days. It could be argued that New Zealanders would readily accept boring rugby in 2003 if it delivered All Black dominance.

It could be argued that the fans who packed the grounds back in the 1950s and 1960s — no live television then — had quite different expectations from today's spectators. Yet *Kings Of Rugby* shows that the New Zealand rugby public of 1959 hungered for a more vibrant and attacking style of play from the men in black. When what they got was more of the same — suffocating forward play and the siege-gun goal-kicking of Don 'The Boot' Clarke — they switched their support to the visitors who sought to win by using their backs to score tries.

Of the first test at Carisbrook which the All Blacks won 18–17 — six Clarke penalties to four tries by the Lions' outside backs, McLean wrote, 'Shall one ever forget the cry of "Red! Red!" which burst from 40,000 throats when D.B. Clarke had placed his sixth and what proved to be the winning penalty goal of the match? Here was an expression, from a community which had always honoured forward play, of a distaste for forward play supplemented by goal-kicking, which had produced so fortuitous and distasteful a result. Not one person in the crowd, perhaps not one true lover of rugby in New Zealand, would have been in the least distressed or dismayed if the Lions had scored the try the tremendous chants so much encouraged them to attempt.'

In his final chapter, McLean described crowd behaviour during the fourth test at Eden Park that would be unthinkable today: 'Now and again, through the second half, the cries would take up spontaneously among the thousands of spectators on the terraces. "Red! Red!" The chant would begin in a small group. Like a flame, it would spread until, in a minute or two, thousands would be uttering the cry of encouragement. It was the ultimate tribute. More, it was a signpost into the future; for if thousands upon thousands of New Zealanders could bring themselves freely and voluntarily to encourage the foe, it demonstrated the widespread belief that New Zealand was embracing unfortunate ideas and tactics.'

Five minutes from time, with the Lions, who were down three–

nil in the series, ahead 9–6 (three tries to two penalties), Clarke lined up a penalty kick to draw the game 'in utter, one might almost call it miserable, silence'. When the kick went wide 'a deepening roar broke out around the ground . . . the strain in the sounds around the ground was relief — relief for the Lions' sake'.

Reflecting on the phenomenon of a New Zealand crowd willing one of their superstars to miss a kick that would have saved the All Blacks from defeat, McLean concluded, 'The unpleasant, unpalatable and unavoidable fact was that the world champion nation was neither playing a game suitable to its station nor looked capable of playing such a game.'

It was, said McLean, 'the greatest tour — as measured by public interest — of antipodean history'. Clearly many, if not most, of those spectators parted with their money to see the visitors rather than their own side.

For a variety of reasons, not the least of which is that the public today simply wouldn't turn on their televisions let alone buy a ticket for the dubious privilege of watching 10-man rugby, the game is now much more of a spectacle. (Law changes, particularly those which discouraged kicking into touch on the full from outside the 22, increased the value of a try relative to a penalty goal and permitted lifting in the line-out, obviously played their part.) However, what McLean's reporting makes plain is that it was possible to play attacking ball-in-hand — and effective — rugby well before the penny dropped in this country.

Even though the paradigm shifted in the 1960s, particularly under the influence of Fred Allen who imposed 15-man rugby on the All Blacks, in 1971 another Lions team entranced the public and made the All Blacks look pallid and pedestrian. And this time there was no superboot to save them.

The following year, in a slim paperback called *The Lions Speak*, the Lions' coach Carwyn James delivered a withering assessment of our game: 'I thought [the New Zealand pattern] was fairly predictable. It hasn't changed much in the last ten years. We were very lucky that this kind of archaic thinking was still persisting in New Zealand. [New Zealand has] lost sight of the value of the quick transference of ball from scrum-half to wing. They could not do this — none of them could do this. It was interesting to watch some of the film of the tour and see how bad the New Zealand handling was.'

Although men such as J.J. Stewart, Jack Gleeson and Graham Mourie strove to expand the All Black game, the teams of the 1970s rarely ignited. The pyrotechnics still tended to be imported. No one who was there will forget the All Blacks being run ragged by a supercharged Australian team at Eden Park in 1978 or the action replay courtesy of the French at the same venue a year later. For all their honest endeavour and good intentions, the All Blacks were, on both occasions, outshone by opponents whose attack was on an altogether different level.

The wheel has turned. It's not such a stretch to suggest that New Zealand is now the Brazil of rugby and only a very befuddled Welshman very late at night would even contemplate the old jibe of last resort: 'Well, you might be good but you're boring.' Former Welsh fly-half Jonathan Davies regarded the back-play of the 2002 All Blacks who toured Europe as the most exciting and innovative he'd seen since 1995, when New Zealand electrified a watching world and in the process persuaded Rupert Murdoch to underwrite the professionalisation of Southern Hemisphere rugby.

It's easy to forget that we were served some pretty dismal fare in the good old days just as it's easy to take for granted the spectacle now dished up week in, week out. As former All Black captain David Kirk wrote in his 1997 autobiography *Black and Blue*: 'Watching the recent Super 12 games we are watching games that almost routinely include passages of play that would have astonished and ravished spectators when I was growing up.'

The Not-so-good Old Days

'Good, old-fashioned forward play' is often a euphemism for a bit of how's your father, which in turn is often a euphemism for dirty play of which there was far too much in the good old days. While some former players suffer from a need to complain at regular intervals that the game is 'going soft' and some journalists demand the injection of 'mongrel' from the safety of their ergonomic chairs, the game is far healthier for having been cleaned up. Thuggery was a two-fold blot on the game: firstly in the ugliness of the fouls committed and, secondly, in the acrimony and dispute they provoked.

Just as shamateurism made serial deceivers of players and administrators alike, dirty play generated hypocrisy like a rubbish tip generates stench. It was the age of the double standard: everyone found ways to excuse or downplay — or simply deny — their own players' misdemeanours while condemning those of their opponents.

Steve Finnane played prop for New South Wales and the Wallabies during the late 1970s but is largely remembered by many for what he achieved with his fists. While obviously an accomplished technician, Finnane was also a master of the black art of the phantom punch, the one the victim never sees coming, the one boxers fear. In Wales they remember him for breaking Graham Price's jaw in the first scrum of a Wales-Australia test in Sydney in 1978 and, for an encore, laying out halfback Terry Holmes. He outraged Aucklanders by poleaxing a promising young lock named Allan Craig with an over-the-shoulder punch at Eden Park. The injury which resulted effectively put an end to Craig's career. The Auckland Rugby Union sent film of the incident to their New South Wales counterparts, demanding that action be taken. Nothing happened. One man's thug is another man's warrior and many of his countrymen regard Finnane as a key figure in the rise of Australian rugby. By fighting fire with fire

A WHOLE NEW BALL GAME

— never mind that it was often a case of his flame-thrower against the other bloke's throwaway lighter — Finnane supposedly dissuaded players in other countries from the notion that Aussies were susceptible to intimidation.

(On his retirement Finnane, a lawyer who was known to warn journalists that they should keep the laws of defamation in mind when writing about him, produced an autobiography entitled *The Game They Play In Heaven*. If they play it the way he played it, then heaven is a rather different place to the one we learned about at Sunday School.)

On the flip side, during a decade in Sydney I didn't meet a single Australian rugby follower who could be persuaded that Colin Meads was a great player. In their eyes he was a dirty player, end of story. Australians associate Meads with one thing and one thing only: his apparent attempt to tear Wallaby scrumhalf Ken Catchpole limb from limb. Catchpole had one leg trapped in a ruck and when Meads got hold of the other one and yanked on it, 'I was driven into a splits position under enormous pressure. I could feel the muscles stretch like rubber bands reaching the end of their elasticity and snapping.'

The resultant injury effectively ended Catchpole's career.

In 1976 New Zealanders were rightly appalled by the action of the Springbok lock Moaner van Heerden who planted his boot on Peter Whiting's head while he was pinned in a ruck. Yet two years later when the great Welsh fullback J.P.R. Williams, captaining his club side Bridgend, had his face punctured by an All Black's sprigs, the management and team closed ranks behind the perpetrator, John Ashworth. A number of paper-thin and contradictory explanations were proffered, including that Ashworth had mistaken J.P.R.'s muddied head for the ball. The nature of the times and the heat generated by the incident were such that as intelligent an observer of the game as New Zealand writer Spiro Zavos devoted several pages of his 1979 book *After The Final Whistle* to clearing Ashworth of any responsibility and laying into J.P.R. and Welsh rugby generally. As the New Zealand management did at the time, Zavos came dangerously close to suggesting that Williams got what he deserved — not that it was in any way intentional, of course. Some of the supporting evidence — for example, assertions that Williams was an 'ultra-physical' player and prone to 'hollywoods' — has more than a faint whiff of an accused rapist's lawyer dwelling on the shortness of the victim's skirt.

The simple fact of the matter was that if the Williams whose face was stamped on had been B.G. rather than J.P.R., if the incident had taken place at Eden Park, if the opposition camp had subsequently been not merely unapologetic but defiantly, provocatively so, it would have caused fury.

But that was how it went in the good old days. We were hard — uncompromising even — but fair; the thugs were all on the other side. Ugly incidents were commonplace and the aftermath — the accusations and counter-accusations, the refusals to acknowledge a degree of fault or express a hint of contrition, the mealy-mouthed defences of the indefensible — was even uglier. We are well rid of it, whatever the old war-horses might say. Now when Troy Flavell stamps on Greg Smith's face, the deed is seen for what it is and no one tries to give it another name.

But these things were mere blemishes on the face of old rugby. The South African connection was a hideous disfigurement.

The tide began to turn against our liaison with apartheid in 1960 when 150,000 New Zealanders signed a 'No Maoris, No Tour' petition. But rugby hung tough for another two decades, determined to preserve the great rivalry whatever the cost to the game and the country. Prime Minister Norman Kirk stopped the Springboks coming here in 1973, a decision that came back to haunt Labour at the 1975 election. Given Robert Muldoon's combative personality and populist instincts, his refusal to stop the All Blacks going to

South Africa in 1976 was inevitable from the moment various Commonwealth countries, some of whose democratic credentials didn't bear close examination, threatened New Zealand with retribution if the tour went ahead. It went ahead and was a diplomatic disaster.

Muldoon's populism and damn-the-torpedoes style encouraged this unhealthy love affair to proceed to its traumatic conclusion during the 1981 South African tour. Between the extremes of redneck — and Red Squad — bloody-mindedness and the self-righteous fanaticism of the anti-tour movement's radical wing, women and the middle class, as James Belich has noted, came out onto the streets for the first time. Rugby would pay a heavy price, in terms of youngsters steered away from the game, for getting offside with all those middle-class women.

After protesters forced the abandonment of the second match of the tour, in Hamilton, Colin Meads told reporters from *The Listener*, 'I wish all those guys had to wear a sign on their chest saying "protester". I'd like to kill two or three of the bastards.' This was the dead end of the cul-de-sac down which rugby had been driven by its obsession, a truth acknowledged 15 years later by another King Country farmer, the then Prime Minister Jim Bolger, a Muldoon protégé. The tour, he said, was a mistake that had 'reached into — and often divided — families, friends and communities throughout New Zealand, perhaps more than anything else in our recent history'.

In *Paradise Reforged*, Belich wrote that were 'seven major issues of contestation and protest in the 1967–85 period: homosexual law reform, Vietnam, abortion, nuclear power, Maori, environment, rugby with South Africa — the last of the big seven liberal v conservative contests and arguably the most intense.' Rugby — predominantly white, almost exclusively male, with a gerrymandered electoral system weighted in favour of the smaller, rural unions — was always going to back the conservative horse which, as it turned out, ran second in all seven starts.

This tumultuous saga had a sleazy footnote in 1986 when the Cavaliers slunk off to South Africa behind the NZRU's back. They received little support, even from within the die-hard rugby community. The stalwarts understood that this particular game was up. Besides, this was no doomed crusade, admirable — despite its folly — for its principled self-sacrifice.

'[The public] didn't see [the Cavaliers] as honourable,' wrote David Kirk who was demonised by some of his once and future team-mates for opting out and becoming the poster boy for New Age rugby. 'How could they be fighting for our honour when they had their back pockets stuffed with cash? Perhaps the memory of the angst and violence from the previous tour had an effect. For all that grief and moral self-examination to be reduced to a mercenary exchange — it hit the wrong note.'

'Mercenary' is the appropriate word, for what were the Cavaliers if not guns for hire in mock uniforms shoring up a beleaguered and discredited regime?

Although they were only a footnote to the South African drama, the Cavaliers did foreshadow the last great upheaval of the pre-professional era — the WRC attempt to asset-strip rugby and create a rival game. As Kirk wrote, if the All Blacks had gone to the WRC 'they would have been 15 guys in hooped shirts called the Kiwi Cavaliers or whatever and they wouldn't have felt they owed their supporters anything and their feeling would have been reciprocated'.

Just as the Cavaliers attempted to justify their covert action by claiming they were striking a blow for freedom, so the All Blacks in 1995 glossed their defection to the WRC with a lot of self-serving guff about their frustration with the inertia and short-sightedness of administrators and their desire to take the game to a new level and a global audience. The reality was that they were driven by the money and their contempt, bred by familiarity, for those running the game.

In his biography *On The Loose*, Josh Kronfeld described how Laurie Mains laid it out for the players: 'Mains told us he had our interests at heart, that the WRC deal was a good one and that the NZRU had mucked players about for too long.' With deadpan understatement, Kronfeld added, 'As Laurie was still All Black coach, I thought that was a surprising position to take.'

With the self-revealing candour and rough language that permeate his biography, Norm Hewitt pronounced this dismissive verdict on the NZRU's efforts to persuade the players not to defect: '[Brian] Lochore gave the "ra ra" speech but seemed out of touch with where the game should be going. I mean, I know the guy was a great AB and a legend and all that but we needed more than a call to tradition. If you live in the past then you get buried there . . . Jock Hobbs I found really off-putting. He begged the players to stay. It seemed really weak to me. It was all "the game will die without you" crap instead of "look we've got something better for everybody".'

When Jeff Wilson and Kronfeld broke ranks to sign with the NZRU, Hewitt's first reaction was '"You Judas bastards." All that crap about loyalty to the game was just so much bullshit. They signed for the NZRU because that was the best option for them personally. When I thought about it, I thought, "Well, fair enough. I guess we're all doing the same. Doing what's best for us."'

Professionalism has landed rugby with a new set of problems, but it is a more honest and humane system than the head-in-the-sand callousness of loading an ever greater training and playing burden on unpaid sportspeople, of expecting the players to be professional in every respect except remuneration. As Hewitt put it: 'I was expected to be a professional, I was expected to train like one, play like one, put myself at risk of permanent injury, give up all work opportunities, face long separations from family and friends . . . but still remain an amateur.'

Professionalism did not create player greed. The players had long since ceased to be selflessly pristine, playing the game for the joy of it and the honours one could aspire to. The challenge facing administrators is to resist that greed when it threatens to consume resources needed to maintain and nurture the base of the game and to safeguard rugby's place in our hearts so that boys continue to dream of being All Blacks rather than millionaires.

4

End of the world, part one

The iron law of sport and gravity is that when you stop going up, you start coming down.

In 1997 the All Blacks were all alone on the mountaintop. In 1998 they lost five tests in a row. The sudden, steep decline shocked a public who had gorged on success during the previous three years and come to believe that New Zealand dominance was the natural order of things. In hindsight there were warning signs: the All Blacks had conceded 24 points without reply in the second half of their final 1997 Tri-Nations match and were stretched by England on their successful but problematic end-of-year tour.

Ironically some of the problems stemmed from the presence on tour of two players who had been the key components of the all-conquering team: captain Sean Fitzpatrick and his lieutenant Zinzan Brooke. Fitzpatrick toured despite a knee operation that had caused him to miss the NPC and Brooke was selected even though he'd announced that he was retiring from international rugby. When Fitzpatrick struggled — mostly in vain — to get on the field and Brooke treated the tour like a long goodbye, coach John Hart and his selectors were exposed to the charge of short-term thinking, of allowing their loyalty to and reliance on these great players to get in the way of a cold, dispassionate judgement about what was best for the team going forward. Or as one or two malcontents on the fringe of the test team chose to see it, they were guilty of favouritism.

At that time Hart's co-selectors and assistant coaches were Ross

Cooper and Gordon Hunter. When I interviewed Hunter, the one-eyed Dunedin detective, in October 2001, he was already suffering the ravages of the cancer that would carry him off within a matter of months. He was hatchet-faced and thin and barely able to eat solid food. He had found religious faith — which, as he sardonically noted, had done little to stem the flow of vivid profanity from beneath his cowpuncher moustache — and insisted that he would overcome the disease. Occasionally one saw a shadow of despair fall across this most robust and positive of men but he was too alert, too emotional, too tough to withdraw into it. If ever a man raged against the dying of the light, it was Gordon.

With characteristic generosity, Norm Hewitt dismissed Hunter as 'a nodder' — a yes-man, a Hart stooge. In fact, he had far too much confidence in his own knowledge and understanding of the game and his relationships with players to be anyone's acolyte. Indeed, almost four years on, Hart's decision to, as he saw it, reinvigorate the All Black coaching set-up by replacing Hunter and Cooper with Wayne Smith and Peter Sloane still rankled. But Hunter was a soldier; he bit the bullet and got on with the job of selecting. And he stood by every decision he was party to with a splendid disregard for the second-guessing and Monday morning quarterbacking of what he called 'the minnows'.

His view of those contentious selections was that 'leadership was an acute issue. For years Zinzan had been the mastermind behind the magnificent Auckland performances and he'd been a key figure in our planning and execution. In hindsight, maybe we should have made him captain when Fitzy couldn't get on the track. He certainly took every opportunity to enjoy himself and took some of the younger ones along with him, but if we have to take flak for supporting him, so be it. Maybe it cost a victory in the last game but we got a draw and if you look at the majestic performances this man put in, it's a bit sad if we're going to be slagged for that.

'It's all very well in hindsight to say that Fitzy shouldn't have gone but the medical advice was that he was up to it. We'd seen him play 80 minutes at the Melbourne Cricket Ground when beforehand we were being told he had no show. Of course we backed Sean: he was such an intimidating figure, a leader and a winner, why wouldn't we?

'We compromised on the basis of loyalty in the cases of Michael Jones, Zinzan and Frank Bunce and perhaps in the end it cost us. Perhaps we weren't close enough to the players to know how they were feeling about it because we were doing our job, and John was going through the anxiety of building up to shafting me and Ross — it's hard being close to people you know you're going to do over. I knew that John's philosophy was continual improvement and the team needed specialist technical assistance, for instance in the information technology area, that he knew I didn't have.'

For his part, the only thing Hart would do differently if he had his time over again is make Brooke captain: 'He was obviously the best person for it. We discussed it with him at length but in the end we decided we had to move forward. I should have managed it better but whatever people say about Zinzan on that tour, it's not an issue with me. I have great respect for that man. [Justin] Marshall was playing with real authority but that was an interim appointment. Our view was that we just had to get through the tour, have a break and regroup with Fitzy back in harness. At that stage no one saw his injury as career-threatening.'

But the apparently indestructible Fitzpatrick, the round-faced youth who went from Baby Black to the dominant personality in the international game cowing one opponent after another with his unquenchable appetite for confrontation, had reached the end of the line.

Fitzpatrick, Brooke and Frank Bunce were the All Blacks'

heart, soul, muscle and mind. They were the thinkers and the leaders who inspired team-mates and intimidated opponents. While it was appropriate in a way that Fitzpatrick and Brooke, comrades-in-arms in so many battles for Auckland and the All Blacks, should bow out together, it was a massive blow to Hart who had overcome their initial suspicion to form a strong, mutually beneficial relationship. He developed their leadership skills by bringing them into his management process and exposing them to his planning and organisational expertise; they, in turn, made major contributions tactically and on the training field. They were also an important bridge between the management and the team. That connection was never as strong after their departure when the results deteriorated and the remaining veterans came under pressure from the new generation.

While the management was still coming to terms with this double whammy, the third member of the leadership triumvirate disappeared. Frank Bunce had also made a significant tactical contribution, in addition to patrolling the midfield like an aircraft carrier, as the platform for strike weapons like Jonah Lomu, Jeff Wilson and Christian Cullen. In Hunter's opinion, 'Bunce was more important than the other two — we never replaced him.'

'We'd lost Zinny and Fitzy,' says Hart. 'Then we lost Frank in unfortunate circumstances: he went to look at an overseas contract without telling us. When the media got hold of it, they hammered us. Michael Jones was near the end but still an important part of the team; Ian Jones was coming under pressure to hold his place. You don't plan to lose four or five of your leaders in one hit and we lost a lot of strength and struggled to rebuild.'

The 23-year-old Taine Randell succeeded Fitzpatrick. In an ideal world, his elevation would have come two years later but it nevertheless met with general approval. He'd had a wonderful year in the test team, he was intelligent, personable and seemed to have been groomed for the role, having captained teams from an early age and led the New Zealand Under-21s and the Highlanders.

'We didn't make him captain on the 1997 tour,' says Hart, 'because at that stage we thought it best to let him continue to develop as a player. Everyone could see Taine's leadership potential so he was the logical person to step up. Age wasn't the issue, experience was. He'd been an All Black since 1995, been on three major tours and made himself part of the All Black test set-up.'

The team that took the field for the first test of 1998 — against a second-string English team at Carisbrook — still had a familiar, formidable look to it. The somewhat scratchy performance — the All Blacks won 64–22 after an English forward was sent off on the half-hour — was put down to rustiness, but there had been no rust evident in the Australian system when they'd flogged the same opposition 76–0 a fortnight earlier. When the trans-Tasman rivals met in Melbourne three weeks later, the All Blacks went down 24–16, the first of the infamous five defeats. It seemed to me a game that could have gone either way but when I saw Hart afterwards, he wasn't inclined to look on the bright side. Perhaps he'd seen the future and it wasn't a pretty sight. Or perhaps he sensed that the All Blacks were running out of luck. They'd had a try disallowed during a period of play when they seemed to be gaining the upper hand. To the naked eye, it looked like the correct decision but replays suggested that Joeli Vidiri didn't knock the ball on in the lead-up.

Luck had gone the All Blacks' way during the previous two years: the coaches' analysis of the 1996 results showed that instead of nine wins out of 10, it could very easily have been five wins, four losses and a draw. They'd also fared significantly better on the injury front than their Tri-Nations rivals. In 1998 the wheel turned.

'We might have won a couple of those games with the video replay technology they employ now,' says Hart. 'Jeff Wilson would have been awarded a try when he dived on the ball just short — as the replays showed — of the dead ball line in a very tight game in Wellington and James Dalton was awarded the winning try in Durban even though he clearly dropped the ball. That was a crushing loss for us because we'd brought some new guys in and prepared well. We were under siege then and it got to Taine. It would have got to anyone, I don't care who they were.'

(Another crushing blow came out of that game in the form of the injury that ended Olo Brown's career. His departure was felt every bit as much as those of Fitzpatrick, Brooke and Bunce. According to Hunter, 'Olo was a huge loss — your tighthead prop is the most important player in the team.' And in Brown the All Blacks had the best in the business. The evergreen England prop Jason Leonard described him thus: 'He was squat and immensely strong. All he wanted to do was drive your head through your spine — every scrum, relentlessly. You had to meet him head on, every scrum.' The tragic death of the Waikato loose forward Aaron Hopa, who'd gone on the end-of-year tour and featured prominently in Hart's World Cup plans, was yet another blow. Said Hunter, 'John had a vision for Aaron because of his height, ability and high standards.')

How quickly it unravelled. In 1996/97 the All Blacks had won six out of seven against South Africa and five out of five against Australia. Now they couldn't buy a win over the same opponents. The losing streak included a drubbing at the hands of Australia in Christchurch. Although a couple of late tries made the score respectable, it was one of those rare games that the All Blacks never looked like winning and it forced the selectors' hand. Out went Walter Little, Michael Jones, Ian Jones and Craig Dowd.

'The old guard were getting old,' said Hunter. 'They weren't good enough.'

After five losses the national mood was deeply sour. The Taliban of Talkback — as some brave soul dubbed Murray Deaker and his cohorts — bayed for blood and a faction on the NZRU board launched a push to remove Hart. Shortly before the decisive board meeting, the viscerally anti-Hart rugby writer Bob Howitt proclaimed that Hart was history — the numbers were against him. Perhaps one or two board members did what people often do in such situations: told the lobbyists what they wanted to hear, then went and did the opposite.

Hart survived, not quite intact. The perception was abroad that he'd expanded his role beyond that of the traditional rugby coach to something akin to a soccer manager, overseeing all aspects of the team's programme on and off the field. He'd got too big for his boots, in other words, and needed cutting down to size. The board's response was to instruct Hart to leave management to the manager and focus on coaching.

'The NZRU made us change the way we operated,' says Hart, 'with Mike Banks being the man in charge as manager, and me being required to coach the backs instead of Wayne Smith. It was silly and knee-jerk because it didn't take into account why we'd structured the thing as we had and what our strengths were. We'd structured a good management team and we would have got better.'

Even at the time it seemed perverse that the board should conclude that the solution lay in curtailing Hart's involvement in the area he regarded as his strength — management — and increasing it in the area he regarded as his weakness — hands-on technical coaching. He had, after all, brought in Smith and Sloane, two highly regarded technicians, to upgrade the technical coaching element of team preparation but now, at the board's insistence, Smith's role was downgraded to that of technical analyst. Scarcely a year later the board would decide that Smith was a good enough coach to be put in charge of the All Blacks. It's hard not to draw the conclusion that the board got it wrong on both counts: if they really believed that a greater degree of technical coaching expertise was required, they should have followed through on their own logic and either pushed Hart into an overall management role, leaving Smith and Sloane to train the team, or removed him altogether.

The fallout also engulfed the young captain. Randell had led the All Blacks to defeat after defeat, he'd had to face the media music afterwards, he'd had to soldier on without much support from the shrinking core of senior players and he'd been in the eye of the storm of criticism. He was not yet 24. It would indeed have been extraordinary if he hadn't wondered what he'd got himself into.

The ensuing imbroglio is one of a number of sad or messy episodes that occurred during the grim years of 1998/99. Hart, obviously enough, was always somewhere near the scene of the crime and that was usually enough for his detractors. Some of them had been awaiting their opportunity for years and were determined to make the most of it while those who jumped on the bandwagon often did so with the zeal of the convert. Their version of events was that Hart, having decided that he wanted to rid himself of Randell, hawked the captaincy around the other contenders. When they all declined the poisoned chalice, he reluctantly went back to Randell, thereby compounding the original humiliation.

This is Hart's version: 'At the end of 1998, Taine told us that he didn't really want the captaincy and he repeated that early in 1999. I said let's wait and see how you go in the Super 12 and how you feel after a few games but, obviously, once he'd said that and repeated it, we had to start looking at alternatives. Peter Sloane, Gordon Hunter and I met Taine in Christchurch and told him we were looking at other options but that he was still in the picture. Robin Brooke's name was mentioned. There were only three options: Taine, Robin and Anton Oliver. I talked at length to Jeff Wilson but there was no way I offered him the job. He knew he wasn't the right person; he was, in fact, a strong supporter of Anton. At no stage did we discuss the captaincy with Robin, let alone offer it to him.

'Robin was coming to the end of his career but he was a hard man and had experience and was respected by the team, although whether that would have extended to him as captain is another matter. People said Anton was young but he was a leader and we would have put a whole structure around him. Sloane had had him in the Colts and was a strong supporter. Then a few things happened: Robin was seen to be one of the ringleaders of the opposition to Jed Rowlands at the Blues; Anton's father Frank and [Highlanders coach] Tony Gilbert talked him out of it and one can understand their rationale; unfortunately no one was looking at the rationale we were faced with. Taine was playing well and captaining the Highlanders well so we went back to him but the circumstances were sad.

'The SAS camp was about teamwork, leadership and seeing how people responded under pressure. They gave us a detailed assessment of people's leadership qualities and Taine was their strong recommendation. He's a highly intelligent rugby player and did a good job under difficult circumstances on the 2002 tour when he was on a hiding to nothing. I have regrets that we couldn't put the resources and strengths around him to make him successful because leadership is not about one person, it's a collective thing. But the point to note here is that if he hadn't come to us and brought up the issue, the whole question would never have arisen. We'd made our choice and he was it, through to the World Cup.'

Hunter, who was close to Oliver, 'went into his bedroom in his flat and pleaded with him to consider the captaincy. It was my belief that he was the only person who could've led the team to success at the World Cup and I still believe that even though he was young and inexperienced.'

Hunter considered the SAS boot camp to be 'a mad idea — the players lost so much weight. It was preparing them for war not to play rugby.' He did concede, however, that in early 1999 the All

Black management had to be — and be seen to be — innovative and proactive.

But controversy now attended everything Hart did. His sending home of three large Polynesians — Lomu, Vidiri and Isitolo Maka — was criticised as harsh and insensitive. Despite his lack of enthusiasm for the camp, Hunter saw it differently: 'They couldn't have done it, mentally — going into the bush and cooking up a feed on their billy cans. That's not their way. Hart had the brains and compassion to see that some people couldn't meet the fitness criteria but could still meet overall criteria.'

However Maka, the 120-kg Highlanders number eight who'd made such an impression during his 50 minutes on the field at Durban the previous August, did not reappear in the All Black frame and subsequently took himself off to France. The public humiliation, it was argued, destroyed his confidence and deprived the All Blacks of a 'go-forward' powerhouse who might have made all the difference at the World Cup.

Perhaps because Hunter's coaching career was over — he'd been deeply hurt when forced to stand down as Blues coach and was darkly unforgiving of all those involved in that decision — he was unwaveringly frank about players' shortcomings, both on and off the field. In my experience, coaches usually bite their tongues. Interviewing Hart, for instance, I was struck by his protectiveness, several years after the event, of players who'd done little to deserve it and, in some cases, gone out of their way to fan the flames of rancour in which he's been slow-roasted since 1999.

Hunter's verdict on Maka: 'Hart didn't drop Maka; Maka chose to drop himself by reneging on his self-discipline.'

The All Blacks rebounded. They put 70 points on Samoa and hammered a distracted French team by the eyebrow-raising scoreline of 54–7. Afterwards, the French coach Jean-Claude Skrela called them unbeatable, a poignant exaggeration given what lay ahead.

A WHOLE NEW BALL GAME

A Springbok team unsettled by the rift between coach Nick Mallett and captain Gary Teichmann was cleaned up by a record margin and the Wallabies were shoved around Eden Park in what was one of their two most emphatic defeats in the Rod Macqueen era (the other coming at the hands of the British Lions in 2001). The Tri-Nations championship was secured in Pretoria with Cullen, playing at centre in a reshuffled backline, scoring two tries.

Five convincing wins gave Hart some breathing space and muted debate about the merits of the positional switch involving Cullen and Wilson. Hunter, whose baby it was, argued that it was 'a fantastic idea. We saw the centre as first fullback, left wing as left fullback, right wing as right fullback and fullback as back fullback. The idea was that they should be interchangeable and have the same skill sets — the ability to kick a long ball, vision, strength on the tackle and the skill to move the ball back and forth across the field to retain possession.'

As Lomu worked his way back into form, the selectors were faced with the dilemma of 'four into three won't go'. The only way to get all four superstar outside backs — Cullen, Wilson, Lomu and Tana Umaga — into the starting line-up was to play one of them out of position and at the World Cup they opted to shift Cullen into centre. Once again with the benefit of hindsight, it could be argued that while the theory was okay, they got it wrong in the implementation and Umaga should have gone to centre, as Bunce suggested at the time. On the other hand, there's no shortage of pundits who continue to insist that Umaga is wasted at centre.

To Hunter, the whole issue was an irrelevance that only served to demonstrate that those who were preoccupied with it had failed to understand how the game had moved on: 'The point is players shouldn't allow themselves to be concerned with the number on their backs and that applies to the whole silly debate about whether Randell should be picked as a number eight.

End of the World, Part One

Taine did an outstanding job at six in 1997 when Michael Jones was injured but when Zin went, he got his chance at eight where he was capable of playing very well because of the way the game was going because of rule changes.

'Did it cause anxiety among all the minnows in our rugby fraternity? Tough. We didn't have time to go around explaining to everyone who doesn't understand these things.'

Hunter has a point. In the modern game, once the play moves away from the set pieces, players frequently take up positions that don't correspond to the numbers on their backs. George Gregan, for instance, often positions himself at first receiver. When the opposition is in possession, Andrew Mehrtens frequently drops back to fullback; when his team has the ball, Cullen frequently plays up in the line like a rugby league fullback while wings are as likely to be found sniffing around the back of the ruck as standing hands on hips out by the touchline, waiting for someone to give them the ball. Loose forwards are used as midfield ball carriers and midfielders compete for the ball at the breakdown like loose forwards. Those who believe Umaga is wasted at centre should consider his value as a midfield defender and contestor of possession in the tackle area. His immense contribution reflects the fact that he is virtually two players in one — midfield back and loose forward. Cullen did well at centre in the first big hurdle of the World Cup, the pool match against England, and I don't recall much criticism of the selection then. He didn't shine in the semi-final but then neither did too many of his team-mates, most of whom were playing in their preferred specialist positions.

But that ambush was still to come. With the Tri-Nations already won, the All Blacks breezed into Sydney bubbling with youthful confidence. Most New Zealanders assumed victory was a mere formality, and that complacency infected the team. Hart was uneasy after a slipshod final practice and his worst fears were borne out as the Wallabies repaid the thumping at Eden Park. The All Blacks got behind, then the heavens opened, making catch-up rugby even more difficult, but there were ominous signs nonetheless. When the pressure came on that night, they did not display the composure to warrant World Cup favouritism.

Which makes the hype, hoop-la and swagger surrounding their campaign all the harder to understand. Which brings us back to that symbol of everything that went wrong, the painted plane. People associate it with Hart but from all accounts it was the brainchild of Kevin Roberts, the Lion Breweries boss turned advertising man and NZRU board member. Although Hart got the blame, he was one of the last to know.

Hart: 'Although Mike Banks and I had monthly meetings with [NZRU chief executive] David Moffett and NZRU people, it wasn't until the meeting two days before the end of our final World Cup camp at Palmerston North that we were told about it. Moffett and Bill Wallace, the operations manager, informed us that they wanted 10 players released on Friday to go to Auckland for the unveiling of the plane and have their photos taken in front of it. That was the first time I'd ever heard of it. When he explained that the front row was on the plane I lost my cool. I've only had one worse stand-up row in rugby. I asked whether the players had been approached. They hadn't; maybe their contracts enabled the NZRU to do that without reference to them. I just wanted to know why the hell they'd done it, given that it ran counter to what we were about. I asked them to pull it back but they were committed to it. Then we had to talk to the players. I was in an invidious position: the players looked to the management to guard their interests but, on the other hand, I couldn't stand up in front of them and berate my — and their — employer. But the fact was I'd never been involved in any discussion about it and would never have supported it. That's why they didn't tell me.

End of the World, Part One

'We managed to get it down to five players. They wanted the front row but we made them take Auckland players who were heading up there anyway. The players said they wouldn't be photographed in front of the plane, which made a mockery of the whole exercise. They were pissed off and blamed us; perhaps they still do. I don't condemn Air New Zealand — they showed initiative — but it was a source of great discontent, particularly when we got over to the UK and the media made a meal of it. It certainly didn't help our campaign. We had a strong desire to protect our culture — humility was something we talked about a lot — but the plane blew us out of the water. Then when we got to the UK, we were ambushed by adidas — their stuff was everywhere.

'Marketing must match the culture and if you have a culture of humility, the way the team is marketed must reflect that. Clearly the painted plane didn't do that. Like everything else about that World Cup, it was easier to simply dump it on me. The NZRU never came out and said it was their idea. I was dumbfounded by their silence on this and other issues.'

The biggest of the 'other issues' was the break in the south of France. Mike Banks confirms that this was unanimously approved by the NZRU board before the team even left New Zealand.

'John and I wrote a comprehensive strategic plan that went in bound form to the board. Part of it included the time-out window and we chose the south of France because it seemed to offer a complete change of environment. That was understood by the board and there were certainly no questions raised.'

It might have stayed that way if Lomu's girlfriend hadn't crashed the party. When shots of the young lovers strolling hand in hand hit the media, all hell broke loose.

'We weren't aware that Jonah's girlfriend was coming,' says Banks. 'No one was more startled than the management team and it was an enormous disappointment and annoyance to us. I remember it very well: we were going somewhere in a van and Hart asked me what I was going to do about Jonah's girlfriend as if it was somehow my fault and responsibility. It pissed me off no end and was one of the very few times I got cross with John.'

'Every team had a gap of a week and did different things,' says Hart. 'Rod Macqueen gave the Wallabies three days off to do whatever they liked and some of them got into all sorts of shit which never came out. Going to the south of France seemed a way of breaking the monotony of being based in England and offered the prospect of some better weather. We stayed in three-star accommodation, not the bloody Ritz, and trained every day. Wives and girlfriends were excluded but that blew out when Jonah's girlfriend turned up unannounced. We had to send her away. People objected when they saw photos of the guys swimming in the sea but that was what we were there for.'

The degree of denial and backside-covering surrounding this episode was illustrated when Banks, at the behest of his union, subsequently stood for reappointment to the board. In the course of his presentation, one candidate delivered a call for transparency, citing the 'holiday' in the south of France as a glaring example of the lack of it and heaping ridicule on the management team. Banks didn't have the right of reply and no one else felt the need to set the record straight.

As if all that wasn't enough, Hart took a third hit when it was reported in the British press that a post-tournament victory parade was being organised in Auckland.

'It was raised at that same meeting with Moffett and co,' says Hart. 'It was the last thing we wanted to be talking about but they said the money side of it had to be organised in advance. I said it was nothing to do with the team. There were some discussions with the mayor and it leaked out and hit the papers so we had stories in the UK that the All Blacks were organising a victory parade before the tournament had even started. Who copped the blame? Me.'

But for the moment these things were rumbling away in the background, like a volcano trying to make up its mind whether or not to blow. What triggered the eruption was the semi-final loss. If that game had been won and the All Blacks had gone on to win the tournament, it all would have been forgotten. It's arguable that if the circumstances of the loss had been different — had the All Blacks just fallen short after a desperate see-saw battle, for instance, rather than inexplicably collapsed — the eruption would have been on a smaller scale. Of course, it hardly helped that the All Blacks were unbackable favourites and seemed to have the game under control at halftime.

In the lead-up to the tournament, former Wallaby coach Bob Dwyer labelled the French 'shot ducks'. A leading British rugby writer declared before the game that a French victory was simply beyond the realms of possibility. If neutrals saw it in those terms, one can only imagine the serene confidence with which New Zealanders settled down in front of their TVs.

Objectively, the widespread belief that the result was a foregone conclusion was hard to fathom, even given the 54–7 hiding earlier in the year and France's patchy form. France is, after all, one of rugby's big five and has a history of bucking the form guide. Besides, had everyone forgotten the rout in Sydney? Had anyone bothered to check the record-book? That victory took France's win/loss ratio against New Zealand during the 1990s to 50 per cent — four wins in eight games. Australia, by comparison, had won 10 of its 23 games against the All Blacks — 43 per cent — and South Africa, traditionally the hardest nut to crack, a measly four out of 15 — 26 per cent. Had anyone bothered to check France's World Cup record? In 1987, they knocked out the favourites, Australia, on their home patch to make the final. In 1991, they went out to eventual finalists, England, in the quarter-finals after a titanic physical confrontation. In 1995, they won the play-off for third place after coming desperately close to ousting the hosts and eventual winners, South Africa.

One writer called it 'the biggest upset in the entire history of rugby union'. Really? The record of the past 30 years should tell us that it is realistic to assume the All Blacks will lose one in three matches against France. The most sensible pre-match comment was that of the French player who said, 'The All Blacks often win but they don't always win.' At first glance, this seems like a Forrest Gump-style inanity masquerading as hick wisdom but in fact it's an eminently sensible attitude for anyone about to take on a better-credentialed opponent. It is certainly a far more rational approach to a two-horse race than taking it for granted, as so many people did, that one of the horses didn't have a hope in hell. The French are realists. They understand that you win some and you lose some. They accept that sometimes the force is with you and sometimes it isn't. And for reasons that even they couldn't fully explain, it was with them that afternoon at Twickenham.

So how did it look from up close? In his autobiography *Seasons Of Gold*, Jeff Wilson said the French 'run hot and cold . . . and on this occasion they were far too hot for us. That's the way it is in sport sometimes and that's what followers have to accept, as unpalatable as it may be.'

Hunter regarded Hart's pre-match team talk as 'the most amazing I've ever heard but the bus trip to the ground took 48 minutes and by the time we got there, the effect had worn off. He tried to get them up again in the dressing room but it wasn't the same. The game plan was flawed, the execution was flawed and the French had the time of their lives.'

And Hart? 'The game clearly raised leadership issues but, having said that, Umaga, Wilson and Mehrtens, probably our three best players at the tournament, played probably the worst 20 or 30 minutes of their careers. What can you do?'

Those seeking an explanation for what happened that afternoon could ponder this passage from Chris Laidlaw's rugby memoir concerning the third test against the Springboks at Lancaster Park in 1965 which the All Blacks lost 16–19, having led 16–5 at halftime. (Just for the record, the All Black pack that day was Lochore, Conway, Tremain, C. Meads, S. Meads, Gray, McLeod, and Whineray, which stacks up pretty well against the starting eight at Twickenham: Randell, Kronfeld, Thorne, Brooke, Maxwell, Dowd, Oliver, Hoeft.)

'"Overconfident!" cried one journalist. "All Blacks contemptuous of opposition," brayed another. Several even pointed to a vigorous Friday morning workout and by a series of deductive brainstorms declared "Overtrained". All this is typical of the journalistic need to provide for the reader a rational reason for an inexplicable defeat. Test rugby, quite apart from any physical contest, is a highly charged emotional contest. "Initiative", that curious commodity which, under normal circumstances, can be held and exploited while the opposition actually "feel" that they are on the defensive, is not so reliable in a test. The tension is such that it is often the most unplanned, even accidental, situation which may turn the game.'

Hart accepted full responsibility and symbolically resigned. He flew home and faced the music on 'Holmes'. But nothing he did or said could placate a section of the public and the media who wanted more than his head on a platter. They wanted a cruel and protracted revenge for what they seemed to regard as a personal betrayal. Either through gross incompetence or dereliction of duty Hart had let *them* down.

And so a rugby magazine put his face on the cover with the single word 'GUILTY' underneath. This is the type of treatment normally reserved for the worst sort of criminal monsters after they have been tried and found guilty by a jury of their peers. He was vilified on talkback radio. He received hate mail, including death threats. At Addington Raceway people threw things at his horse. Think about that for a moment.

Wilson and his co-author Ron Palenski wrote that at Addington that night 'a section of the crowd was crudely abusive to [Hart] and it shook him greatly. No man should have to put up with that, no New Zealander should be subject to the worst of human behaviour, and especially not a man who had achieved things in his life to which his detractors could not even begin to aspire.'

The reputation he had built up over a 25-year coaching career was systematically hacked down. An entire book was devoted to this purpose, using unattributed quotes from anonymous All Blacks. I suppose if you're going to kick a man when he's down, it makes sense to don the mask of anonymity. His successes with the All Blacks in 1996/97 were belittled as just a matter of luck because he'd inherited a great team from Laurie Mains. The same thing could be said about Fred Allen and Alex Wyllie, who also inherited great All Black teams. But it isn't said about them: Allen and Wyllie are rightly given credit for what *they* achieved.

For that matter, Mains himself took over what was, after all, the second-best team in the world, given that at the 1991 World Cup the All Blacks beat the eventual losing finalists England in their pool game at Twickenham. While Mains and his lieutenants, like incoming ministers of finance, made much of the mess they'd inherited, the cupboard wasn't exactly bare given that current All Blacks included John Timu, John Kirwan, Inga Tuigamala, Walter Little, Grant Fox, Graeme Bachop, Zinzan Brooke, Mike Brewer, Michael Jones, Gary Whetton, Ian Jones, Richard Loe and Sean Fitzpatrick.

Worst of all, Hart was abandoned by the official rugby community. He became, effectively, a non-person, a rugby equivalent of the Bolshevik leaders who got on the wrong side of Stalin and were expunged from the record, their faces air-brushed out of official photos. Much of what was said and done by the NZRU and the new All Black leadership seemed designed to put as much distance between themselves and Hart as possible.

Says Hart, 'Part of my responsibility was to grow the succession and I reckon we had a good system in place in the coaching, medical and fitness areas. But we lost one game and people said forget about all that, let's start again. Instead of analysing what had happened at the World Cup, which would have involved talking to me, it was a case of we've got to return to basics and all that claptrap. They appointed a think tank to decide what was required, mainly made up of people who had little or no knowledge of professional rugby, and they didn't talk to us so there was no exchange of information or knowledge transfer. Being All Black coach is a huge job with dramatic off-field pressures. Tony Gilbert is a very nice man and it was probably very good to have him around the team but he wasn't the specialist forward coach who was required and we ended up with the wrong combination. He was put in there for his personal qualities, which fitted with the mood of back to the old virtues, but he didn't have the specific expertise required. Peter Sloane did: he was a hard-nosed, top-drawer forward coach but he was tarred with my brush, which was ironic since Wayne Smith was more part of my team: he had a hell of a lot more say in the tactics than anyone else.'

The great virtue of laying all the blame at the feet of one man was that things could be quickly set to rights by getting rid of him and everything he stood for. With the corporate blight removed and real rugby people in charge, the All Blacks would be back on top in two shakes of a lamb's tail. Except it didn't work out that way. For all the talk of turnarounds, the 1999 All Blacks actually won the Tri-Nations championship and beat England at Twickenham, which no team has managed to do since; the 2000 and 2001 All Blacks did not win the Tri-Nations or regain the Bledisloe Cup. Todd Blackadder, the people's choice, the personification of the return to the good old ways, was dumped after a year. The two coaches followed a few months later.

Thirteen of the 15 players who started the World Cup semi-final were All Blacks again in 2000. The exceptions were Wilson, who sat the year out, and Brooke, who wasn't required. These players were out there on the big stage, playing for a place in the World Cup final and a chance for glory; their destiny was in their hands. They failed but they were forgiven.

According to John Mayhew who, with one break, has been the All Black team doctor since 1988, 'Hart was ahead of the players in terms of identifying the issues surrounding professionalism and attempting to address them. He asked a lot of the players and many of them weren't capable of meeting his standards. Where he went wrong, I think, was that he wanted too much control over their private lives, but he was terribly pilloried for the wrong reasons. It was very disappointing that so few of the players spoke up for him but there might have been things going on between him and various players that I wasn't aware of.'

Hart tries hard to be philosophical: 'Perhaps professionalism has made it harder to develop relationships. The guys in the Auckland team of the 1980s — Haden, the Whettons, Drake, Rich — are mates but you don't seem to end up with the same relationships in professionalism. That might reflect on me but it also reflects on the selfishness of the players — I've hardly heard from most of them. Jeff Wilson's been a great support and Mark [Sharky] Robinson was one who did, even though he wasn't even at the World Cup. Some don't know how to handle it. I still feel a lot for those players but they don't give you much back.'

Andrew Martin, who succeeded Banks as All Black manager and

was himself summarily discarded, describes Hart's treatment by the media and the country as a whole as 'despicable. In many respects he was setting standards of holistic professionalism that were ahead of the administration and the players and therefore they struggled to cope with it. The tragedy is how few people recognise it.'

In his foreword to Hart's first book, John Graham wrote that 'he was not accepted by many rugby people outside Auckland who could not cope with his flamboyant, confident, open, intellectual style. Perhaps . . . he failed to reach the top [this was 1993] because of his tendency to be divisive.'

There is no doubt that over the course of his career, Hart has trodden on toes and made enemies. He didn't hide his light under a bushel: the self-confidence and ambition that were there for all to see caused him to be impatient when he would have been better off keeping a low profile and biding his time. Add in his corporate background and the fact that he's very much an Aucklander and it's hardly surprising that in those parts of the country where to be tongue-tied is regarded as a mark of character, he was seen as up himself, a big-noter.

His rivalries with Wyllie and Mains generated much ill-will and he must accept some responsibility for that. It's no coincidence that two of his most implacable critics are Phil Gifford, Wyllie's biographer, and Howitt, Mains' biographer. Even now, this pair find it hard to resist taking swipes at Hart, however tangential they are to the matter at hand.

Here I must declare an interest. I have written two books with John Hart that were rewarding experiences on a professional and personal level. I don't pretend to be impartial. But there are two aspects of Hart's treatment that would disturb me even if I'd never met him. The first is that whatever his flaws and whatever mistakes he made, Hart was a major figure in New Zealand rugby over two decades and his contribution entitled him to far better than non-person status. Secondly, Hart was kicked when he was down, which doesn't say much for his countrymen.

Hunter, who could and did have his own complaints about Hart's demanding perfectionism, went into his local dairy when the owner was reading Hewitt's book. Taking his cue from Hewitt, the owner proceeded to 'slag' Hart. Hunter told him, 'Every time you see Hart's name in that book, write mine beside it.'

But perhaps New Zealanders like Gordon Hunter are becoming a dying breed.

5

End of the world, part two

A rugby trivia question for the year 2053: Although the Rugby World Cup is held every four years, one country managed to blow it twice in the space of two-and-a-half years. Name that country.

On April 18, 2002 the International Rugby Board (IRB) council voted to award Australia sole hosting rights to the 2003 Rugby World Cup. Not content with stripping New Zealand of sub-hosting rights, the IRB twisted the knife with a media statement that dripped disdain — the NZRU had repaid its 'generous accommodations' with 'wholly inappropriate behaviour' — and skated misleadingly over the central dispute.

Previewing the meeting, the forthright British rugby journalist Stephen Jones wrote that such an outcome would amount to 'a betrayal of New Zealand's contribution and standing and a sad commentary on commercial rapaciousness.'

No doubt many New Zealanders shared Jones' disgust at the manner in which their country had been shafted by the international rugby community — to the extent that it is represented by the IRB — and betrayed by their closest neighbour and supposed partner in the whole enterprise, a country whose emergence as a frontline rugby nation was assisted and accelerated by New Zealand's help. But some sections of the public and media did not see it that way. Even though they had barely finished a frenzy of scapegoating over the 1999 World Cup campaign, they were up for more and duly embarked on another round of vilification of those who had 'let us down'.

Murray Deaker is eager to claim credit for leading the charge: 'Without my personal investigation into why we lost the World Cup,' he says, '[Murray] McCaw and [David] Rutherford would've got away with it. I'd determined that they blew it and consistently said so. I interviewed [IRB chairman the late] Vernon Pugh, the only interview he gave, and what he said was confirmed by [Australian Rugby Union (ARU) chief executive] John O'Neill. It was tough because of the lies coming out of the NZRU. The breakthrough was when I had John Alexander of the Eden Park Trust Board on the show and he revealed he hadn't had a single conversation with the NZRU about clean stadia. They had to deliver but they didn't do the job because they were lazy, then they tried to blame Australia and spread rumours that Pugh and O'Neill were in cahoots.'

Evidentially, the fact that Pugh's and O'Neill's stories matched does not prove much either way: it neither guarantees reliability nor demonstrates collusion. But the man from Cardiff and the man from Sydney — as shiny-eyed a pair of idealists as ever sauntered into a VIP suite — said it was all our fault so there is an end to it. Only it wasn't.

On March 17, 2003, very nearly a year after New Zealand was cut off at the knees, Deaker interviewed O'Neill, who'd just been named Australia's sports executive of the year, on his TV show. Deaker lobbed up a couple of juicy half-volleys with McCaw's and Rutherford's faces stamped on them and looked on admiringly as O'Neill dispatched them with contempt.

Bear in mind that by then McCaw and Rutherford were, in rugby terms, just a couple of faces in the crowd. The ARU was busy exploiting its sole hosting rights to the hilt and the new NZRU board, complete with new chairman and CEO, was picking up the pieces. But neither Deaker nor O'Neill, it seemed, had lost their taste for blood.

(Another declaration of interest: McCaw is also a friend; I help him coach a junior club team).

In *The Judas Game* Joseph Romanos wrote, 'Ultimately, the brouhaha over the World Cup has done New Zealand rugby a favour because it rid us of two lacklustre figures who had been charged with leading the game in this country.'

How casually we question people's motives, belittle their efforts and classify them as failures. How black and white these issues are. As the novelist Howard Jacobson wrote in the English newspaper *The Independent* early in 2003, discussing a subject far more serious that rugby, 'Society is never less to be trusted than when it is in a fit of agreeing with itself.'

Enter His Honour Sir Thomas Eichelbaum. While his review fingered the NZRU board, and McCaw and Rutherford in particular, most of his criticisms were balanced with acknowledgements of the difficulties they faced.

For instance, he concluded that 'a key factor in what went wrong was the breakdown of NZRU's relationships with IRB/Rugby World Cup Ltd [RWCL] and ARU.' But he noted that the ARU played a part in this breakdown and RWCL's 'administrative deficiencies' contributed to the final crisis:

'NZRU found [RWCL] a difficult body to deal with principally because of the apparent need to route all significant decisions through Mr Pugh. RWCL at first stood by while inequities developed between ARU and NZRU thus eroding relations between the unions. It contributed to gross delays in the finalising of Host Union Agreement [HUA] which ran three years over the time originally set. The requirements for boxes emerged slowly and confusingly. The response to the Sub Host Union Agreement [SHUA] of 21 December 2001 was unsatisfactory in its lack of detail and took too long. The venue inspection of March 2002 should have been arranged earlier.'

Given that RWCL was meant to be overseeing the whole process, this is a pretty damning report card.

Eichelbaum concluded that the NZRU should have gone about securing corporate boxes 'vigorously at an earlier stage' while acknowledging that the original definition of clean stadia did not include boxes, that RWCL changed its position on boxes three times, that RWCL made quite misleading public statements on this issue, that the NZRU was unable to deliver the boxes 'because of previous contractual commitments made to boxholders with NZRU's knowledge' and that the NZRU believed that breach of the clean venues conditions exposed it to a liability of A$10 million.

He found that 'until the crisis, NZRU did not strongly press a case for Government funding' but acknowledged that 'it is unlikely any stronger request would have been successful'.

The consensus among NZRU people, past and present, to whom I spoke is that the review did not go deep enough. One, who prefers to remain anonymous, says, 'By and large the Eichelbaum report is very good. It accurately portrays the events which led to us losing the World Cup but it's light in some areas. It only briefly touches on the actions of the IRB and ARU which contributed to us losing out. People like Murray Deaker saw it as a vindication but if Sir Thomas had been given a wider brief, he would've taken a much more detailed look at what the IRB and ARU did. If he'd been able to do that, he would've found that the ARU decided early on that they wanted to be sole hosts and that the IRB's administration of the event was appalling and unprofessional throughout as was evidenced in many little ways — things were never done on time — and the way the ground rules kept changing. There would have been some doubts as to whether Eichelbaum would have had jurisdiction over IRB and ARU records and it could have taken forever but the fact remains that it was an inquiry into the NZRU's handling of the situation rather than a definitive piece of work on how and why we lost the right to sub-host the World Cup.

'There was a massive failure of leadership on the part of the IRB. Instead of saying we are the rugby community, this is our celebration and it must be done in a way that reflects our international brotherhood and values, they stood aside. Rugby values went out the window and it became a case of every man for himself and devil take the hindmost and the definitive rugby nation got shafted.'

'We told [Eichelbaum] we wanted a commercial person involved,' says McCaw 'but that didn't happen and consequently there was a lack of focus on financial issues.'

Eichelbaum struck a studiously neutral pose on one of the most vexatious and hotly contested issues in the whole saga — whether Pugh gave 'nod and wink' assurances that 100 per cent clean stadia and corporate box availability did not really mean that. The NZRU set much store on McCaw's version of his meeting with Pugh in London in November 2001 at which Pugh supposedly talked of 'pragmatic solutions'. NZRU board member and IRB delegate Rob Fisher reported that Pugh told him that 'some shortfall in the 100 per cent would be acceptable'. After Sports Minister Trevor Mallard met Pugh in Sydney in March 2002, he recorded his understanding of what he had been told in a letter: the NZRU had to provide 'suitable top class accommodation for VIPS, sponsors and their guests, including usage of up to 70–75 per cent of corporate boxes and hospitality suites at all stadia.'

Pugh told Sir Thomas that 'in regard to boxes he told the Minister the same as he told Mr McCaw', which is a gem of legal-speak seeing that both men insist he gave private assurances that he subsequently denied giving. At the fateful IRB council meeting, Pugh read out Mallard's letter but excluded the passage quoted above.

What we have here, in layperson's terms, is three people's word against one. Which makes Sir Thomas's disinclination to draw a conclusion a little surprising.

Some of Eichelbaum's most severe comments are directed at McCaw's and Rutherford's public remarks about Pugh after he had given the ARU the green light to withdraw the SHUA and submit a sole bid:

'When the story broke on 8 March, it was obvious there would be a storm of criticism of NZRU. Messrs McCaw and Rutherford tried to deflect this by blaming IRB/RWCL. This was not a viable long-term strategy if NZRU still wished to pursue a case for retaining the sub-hosting, given that a final decision would rest with IRB, acting on the recommendations of RWCL.

'It would serve no good purpose to repeat the numerous comments attributed to Messrs McCaw and Rutherford on and immediately after 8 March. With justification, Mr Pugh, RWCL directors and IRB councillors regarded them as offensive and hurtful.' Elsewhere Eichelbaum described the remarks as 'inexcusable'.

The sharpest arrow in this offensive and hurtful volley was, apparently, McCaw's line that the IRB was being run 'by a Welsh town-planning QC'.

Let's break this slur down to its component parts. Firstly, did Pugh run the IRB?

The NZRU view was that the IRB was effectively Pugh's fiefdom over which he exerted iron control. Eichelbaum noted that, 'For a lengthy period in 2001, IRB functioned without a chief executive. During this time all matters of substance relating to RWC seemingly had to be referred to Mr Pugh. He had a busy professional life as well, involving travel, while RWC and IRB commitments required his presence in many parts of the world. It must have been a demanding time for him, and NZRU's files and statements make many references to the problems of making contact. I have seen telephone records indicating continuous unsuccessful attempts to do so. The frustration was not confined to NZ; for example in a fax dated 14 September 2001 Mr O'Neill said there was no point in Messrs Martin, Neil or Brophy negotiating on HUA: "they keep telling us they do not have the authority to agree to anything".'

There's no dispute of which I'm aware that Pugh was Welsh and a town-planning QC. Are those terms of disparagement? I would have thought most people — and certainly a judge — would regard being a QC as a rather impressive indicator of professional success, whatever one's area of the law. And while the reference to Pugh's nationality might have been gratuitous, it is only offensive if you subscribe to the extreme politically correct view that to be conscious of a person's ethnicity is racist.

'It wasn't meant as a put-down,' says McCaw. 'People got this idea I was scorning the fact Pugh was a town-planning QC. On the contrary, the point I was making was that here was this very busy man also running the IRB and RWC without a chief executive. We made a conscious decision not to criticise the ARU but point to the lack of leadership from the IRB. Eichelbaum made great play of it. One man's dignity seemed to count for a great deal.'

Whether Pugh genuinely took offence — and as a product of the Welsh Rugby Union's fraught brand of politics, it seems unlikely that this was the most vicious denunciation he'd ever suffered — or chose to do so for tactical reasons will never be known. He certainly made the most of it, which included revealing his family's distress. (Did they think he was secretary-general of the United Nations and second cousin to the Queen?)

Having said that, it only made sense for the NZRU to go public if it was washing its hands of the whole business. Having a crack at Pugh and the IRB was incompatible with continuing to press the case for sub-hosting and led to the NZRU losing both at the IRB council and in the court of public opinion. In public relations terms, the apology to Pugh — which proceeded from the decision to fight on — was an unmitigated disaster because it undercut the case that the situation had been created by the IRB's dysfunctional administration and abdication of responsibility.

'The board got woolly in its response to the March 8 deadline,' says one of the participants. 'There was no clarity on what the objective was. They could've decided not to sign, spelt out the reasons and walked away. We had the country with us for the first two weeks. The strategy was to say we can't sign because we can't take corporate boxes off New Zealanders. Then they decided they really wanted it after all — hence the apology to Pugh — and it wasn't surprising that people started asking, "What are these guys doing?" [NZRU board member and IRB delegate] Tim Gresson passed on the advice from his so-called friends at the IRB that we needed to apologise. McCaw and Rutherford did so reluctantly: it didn't change anything. It made them look stupid and turned public opinion against them; and it gave Pugh and his cronies a huge weapon to use against us — if they're right and I'm wrong, why did they apologise?'

'For me, the turning point came when we apologised to Vernon Pugh,' says David Rutherford. 'If we hadn't done anything wrong, why were we apologising? From that point on, the media and public stopped believing our side of the story.'

A collective silliness — at times downright nastiness — gripped the New Zealand rugby community after the 1999 World Cup. The NZRU wasn't immune to it and at times was only too happy to swim with the tide, which was essentially a rejection of everything associated with the John Hart era. The message was: out with hype, commercialism, the corporate approach and the focus on the elite, and in with heritage, tradition and grassroots values. However, this populism became a liability when it influenced thinking and decision making on issues that had nothing to do with the grassroots and the base of the game.

Making Todd Blackadder All Black captain was one example. As John Graham says, 'The choice of Blackadder was more driven by the off-field issues than whether he was the best player in the country.' It was obvious from the outset that, for all his qualities, Blackadder simply wasn't physically equipped to play lock forward at the highest level; in John Mitchell's terminology, he was a 'sawn-off shotgun'. Blackadder was appointed because he wasn't a Hart man, he was popular — particularly in his home province — and he fitted the sentimental conception of what an All Black should be.

'Toddy . . . characterises everything that's good about the Kiwi bloke,' wrote Wayne Smith in his introduction to Blackadder's book, *Loyal*. 'He's humble, he's not sophisticated, but he's wise in a number 8 wire sort of way.' Fine, but what has that got to do with winning lineout ball against the Wallabies?

Knocking back Australia's bid for a fourth Super 12 team, knowing full well how important it was to them, was another example. Says Rutherford, 'Post the 1999 World Cup, that issue became the touchstone for the feeling that if we gave in on it, the Aussies would have beaten us again.'

This was a slow-motion train crash: 'It seemed to me that prior to my arrival there'd been a history of loose understandings with the ARU and that sometimes these understandings hadn't been hammered out by either side,' says Rutherford. 'One surprise to me was that the revenue split on the News [Ltd] contract hadn't been settled — this was in 1999, three years after the deal was done. It was pretty clear to me when I came into the job that the Australians felt they had some sort of agreement from us on their fourth team but there's no background to that in any of the minutes or other material and I can understand why. At my first meeting with O'Neill it was clear he felt he had our agreement to a fourth team; I told him, "That's news to me."

'We got the board to agree to a fourth Australian team and a fifth South African team providing a number of conditions were met: we wanted the broadcaster's agreement and as part of that process we hoped to negotiate away some of our international obligations — the meaningless tests — and we wanted agreement on equalisation by 2005. That was in August 2001. We didn't put that in writing until late 2001, which O'Neill interpreted as part of the negotiating around Rugby World Cup, but we were simply waiting for the meeting with News that the ARU had undertaken to arrange. In fact, the proposition was never put to News. The onus was on Australia to make the appointment; the onus was on us to put the conditions in writing. The board was concerned that the season structure wasn't nailed down to the week for the next 10 years because we didn't want the Super 12 — or Super 14 — to encroach on the NPC window. When we had the meeting in February 2002 the ARU effectively asked us to waive those conditions.

'The issue bedevilled relations through the period I was involved and it wasn't helped by the way administrators on both sides of the Tasman debated it publicly. If we'd achieved agreement on these matters at that Sanzar meeting, both countries would be in better shape than they are now but whether that would have engendered enough goodwill to avoid the World Cup fall-out is a moot point.'

The NZRU's veto went down well with the public and the media. The view seemed to be that, at long last, New Zealand had played hard-ball to protect its interests. The stuck-pig squeals across the Tasman were music to our ears; at that stage, O'Neill did not have a fan club in our media and his outraged splutterings provided much enjoyment. With the mutual admiration society in session, who heard O'Neill mutter darkly that 'What goes around, comes around'? Who paid any attention?

As part of this process of re-establishing the core values, great importance was placed on the NPC — 'the greatest domestic competition in world rugby' as it is routinely described, although seldom on the basis of a rigorous comparison. It was ours and ours alone, it was the heart and soul of our game, it was the real thing — unlike the Super 12, which was as much a marketing concept as a rugby competition — and no one was going to mess with it. And so, until very late in the day, the NZRU insisted on having the right to stage NPC matches during the World Cup.

Eichelbaum reported that, 'although Mr Pugh supported New Zealand's position, he was the only member of the RWCL board who had any sympathy for it. Meeting notes following the 18–20 February 2002 meeting recorded "huge negativity" from sponsors. Other IRB/RWCL persons thought it was ludicrous to have a domestic event competing for attention and ticket sales with RWC, and the NZRU's persistence with the concept caused them to wonder about New Zealand's commitment to sub-hosting the tournament.'

Who could blame them?

These decisions backfired on the NZRU but it should not be forgotten that, at the time, they were met with near-unanimous approval. Many of those who later condemned the NZRU over the loss of the sub-hosting rights were loud in their support of the belligerent mind-set which contributed to that loss.

This is the section of Eichelbaum's review which probably sealed McCaw's and Rutherford's fate: 'A successful RWC 2003 required close cooperation between IRB/RWCL, ARU and NZRU. It was essential that New Zealand maintained good relations with the other bodies. The rebuilding of relationships seems to me to be one of the most important needs unearthed by this Inquiry. A number of persons interviewed referred to the difficulties which Messrs McCaw and Rutherford would face in this respect.'

Given that the NZRU was convinced — with reason — that Pugh

controlled the IRB, wouldn't it have been sensible to have got, and stayed, on side with him? Also, whether they liked it or not, O'Neill was the key to dealing with the ARU so getting on his fighting side doesn't seem all that smart either.

With hindsight, McCaw concedes that he made a mistake in choosing not to be one of the NZRU's two IRB delegates when he became chairman. 'At the time I felt I couldn't run a company, be chairman of the NZRU and be on the IRB.' Whether or not some on the IRB saw this as a snub, it seems likely that there would have been better communication and a little more goodwill floating around had he and his chief executive joined the IRB club.

One of Rutherford's former colleagues describes him as 'a good-hearted person with a spiritual side who believes all the right things for the right reasons and loves the game. He and O'Neill had an acrimonious relationship going back 12 or 18 months. O'Neill was forever undermining him and the NZRU and David would bite back. His first response to any challenge or disagreement was to fire off a legal letter.'

However, Rutherford is surely right on both counts when he says that, 'There was an absolute need for an all cards on the table planning exercise but the suggestion was never taken up. We needed to get past personalities but that's easier said than done.'

With Pugh's death and the departure from the scene of autocrats like Albert Ferrasse and Louis Luyt, there cannot be a more powerful administrator in world rugby than John O'Neill. His supporters would argue that his power is a by-product of his performance — he has delivered growth in player numbers, spectacularly increased the ARU's revenue, raised rugby's profile and presided over a victorious World Cup campaign. He certainly appears to adhere to the view that there is no point in having power unless you exercise it: crossing O'Neill is not the way to get ahead in Australian rugby. Even as laid-back an individual as former Wallaby coach Rod Macqueen must have been driven to distraction by O'Neill's incursions onto his patch but he bit his tongue. Likewise the media: whatever they think of O'Neill, they understand where the power resides.

To give O'Neill his due, his abrasive outspokenness is not simply a reflection of his ego, large and difficult to control though that might be. Whereas in New Zealand rugby can and does take unwavering media interest for granted, in Australia the game has to fight for newspaper space and air time with three other football codes — league, soccer and AFL. Australian rugby needs a recognisable face and a strong voice and O'Neill provides them. It is also the case that Australian public life is no place for the faint-hearted: the give and take is robust, often brutal, and playing the man is just part of the game. What might seem like overkill to a New Zealand audience is par for the course over there. Jonathon Hunt, the dowager aunt-like speaker of the New Zealand Parliament, whose delicate ears are offended by that quaint term 'bugger', would be well-advised to steer clear of Australian parliaments, particularly the New South Wales Lower House where the air turns blue and names are blackened on an almost daily basis.

A curious footnote to this sub-plot is that while McCaw's and Rutherford's lack of rugby pedigree was held against them, that wasn't an issue with O'Neill. With his banker's shirts, high maintenance hair and preening self-satisfaction, O'Neill is about as far removed from the traditional rugby man as it is possible to be. He is, in fact, the quintessential corporate man. As usual, the fault-finders were having it both ways, scorning McCaw and Rutherford for being corporate and then, when they were out-manoeuvred by O'Neill, for not being corporate enough. They savaged the NZRU board for losing sight of what was important to the rugby heartland but rolled over to have their tummies tickled by O'Neill, who pursued his commercial agenda with cold-eyed ruthlessness.

One of the generalised charges against the NZRU was that of

arrogance. Given the frequency with which this complaint surfaced in the UK press, it was obviously the message emanating from IRB headquarters in Dublin. More specifically, it was suggested that the NZRU never really accepted that they were playing second fiddle to Australia.

'Three weeks before the shit hit the fan,' says Hart, 'I got a call from a very senior rugby figure in Queensland asking me if I could get involved because the thing was headed for disaster. I had to tell him that was beyond the bounds of possibility. He said the arrogance of the NZRU was quite breathtaking and that what they seemed to fail to understand was that when they agreed to Australia being the lead host, they conceded a lot of things.'

(On the subject of back-channel communications, NZRU sources tell of messages from ARU board members expressing their unhappiness with what was going on and the way O'Neill was driving the process.)

Eichelbaum picked up on this but placed it in the wider context of the overall organisation and communications: 'While NZRU understood RWCL's formal bid structure meant ARU was the host union, in the early stages I do not think NZRU believed the chain of dealings (RWCL with host union, host union with sub-host) would be enforced as rigidly as turned out to be the case. Initially NZRU liked to regard itself as co-host rather than a sub-host. Over time, it found out that the tail could not wag the dog.'

'There used to be a very strong relationship between New Zealand and Australian administrators,' says Murray Deaker. 'There was a joint committee for the 1987 World Cup. Where was the joint committee this time?'

Perhaps the answer lies in Eichelbaum's comment about the chain of dealings between the various parties being rigidly enforced. Who did the enforcing? Obviously not the NZRU because it was not in a position nor was it in its interests to do so. Besides, if one thing is clear in this sorry saga, it is that the NZRU was unable to enforce its views on any issue.

One of Eichelbaum's more barbed comments is that, 'I have heard a point of view — amounting to a conspiracy theory — that ARU worked towards hosting RWC alone. I have found no evidence to support it.' Elsewhere he wrote that, 'among the many persons I interviewed I heard remarkably little criticism of ARU . . . they played hardball with competence, but I heard few suggestions they deliberately undermined NZRU or were otherwise duplicitous.'

Which is strange given that what he described as a conspiracy theory was, in fact, the collective view of the NZRU board. 'We reached the view,' says McCaw, 'that Australia was absolutely hellbent on getting New Zealand out to maximise their profit.'

In Appendix B to his review, 'Persons Interviewed', Eichelbaum listed 'Australian Rugby Union (written submission, email follow up)'. According to McCaw, 'Australia made written submissions but refused to be interviewed so there was no cross-examination. They supplied their stuff at the last minute — it held up the report — and it wasn't tested against NZRU people.'

Whether Australia had a sinister plan or not, they certainly moved in for the kill with turbo-charged opportunism. On March 8, 2002 the NZRU signed the SHUA agreement, adding clauses protecting itself on the three requirements with which it could not comply: corporate boxes and hospitality areas, catering and the 500 metres clean precinct.

Within 32 minutes of receiving the amended SHUA agreement, Australia withdrew the invitation to sub-host with immediate effect. In that time O'Neill had sprung Pugh out of bed at 4 am to get the go-ahead. We know this because O'Neill told *Sydney Morning Herald* journalist Roy Masters who reported it on February 22, 2003 in a story appropriately headed 'Festival of the booty'.

In the article O'Neill described the A$45 million that the ARU will make from hosting the World Cup as a 'one chance in a lifetime windfall. What keeps me awake at night,' he added, 'is the fear of wasting the opportunity.'

O'Neill did not evince a trace of regret or of sympathy for New Zealand. The opposite in fact. Talking of the final IRB council meeting in Dublin, Masters wrote that 'When the meeting finally resumed on April 18, the first item on the agenda was the World Cup and, according to O'Neill, ARU chairman Bob Tuckey was asked whether he would compromise. Bob, a former rugby league player from Tamworth, simply said, "No".'

If the roles had been reversed, would the NZRU have adopted an adversarial attitude towards its supposed partner from the outset, then seized the opportunity to dump Australia in order to maximise its financial windfall? Would the New Zealand public have wanted them to? One would like to think that the answer to both questions would be a simple 'no'.

One Eichelbaum conclusion with which it is difficult to disagree is that 'NZRU should have pursued obtaining [corporate] boxes more vigorously at an earlier stage'.

The apparent lack of urgency was highlighted by the dramatic degree of compliance that occurred once it became clear that if New Zealand had not already been dealt out, it was in grave danger of being so. On March 8 the availability of corporate boxes at the main grounds was four out of 77 at Eden Park, seven out of 64 at Westpac Trust Stadium, 14 out of 65 at Jade Stadium and three out of 43 at Carisbrook. Three weeks later the availability was Eden Park 64, Westpac Trust 55, Jade 51 and Carisbrook 34. This was the second great public relations disaster because it fed the perception that the crisis would have been averted if the NZRU had just got off its backside.

NZRU staff argue that the rush to cooperate was triggered by the realisation that we were on the brink of losing a share of the event and the resultant public pressure on the boxholders. In their view, if there had not been a crisis, the boxholders would have played hardball. The ARU had to pay A$20 million to secure the boxes; the NZRU got them for thousands of dollars but at that stage the boxholders knew that if they didn't cooperate, there wouldn't be any World Cup rugby to watch.

'Even when the figures showed we weren't going to make any money,' says Rutherford, 'there was no money in the budget for clean stadia.'

All up the ARU paid A$40 million to deliver 100 per cent clean stadia and all the suites and boxes. On March 1, 2003 *The New Zealand Herald* ran an NZPA story that quoted ARU public affairs manager Strath Gordon describing the pay-out as 'a really bitter pill to swallow. This was a very big requirement, but we just took a deep breath and did it. In New Zealand they struggled to take that deep breath.'

What Gordon did not say was that thanks to federal and state government hand-outs to cover this eventuality, the ARU was in the position of being able to throw money at the boxholders and sponsors whose billboards were removed from the stadia and still make a A$45 million profit. The NZRU was not in that position. It was not even in the same ballpark.

There were suggestions that the NZRU could have got the same sort of support from the New Zealand Government if only they had bothered to ask. Well, they did ask and got knocked back. On October 7, 2001 Rutherford wrote to Pugh to let him know that Mallard had indicated that the NZRU would get no direct government funding to help it meet the costs associated with sub-hosting the tournament. There would only be indirect government and local assistance by way of promotion and assistance with event management.

The NZRU did not push very hard because Mallard, as he

confirmed to Eichelbaum, had told them that the Government was not disposed to put taxpayers' money into an event that was going to generate huge profits for Australia and the IRB.

'I can understand the Government's position,' says McCaw. 'They were in effect being asked to cover us for a loss when the figures showed that our supposed rugby partners were going to make massive profits.'

According to another NZRU figure, 'Apart from Mallard, this government doesn't like rugby and doesn't see sport as a driver of economic benefits.'

If anyone got it wrong here, it was the Government, not the NZRU. There were various figures bandied about suggesting that sub-hosting would be worth hundreds of millions of dollars to the New Zealand economy (compared to the A$1 billion which will supposedly flow into the Australian economy now that they have the event all to themselves). Some of McCaw's and Rutherford's accusers barely stopped short of adding economic sabotage to the charge-sheet of crimes and incompetence.

Since when did the NZRU run the New Zealand economy? The NZRU is responsible for rugby; the Government is responsible for the economy. If the Government thought significant overall benefits to the economy were on offer, surely they would have been shoulder-to-shoulder with the NZRU from the word go.

As Pugh put it in his reply to Rutherford, 'The financial benefit of RWC to any country is huge and only the most impecunious or negative agency would not do everything in its power to secure such an event.'

And as Eichelbaum commented, 'Notwithstanding that the financial problems encountered by the NZRU did not arise in Australia, ARU obtained substantial government funding. It seems Australia shared Mr Pugh's philosophy.'

Indeed it does. Even before the Sydney Olympics most

Australian state governments were active internationally trying to entice big-ticket sporting and entertainment events to their states because they see them as generators of significant tourism and hospitality revenue. They do not wait for sporting bodies to come to them cap in hand; they do not have to be talked into it.

The Government's strings-attached offer of $32 million to Team New Zealand — an infinitely more speculative investment — suggests that it might have had a change of heart. Whether the new attitude survives the sour public reaction to the idea of taxpayer backing for an America's Cup challenge in Europe remains to be seen.

Some argue that the NZRU should have simply done what the Australians did: trusted in Pugh's nods and winks that the clean stadia/corporate boxes issue would sort itself out, taken a deep breath, signed on the dotted line and thrown themselves on the Government's mercy if they had ended up in the red.

But the positions of the two bodies were poles apart. The ARU was going to make a killing, the NZRU was looking at a hefty loss; the ARU already had $A20 million backing from state and federal governments to cover those costs; the NZRU's approaches to the Government had been rebuffed. And given that Mallard had legal advice that the NZRU's directors would break three laws relating to fiduciary duty if they signed the SHUA promising 100 per cent clean stadia, it is highly questionable whether the Government would have been inclined to stump up to cover damages incurred for failing to honour a contractual agreement that the directors had known all along they couldn't deliver on.

McCaw and Pugh did agree on one thing: that the original 1997 agreement between the NZRU and the ARU was unfavourable to New Zealand.

Pugh told Eichelbaum that the NZRU had made 'what appeared to be a very poor commercial arrangement'.

'New Zealand did a dumb deal,' says McCaw, 'with each getting the revenue from ticket sales to their games but splitting the costs. There was a lack of documentation and the Australians were aggressive, even rude, in insisting they had agreement on various issues.'

Eichelbaum described the arrangements as 'sloppy', adding that while they might have seemed logical at the time, they 'had the potential to produce a lopsided outcome. Australia with its far larger population base, the growing popularity of rugby and plans for the much larger stadia, stood to profit in a way not open to New Zealand.'

In his opinion, the host-sub host structure was also unfavourable to New Zealand: 'At the New Zealand end it may have been viewed more as two friends going into a venture together, and such a view was more explicable in 1997 than today. However, if that was the approach, it was a naïve perspective. In both respects (financial and structural) the concept was conducive to an "every man for himself" approach rather than a partnership.'

For the record, in 1997 the NZRU chairman was Rob Fisher and the CEO was David Moffett.

As I discuss elsewhere, the public sees the NZRU in a similar light to the government. Among the things they have supposedly got in common is a bottomless pit of money. No wonder then that the NZRU's attempts to locate this whole affair in a financial context did not cut much ice. However, it is apparent that the NZRU's primary focus was on the finances in the form of concern over their potential loss and a sense of grievance, even resentment, at the ARU's and IRB's potentially huge profits. What made it all the more galling was the knowledge that a significant portion of those profits would be generated by the All Blacks.

'Early on the boxes were the last thing on people's minds,' says one insider. 'It was about revenue sharing. Rutherford's view was that, given how important the All Blacks were to the World Cup's financial success, we weren't being offered a fair share.'

'At the start, the projections were that we'd make $10 million and Australia $15 million,' says McCaw. 'Post the 1999 World Cup, Australia came back with revised figures which showed us losing money and them making $30 million but the IRB didn't see the combined figures. When the IRB put $20 million of extra costs on the hosts to be split 50–50, our bottom line was a $10 million loss. At that stage there was panic.'

The loss would have fallen in the 2003/04 financial year, which was already looking rocky. Following a change of management at adidas, there were real fears that the sportswear giant might not renew its $20 million-plus a year sponsorship. The sports broadcasting market was in a downturn, causing anxiety about what would emerge from the Sanzar renegotiation with News Ltd that was coming up in 2005. The NZRU was therefore having to factor into its planning the potential reduction of both its major sources of income and the possibility that one of them might disappear altogether. Regardless of what happened to revenue, existing player contracts would have to be honoured and there was the prospect of having to bump up some key All Blacks' salaries to prevent a post-World Cup exodus. Any loss incurred through sub-hosting the World Cup would have had to have been offset by a corresponding reduction in expenditure, the brunt of which would have fallen on the grassroots in the form of axed grants to clubs and provinces.

'The loss would have placed us in a precarious financial position,' says Rutherford. 'Whatever we lost, we couldn't spend. We have to pay the players and run the competitions so the money would have had to come out of the provinces, trickling down to the club development officers.'

As one NZRU figure puts it, 'Very few of the critics have ever had to make the choice between hosting a feel-good event and potentially losing $15 million.'

Notwithstanding the purge carried out by the provincial unions when the World Cup had gone, the provinces had shown no stomach for cutbacks and austerity beforehand.

McCaw: 'When I went around the provinces, only one chairman and one CEO said we should do it even if it meant making a loss. [Canterbury chairman and new NZRU board member Mike] Eagle, later to become a critic, said we shouldn't do it unless we could make $1 million.'

Rutherford also detects an element of hypocrisy in the provincial unions' NZRU bashing: 'Some of the leaders of these sort of people are often throwing stones at other glass houses when their own aren't in order. I hope the performance management system in the provinces will enable the clubs which want to hold its administrators to account to do so.'

As the net closed, the idea of resorting to high-stakes brinkmanship was floated. One of the most prominent of the leading business people consulted during the end game was adamant that the NZRU should threaten to withdraw the All Blacks from the World Cup. He argued that the NZRU was fighting the battle on commercial grounds and that was the best — if not only — commercial weapon they had.

'The board took the decision that our imperatives were that we wouldn't lose money on it and we wouldn't pull the All Blacks out,' says Rutherford, 'so we went into it with our biggest card out of the deck. Without the All Blacks, no one would make money.'

McCaw considered the risks were too great: 'We might've been tossed out of the IRB and our sponsorships would have been up in the air — would adidas have wanted to sponsor a team that wasn't there? Long term though, we might have to consider it because if there's no equalisation of revenue, it will simply promote the trend of the All Blacks making money for others.'

The board clean-out brought to an end political manoeuvring centred on Otago's John Spicer, the deputy chairman. Spicer, who had previously been deputy to Richie Guy and Fisher, had had his eye on the seat at the head of the table for some time and had unsuccessfully angled for it after the 1999 World Cup. The ongoing crisis was almost guaranteed to bring rivalries and tensions to the surface and NZRU sources talk of backstabbing, plotting and investigations into leaks.

The board met on July 14, 2002 to discuss the draft of Eichelbaum's review. The story goes that Spicer approached McCaw beforehand to tell him he had to stand down. McCaw and Rutherford marched into the meeting and whatever they said stopped the *coup* dead in its tracks.

'I assume they had something on Spicer,' says one observer. 'The point is that the whole thing was caught up in the political battle that was going on within the board.'

Jock Hobbs, who succeeded McCaw as chairman, chooses not to discuss the loss of the sub-hosting rights because his emphasis is on 'looking forward not back'. Of the aftermath he says that, 'the rugby community represented by the key stakeholders made the decision and the decision was that everybody involved had to go. There were real concerns about how it was handled but it was definitely a catalyst which brought issues that had been festering to the surface. What I said as chairman was that there was no point in thrashing ourselves over it — there are lessons but we need to move forward and set a vision which everybody can understand and embrace.'

He believes the damage to New Zealand's standing and influence in the international rugby community is temporary: 'I've sensed at the IRB that there's enormous respect for New Zealand and our contribution to world rugby. Likewise with Sanzar I feel that the damage is temporary. We have common objectives and goals and we're better off working together to achieve them.'

Fine sentiments and no doubt sincerely held, but among the lessons of this affair are that the common goals are not clearly defined, there is no coherent plan in place for achieving them and when lofty ideals and material self-interest come into conflict, the lofty ideals do not stand a chance. A further lesson is that, for all New Zealand's contribution to world rugby, in an international professional game driven by financial imperatives our smallness and geographical isolation leave us vulnerable. The current system, whereby international fixtures and the World Cup are controlled by the four home unions-dominated IRB, does not operate to New Zealand's advantage. And if, as seems entirely possible, the rights to stage future World Cups are rotated among our four major rivals, the strategic implications for New Zealand are grim.

'What is the policy underpinning the World Cup?' asks Rutherford. 'Is it to make as much money as possible or to balance that against the development and expansion of the game?'

McCaw believes that decision has been made by default: 'Under the current model, no one but the host and the IRB makes money. If you're serious about building a global game, you're not going to do it by structuring things so that a handful of already rich nations just get richer.'

Andy Haden is on the board of the Fiji Rugby Union. 'The unholy alliance between Pugh and O'Neill represented self-interest rather than the interests of providing a good funding base for developing countries,' he says. 'Where does the money generated by the World Cup go, because it doesn't find its way down to the likes of Fiji? Pugh's solution was to stage a Northern Hemisphere versus Southern Hemisphere game — why should we need to do that? A lot of the money seems to go on first-class airfares and hotels in places like Bangkok and the Bahamas where they meet to discuss who'll stage the next World Cup. It's pretty easy to work out that it's the North's turn, which is a choice between England or France, so why do they need to traipse around the world to make that decision?

'Surely Fiji is one of the countries that should be developed.

When Brad Johnstone was the coach he found great athletes but only two of the forwards could do more than two chin-ups. They have great strength for playing on the wing but not for scrummaging. They need gyms but they're scratching to find a rugby ball. It could be worse — the Romanians can't afford a set of jerseys for their national team. The IRB either doesn't know or doesn't care what's going on. Little wonder that Michael Lynagh resigned from his IRB development role, which was announced with a great deal of fanfare — he simply couldn't do anything.'

So what is to be done? Some observers believe that the process of change is already underway as more national unions' CEOs become IRB delegates, replacing 'blazers' — amateur era administrators who have come up through the political process. If a loosening up process is underway, it is likely to be accelerated by Pugh's death. Perhaps because of these developments, Hobbs is said to be optimistic that evolutionary change is possible, that the IRB can be reformed from within by persuading the members to adopt a more democratic system of representation that would give developing nations greater say. They would surely use that to press for a fairer division of the spoils and more emphasis on development.

Others, however, believe that nothing short of a revolution will persuade the Celtic nations to accept any diminution of their power and privilege.

Although the decision to award the 2007 World Cup to France rather than England was preceded by horse-trading resulting in the multi-host arrangement that detracted from the 1999 tournament, it might have represented a step back from the approach of seeking to squeeze every last dollar from the event. England had projected a profit of £111 million compared to France's guaranteed minimum of £70 million backed by £15 million of government support. Cynics might point out that a decision in England's favour would have amounted to a calculated and potentially destabilising slap in the face for France, given that England have already hosted the tournament and that, after this year, France will be the only one of the big five rugby nations that has not. It is also worth mentioning that the IRB's audit cast doubt on England's upside and indicated that there was not much financial difference between the bids.

The acid test will come, one feels, when the decision is made on the hosting of the 2011 tournament, which logically should be sole hosted by New Zealand. South Africa is already making noises about putting in a bid.

McCaw does not believe New Zealand will ever host the tournament under the current model because 'we're in the wrong time zone for European and South African TV audiences and we don't have the stadia or the economic infrastructure to generate the income the IRB wants. And if the World Cup is going to be rotated among our biggest rivals — England, France, South Africa and Australia — then we're going to be in a situation where we're being frozen out while one of our main competitors is getting a massive financial windfall every four years and all of them are getting one every 16 years.'

'If the government won't put in $100 million,' says Rutherford, 'I can't conceive of how we can ever host the World Cup. And if we're never going to host it, why are we playing in it?'

6

Society is to blame

In 1924 the number of members of club and school teams was equivalent to about 20 per cent of the male population aged 10 to 29 — large but far from universal. Horse racing coverage overwhelmed rugby in Truth *in the early 1920s; billiards, boxing and even soccer and hockey contested the minor placings with it . . . What protected, entrenched and increased the dominance of [rugby] union and magnified its importance well beyond the numbers participating was its role in collective identity.*

— JAMES BELICH, *PARADISE REFORGED*

The grassroots are the scene of the alleged crime. This is where New Zealand rugby was supposedly betrayed. The evidence is everywhere: the near-empty clubrooms; the schools where goals have replaced goalposts; all those snowy-haired, blue-eyed soccer players who once were warriors.

The accusers maintain that beneath the shiny surface of the elite professional game, with its highly paid stars and packed stadia, rugby is in retreat. The schools and clubs that have always churned out tomorrow's stars are cutting back production because of the neglect of administrators besotted with the glitz and crass commercialism of globalised professional sport in the 21st century.

The administrators don't pretend that everything in the garden is lovely but they do object to being cast as arch-villains in what are often little more than conspiracy theories.

'We have some problems,' says Steve Tew. 'An ageing population, a browning population, a declining rural population except for dairy farmers who don't want to play. Having said that, rugby in New Zealand enjoys a place that no other sport in no other country enjoys, except perhaps for soccer in parts of Latin America that I haven't visited. As a result, we've been able to generate player numbers and funds well beyond what we should. Rugby's played by working-class people and QCs. It's a huge part of what we are as a people. The game we have is a consequence of its economic and participation base.'

'There's an interesting myth here,' says David Rutherford, 'because there's absolutely no choice between looking after the grassroots and being the most businesslike and professional organisation that we can possibly be because if kids aren't coming in at the bottom end, we won't have All Blacks coming out the top in 15 or 20 years time. It would be bad business practice to ignore the grassroots.'

Administrators refer to the pyramid. The base is junior club rugby and primary schools; the second tier is secondary schools; the third tier is senior club rugby. From there the ladder extends through age-group rugby, NPC and Super 12 all the way to the All Blacks.

'The break comes when people go from club to secondary school then back to club,' says Murray McCaw. 'That's where a lot of people get lost to the game as players. There's a dislocation when the schools get involved; the rest of the structure is logical. About 57 per cent of boys under 13 play but by the time they get to 17, that figure has dropped to 11 per cent. There's a societal element to that but schools don't press it with the same rigour as clubs — it's not their main game. We lose players going in and coming out at both stages of the move from club to school and back to club. When a boy's

Society is to Blame

in his college's first fifteen he's a hero. When he leaves school and goes back to his club, he's no longer a hero, he's just one of a bunch of young guys. I don't think we manage that well as a rugby nation.'

While these current and former administrators acknowledge the problems, they also point out that participation can take many different forms and, in the professional era, they all count.

'The base drags people into the game even if only as couch potatoes,' says McCaw, 'but that's important because if you don't have the audience, you won't be on TV and if you're not on TV, you don't get sponsorship. The broadcasting revenue is fundamental to our future in terms of the sustainability of a professional game here. If we lose people as players, they may become supporters, administrators, referees — they're still absolutely critical to the game so we ignore them at our peril. Because the game is socially based, we need to have a very fat base. People worry about losing NPC players offshore but that's a minor issue compared to losing them at a lower level because it doesn't affect our sustainability.'

While it might be a shame that people no longer watch club rugby in the numbers they used to, that doesn't necessarily indicate a problem for the wider game. Most people watch sport for one of two reasons: to support a team and/or an individual with whom they have a personal connection, which accounts for the majority of spectators at amateur, essentially participatory sporting events, or to be entertained. If it is entertainment they are after, who can blame them for seeking out the best on offer? By plonking themselves in front of TV to watch a Super 12 match, they're indirectly bringing revenue into the game, which can be used to assist the grassroots.

'The bigger the base, the stronger the game,' says Graham Mourie. 'The aim has to be to have as big a base as possible, which means focusing on the game for everyone. While the numbers may have dropped, most Kiwi boys still play it, whether in the form of fifteens, sevens or touch. A lot come in and move out again but

I think rugby's still capturing them and those that are good will stick with it.'

The section of *The Judas Game* covering secondary schools rugby was headed 'The Greatest Threat' and Joseph Romanos described the results of his survey of our major rugby schools as 'frightening'. The figures speak for themselves: it's quite clear that rugby's hold over secondary school sport has loosened. Our greatest rugby school is Auckland Grammar. Romanos' research shows that in 1940, when Grammar's roll was 874, the school had 15 rugby teams and no soccer teams. By 1990, the roll was up to 1885 and there were 26 rugby teams and 20 soccer teams. A decade later, soccer had 32 teams to rugby's 17.

John Graham, Auckland Grammar's headmaster from 1973 to 1993, takes some credit for that: 'The practice of compelling people to play rugby has gone and that's a good thing. A lot of those playing 30 years ago didn't want to. Some of them stayed with the game but a lot hated it and continue to hate it. I made a conscious decision not to push rugby. Playing for the senior sports team gave you access to the tuck shop queue, which was highly prized, and I extended that to musicians, chess players, table tennis players. When I gave an award to a musician, there was a surly rumble from assembly. I took off my glasses and gave them a look and pointed out that he would have put more time into learning his instrument than any sportsman. We were honouring excellence, which isn't the exclusive province of sport. It didn't help but the thinking was accepted in the end.

'Of course, that's changed dramatically. There's now a strong push in society to honour those involved in cultural activities that are seen as crucial to a wholesome society. Rugby is no longer seen as the essence of what is New Zealand but as a sport in which we should and do excel and which is important to our way of life.'

Romanos acknowledges that the situation at Auckland Grammar

reflects its unique standing as the school of choice of Auckland's Asian community. He quotes a figure of 40 per cent of the 2002 third form intake being Asian; my understanding is that the school as a whole is now 40 per cent Asian. Most of those Asian students who do play sport play soccer.

Graham draws the obvious conclusion: 'Grammar won't remain a strong rugby school if the present enrolment policy continues. We're already not as strong as we used to be.'

Romanos demonstrates that the numerical decline of secondary school rugby isn't confined to Auckland Grammar or even Auckland, although the trend is less pronounced in provincial regions. One obvious contributing factor is school teachers' increasing reluctance to coach. This may indicate that teaching is no longer seen as a vocation or that we got an incredibly good deal out of the teaching profession for a long time but, like all good things, it has come to an end. Professionalism didn't help either.

'Professionalism has excluded players who were school teachers,' says Graham. 'You used to have guys who taught, coached at school and played rep football. At one stage at Grammar we had on the staff myself and Graham Henry plus two members of the Auckland front row — Steve Watt and Dave Syms — as well as four or five others who were playing senior club rugby. There were 30-odd rugby teams and these guys coached the coaches. That won't happen in the modern game. When I taught at Christchurch Boys High, there were three All Blacks on the staff — myself, Pat Vincent and Tony Steel. This must have an impact on the game eventually.'

Add to that the feminisation of the teaching profession and it seems likely that, as with junior club rugby, coaching school teams will increasingly fall to parents, although that will run up against the constraints of Saturday work and Saturday shopping. The NZRU and the provincial unions may need to be more proactive in relation to secondary school rugby. As a group, teachers take the view that

A WHOLE NEW BALL GAME

they are not paid to coach so perhaps it is in rugby's interest to step into the breach and pay outstanding teacher/coaches both to coach school teams and train other teacher/coaches and parent/coaches. Schools that do not have keen and capable coaches on their staff would need assistance from professional coaches employed by the provincial union or a local club.

New Zealand rugby fans no doubt struggle to take seriously the notion that their game is under threat from soccer, long lampooned as the languid refuge of males who never leave home without their eyebrow tweezers. McCaw, however, doesn't take the threat lightly: 'I think the best athletes are still coming to rugby and the way the game has changed fits quite neatly with the changes in our physical make-up, but soccer is getting high participation. It won't get stronger until they have strong team brands and strong competition brands but the stuff they're doing for kids — registration packs and player-of-the-day awards — is absolutely fantastic. The TV audience can watch good quality soccer from Europe, and clubs like Manchester United and Liverpool have done a good job of selling their brands internationally — look at the number of kids here running around in UK soccer club apparel. If Manchester United came here, there'd be a huge number of kids wanting to see them. If those games were on in prime time, what sort of audience would they get? It may be our salvation that the timing will never be ideal.'

Casual observation indicates that soccer's participation levels are inflated by those who see it primarily as recreation rather than competitive sport and a 180-degree variation on the 'real men play rugby' compulsion that used to drive up rugby's player numbers. This is the Soccer Mum phenomenon: assertive mothers steering their little boys away from what they regard as an overly physical sport with an overly competitive ethos.

'Social change has actually helped other sports,' says Mourie.

'South Africa was a factor but social change and changing social attitudes much more so.'

'A lot of kids are playing soccer because they've been told to,' says Murray McCaw. 'Soccer is a good game for people who aren't physically suited to or interested in sport. But they're active in identifying young talent with the objective of strengthening teams.'

'Soccer has worked pretty hard,' says Mourie, 'and there's a greater awareness of other sports, some of which are easier for teaching structures to cope with — rugby takes some organisation and coaching knowledge.'

Soccer may or may not be the beautiful game but it's certainly the simple game and therefore a far less daunting proposition for novice players and coaches than rugby. By comparison rugby is fiendishly complicated: the tackled ball area continues to be the plaything of the refereeing freemasonry, enabling them to influence the outcome of matches if not exactly on whim then certainly on the basis of highly subjective snap judgements. (If this complexity is a negative in rugby-mad New Zealand, one would suggest that the game's leaders are deluding themselves if they think rugby can become a genuinely global game with its current set of laws.)

John Hart believes it's time for an all-out assault on the law book. 'We've got to simplify the game because it's too complex for people to understand. If referees have to talk all the time, then there's something wrong with the laws. We should rip up the book and start again. We shouldn't stop games for marginal things like a forward pass if it doesn't affect play, or a crooked lineout throw if the opposition don't compete. It's a hard game to coach. You find representative players saying they don't want to coach because it's difficult.'

Because we have a much smaller population than our main rivals, New Zealand rugby needs a high participation rate and we have one: 3.4 per cent, according to the Boston Consulting Group's

2000 report *Ensuring the Future Success of New Zealand Rugby*. To put that in perspective, only one other country — Wales — is above 2 per cent. The report's authors seem to think that, in this day and age, 3.4 per cent is about as high as can be expected, commenting that 'current participation rates suggest limited potential to significantly increase player numbers'.

The danger is that, given their comparatively low participation rates and large populations, those countries that already have more players than we do — England, South Africa and France — have the potential to build massive player numbers. Extrapolating from the report's figures, if these countries could lift their participation rates by just 0.5 per cent, England would have 879,000 players, South Africa 560,000 and France 517,000. A similar increase would give Australia over 200,000 players. In case you need reminding, in 2002 New Zealand had 122,280 registered rugby players.

While our administrators accept that looking after the base of the game is critical to its long-term health, the reverse is also true. Australia, for instance, has pursued a 'top down' approach, leveraging off the Wallabies' success to promote the game to a wider domestic audience and increase participation levels. The critics can bemoan the focus on the elite but spectacular All Black success will attract more youngsters to the game than any amount of club open days. As Andrew Martin points out, 'If you don't get it right at the top, the base will suffer.'

While there's much wailing and gnashing of teeth over the state of club rugby, it's hard not to conclude that, like Mark Twain, reports of its death have been greatly exaggerated. It's certainly a lot different to what it used to be but then so are most things.

'When I played,' says John Mayhew, 'the rugby club was the centre of your life. Now it's somewhere to get changed before the game and maybe have a quick beer afterwards. There's a host of reasons for that, most of which are beyond rugby's control.

In Auckland there's plenty of stuff to do rather than go to the rugby club and I suspect that's even true in Invercargill. It may be regrettable but it's reality and we have to accept it and adjust to it.'

'People don't live in some of these provincial areas like West Coast and North Otago in anything like the numbers they used to,' says McCaw. 'There's no rugby club in Hunterville now because there isn't the same requirement for shepherds. It doesn't mean to say we couldn't be doing more to grow the game in provincial areas but people have to get real about it.'

Perhaps too, people need to start taking responsibility rather than moaning about the situation and demanding that the NZRU do something about it. Surprisingly, given that attributes such as tough-mindedness, adaptability and self-reliance are supposedly ingrained in the New Zealand rugby culture, this debate is permeated with sentimentality and there's more than a whiff of welfarism in the constant demands for the NZRU to put more 'resources' — that's money to you and me — into club rugby.

McCaw: 'Many provincial unions haven't recognised that it's their responsibility to promote and grow the club brand because if they don't, people will do something else and that doesn't mean watching a rugby match on TV because there are very few Super 12 games or test matches on Saturday afternoons. People have many more options today, assuming they don't work or go shopping on Saturdays; they don't necessarily put on the cloth cap and stroll down to the local club ground to watch a game of footy.'

'You don't go to the club for a beer and a pie and the disco,' says David White. 'Young people go to cafés; they don't go out till midnight. Clubs have to be flexible to provide what people want.'

However, both McCaw and White readily accept that the profile of club rugby has been downgraded as a result of being deprived of the 150 top players for half the season. All Blacks now only turn out for their club teams to test their fitness after injury or if the coaches have decided that a dose of public humiliation is in order, as when Christian Cullen was sent back to club rugby to improve his on-field communication. Received wisdom holds that this is a fundamentally bad thing or, to put it another way, that there is intrinsic merit in All Blacks playing club rugby. Not everyone sees it that way.

'Some All Blacks will find time to go down to their clubs and if they're able to squeeze in a game that's fantastic, but turning out regularly is no longer doable,' says Andrew Martin. 'It's like expecting Tiger Woods to play a pro-am every second week.'

Andy Haden takes the analogy further: 'I played in a pro-am golf tournament in Sydney and the demarcation between the amateurs and the pros was absolutely clear. I don't get this idea that it's good for All Blacks to play club rugby. Why? Amateurs shouldn't be playing pros. The player who earns his living from rugby should be concentrating on performing at the elite level.'

It is unrealistic to expect an All Black to approach a club game as if it was a test match. If he fails to do justice to his ability — whether from lack of motivation, unfamiliarity with his team-mates and the game plan, or a failure to make allowances for the other players' inferior skill levels and reaction times — the spectators who have turned up to see him decide he is overrated or precious, which undermines the public relations component of the exercise.

The desire to have All Blacks play club rugby is an example of the confusion over the place of the grassroots in a professional game. The whole grassroots thing is mired in the misconception that rugby is rugby whether it is the All Blacks or a club game out in the sticks. As a result of professionalism, there are two games under one umbrella — the elite professional game and the mass participation amateur game. Contributing to the confusion is the fact that the two converge in the NPC, so the divide is not as clear-cut as it is in most sports in most parts of the world. Be that as it may, the two parts are quite different and to insist on lumping them together out of nostalgia or chip-on-the-shoulder egalitarianism or narrow self-interest will only perpetuate the confusion. Until New Zealand rugby fully comes to terms with the reality of a two-tier game, the hiccups and problems of recent years will continue to occur and the malaise afflicting sections of the rugby community will persist.

The real debate should be about player development: how 'the factory' operates in the professional era.

Mourie: 'If a player comes through the club system and he's any good but can't make it through to NPC, he goes overseas and plays for money. There are hundreds if not thousands of New Zealanders playing in small clubs, getting some OE and being paid for it. One of the things we need to look at is what's happening with the player development that was traditionally done through the club system. The older players who used to go through into coaching are overseas; we have young club sides with coaches who may be well trained but lack playing experience. We don't have the experienced coaches to bring the young guys through.

'Leadership is lacking in the [modern] game. In the past, you've had players who were club captains or provincial captains so when they all came together, there was a good base of experience. But most top players hardly ever play club rugby these days and if they do, they don't captain their teams. The increasing influence of Polynesian players is also a factor. They're marvellously skilled players but leadership is not their thing. They don't feel comfortable with responsibility.'

Graham makes the point that he learnt to captain 'by captaining my club side where I could make mistakes. It's harder to captain a club side than the All Blacks because at the top level most of the players know what they're doing. I progressed through the ranks and played under great captains like Tiny Hill until I was ready — there was no way you'd be captaining a provincial team after three seasons of rugby; you had to have a track record. That doesn't happen now.'

In 2001 Ross Brown, the president of Dunedin's famous University club, called for the resources going into high-performance rugby to be redirected into club rugby. 'The [NZRU's] high-performance policy is saying in essence that the traditional method of developing rep players — via club rugby — is no longer good enough.'

Well, yes. Take out the 140–150 Super 12 players, take out the hundreds if not thousands of New Zealanders playing overseas, factor in the decline of empirically based coaching and it is reasonable to ask if club rugby can continue to play its traditional development role. Representative rugby can mean different things to different people but if we are talking about developing players for the top NPC first division sides and their Super 12 franchise alter egos, then club rugby may no longer be up to the job. Which is where the high-performance policy with its talent identification and development programmes, its age group teams and academies, comes in.

White cites the example of the talented young Aucklander Ben Atiga, who, in his last year at school, played for the New Zealand Secondary Schools, New Zealand Under-19s and New Zealand Under-21s before taking a break from the game because he'd played too much rugby. Atiga, who had never played club rugby, is following the career paths of the likes of Daniel Braid and Sam Tuitupou who have won a Super 12 championship — and, in Braid's case, made the All Blacks — with virtually no experience of club rugby.

'The bulk of young players are coming through the age-group teams and academies,' says David White. 'It would be good if they could have some grounding in club rugby but where do you fit it in? They're all in a hurry because there's all this money out there; they want it to happen tomorrow and if they don't crack it here, they'll go overseas.'

John Plumtree, the new Wellington NPC coach who spent four seasons coaching Swansea, compares the 'stuffed' Welsh system — recruiting from rival clubs — with Wellington where the academy is seen as the primary source for the NPC team. 'Young players aren't being pushed forward because they're young but because they're good enough. I think they're maturing physically and mentally at an earlier age because they're coming through good systems.'

Mourie believes we need to put even more emphasis on talent identification and development or risk falling behind our major rivals who are making huge investments in these areas. 'There are four aspects to professional rugby: governance, marketing and finance, competitions, and players and coaches. A huge amount of effort has been put into the first three but we've probably taken our eye off the ball in terms of player development, which is the research and development side of the game. Some players go from under-16s through to All Blacks but they're in competitive situations throughout and, in the end, they'll only progress if they're good enough. They don't all go through.'

While some current All Blacks — Dave Hewett, Marty Holah, Reuben Thorne — didn't play age-group rugby, most future All Blacks will stand out from the pack by their mid to late teens, especially if rugby is indeed becoming more and more a young man's game. While there will always be the odd late developer — Nick Farr-Jones, for instance, didn't make his school's first fifteen — and those who, for whatever reason, slip through the net, common sense tells us that players who are going to be starting All Blacks when barely out of their teens — like Richard McCaw and Aaron Mauger — will make their mark in schools and age-group rugby. Nineteen of the 28 players in the 2001 New Zealand Under-21 team gained Super 12 contracts for 2003.

A WHOLE NEW BALL GAME

The argument for an apprenticeship in club rugby that will always strike a chord is that club rugby has been a key factor in our ability to churn out generation after generation of physically and mentally tough forwards. Club rugby was where up-and-comers ran into hardened campaigners who liked nothing better than giving them a crash course in the facts of rugby life. Age-group rugby and the academy system, it is argued, can never replicate the harsh, often painful, lessons that toughened young men's bodies and minds. A steady diet of age group as opposed to club rugby can be viewed as a way of putting off the evil day when the young stars have to go out and compete against fully grown men. On the other hand, our best young forwards — the likes of McCaw, Ali Williams, Jerry Collins, Rodney So'oialo and Corey Flynn — seem to have coped with the physical demands of Super 12 and even international rugby. In fact, while it is still early days, one gets the distinct impression that the new millennium generation of forwards are more physically assertive and have a steelier attitude than those who came into the All Blacks between the 1995 and 1999 World Cups.

John Mayhew says, 'We hear old players going on about hardness — so and so was a hard bastard — and I'm not sure what they mean. Do they mean that he kicked guys or that he played through injury or that he was mentally tough? If you want to compare props, Greg Somerville [New Zealand Under-19, New Zealand Under-21, the Rugby Academy] is certainly much stronger than the props 10 years ago. Some say today's props aren't as hard because they haven't been put through the mill in club rugby but someone like Tony Woodcock [New Zealand Under-19, New Zealand Under-21, the Rugby Academy] has had to front up against some of the best props in the world in Super 12, so isn't that the same process? Some of these guys are going to be very experienced players by their mid-20s. Woodcock is strong enough and good enough technically at 21. The question is more about the mental capacity for playing in very high pressure situations. Some people can cope with that at a young age — Sean Fitzpatrick never came across a player better than himself and I'd guess the same could be said of Richard Loe — but not everyone's like that.'

Another crime against the grassroots is the disparity between the big urban-based unions and the rest, which is supposedly ruining the greatest domestic competition in world rugby. These unions have, so the argument goes, been hugely advantaged by the advent of Super 12 because they assemble squads of out-and-out professionals which, with a few exceptions, are redeployed in the NPC against the semi-professionals of the non-Super 12 unions. Those smaller unions are putting themselves under increasing financial strain trying to keep up with the big boys but the gap just keeps getting wider. As a result the smaller, rural provinces — the Northlands, Taranakis and Southlands — have virtually no chance of winning, which deprives the tournament of much of its excitement, intrigue and romance.

The first thing to be said here is that big-city union domination of the NPC is not a recent phenomenon and therefore cannot be attributed to professionalism or the advent of Super 12. They may not have helped the situation but they didn't cause it. The NPC began in 1976 when the first division champions were Bay of Plenty. Counties won it in 1979 and Manawatu the following year. Since then, only the five big-city unions on which the Super 12 franchises are based have been first division champions. In the 15 years before the game went fully professional, Auckland won the first division championship 10 times. Wellington won it twice and Otago, Canterbury and Waikato once. Since then, Auckland have won it three times, Canterbury twice and Otago and Wellington once. One could draw the tentative conclusion that professionalism and the Super 12 have actually evened things up at the top of the first division by countering Auckland's natural advantages.

Colin Meads, hardly an apologist for new rugby, grasps that this is not, fundamentally, a rugby issue: 'To Meads, the main reason for the decline in the competitiveness of the country unions is the population drift to the big urban maws,' wrote his biographer Brian Turner. 'When he was a gung-ho young player in the 1950s and 1960s, every little town or village had a mill. Many of these villages are gone now.

'[Says Meads] "In a mill, there is half a rugby team. Some of them were real tough, hard men. Pureora used to have a team; there was a whole village there, and two or three sawmills all within about ten miles of each other. Now there's nothing. The same applied to those little places in the south of the King Country — Owhango for instance — they all had teams. They have gone. Instead of sawing logs in local mills, the logs are all transported elsewhere."

'Changes in farming have also meant the loss of young men who used to be employed on farms. "Every four-wheel farm bike represents the loss of one young fella who used to work on the farms. Technology has replaced workers."'

Social and economic change is the root cause of the big five's dominance and the decline of the rural unions. Reversing this trend will require radical, if not extreme, measures: salary caps, drafts, highly centralised NZRU control. But even all that would not necessarily guarantee a successful outcome.

These measures have had some success in Australia but it is worth remembering that the majority of NRL and AFL clubs are in the one city. With most of the teams in greater Sydney and greater Melbourne respectively, player mobility is not an issue. It is one thing to move across town from Manly to Cronulla or from St Kilda to Essendon, quite another to expect a player with a young family to pull up stakes and relocate from Auckland to Invercargill. On top of which, there are legal issues involved in forcing players to go where they don't want to go or preventing them from going where they do want to go.

Says Rutherford, 'In the 1997 Rugby Union Players' Association versus NZRU case, you had people like Brian Lochore giving evidence to say that it was essential for the game that players' freedom of movement be constrained, but it didn't work in the long run. The Players' Association lost the case but history has proved them more right than wrong.'

It is a fact of life that professional athletes will seek to maximise their earnings. That should not come as a surprise: that is what the rest of us do; that is how it works in every other walk of life. It is a fact of life that the big-city unions have a head start through their large player bases and financial muscle, which enables them to bolster the talent at their disposal via selective recruitment. And it is a fact of life that for a professional sporting organisation, the only restraint on recruitment is financial because you can never be too strong. Think of Manchester United who, on any given Saturday, have better players on the bench than most premier league clubs have in their starting line-ups. Think of Canterbury/the Crusaders with their All Black bench.

'You can't underestimate the need for depth on the bench,' says Tew, who as a former CEO of Canterbury Rugby remembers the dark days of 1996 when they finished last in the Super 12. 'Think of the people who came off the bench for the Blues in the early days. You're only ever one injury away from having a problem.'

Tew believes the goal is to 'increase depth rather than spread it' but it is questionable whether this country will ever have sufficient depth for every team in a 10-team first division to be a potential winner. If one accepts the central premise of professional sport, that it's about the best playing the best, then there's an argument for accepting that the big five have an inherent and probably unbridgeable advantage over the rest, rather than clinging to the fairy-tale notion that a Bay of Plenty can compete with an Auckland, that semi-professional journeymen can compete with fully professional elite athletes.

The big five could take part in a two-round, home and away 'premier league'. Alternatively, if it was felt that five teams were not enough for a successful competition, the three Australian states could be invited to take part. No doubt that would be vehemently opposed on the grounds that we should not lift a finger to help the Aussies, but the reality is that, like it or not, Australia and New Zealand are joined together. We form a natural sporting market and will ultimately sink or swim together. It is in New Zealand rugby's interest that Australia is strong since, at the end of the day, we want exciting, high-quality contests. The Bledisloe Cup is now the greatest rivalry in the game and a commodity that, one suspects, will become more and more valuable, providing it continues to produce close and pulsating matches. (It is surprising, therefore, that the two countries have not agreed on a third and deciding game in the event of a deadlock, as has happened in three out of the last four years. One would have thought that a decider at a venue of the holder's choice with shared gate-takings and television rights would be a nice little earner for both parties.)

Below this elite tier, provincial rugby could get back to what it used to be and probably should have remained: an essentially amateur game.

'When they offered $65,000 to provincial players,' says John Hart, 'they effectively and immediately made the NPC a professional competition. Only Super 12 and academy players should be getting money to play NPC; the rest should be doing what they did 20 years ago, which is training twice a week and playing at weekends. We've encouraged a whole group of players to see rugby as a career, which means they become greedy and run off overseas if they're not getting enough money. They've widened the gap between the provinces; all the provinces are paying players and they're all going broke. It became too easy to pay everybody and some of the money was ridiculous. I've seen the other side of it with the Football Kingz: if they got $30,000 or $40,000, they thought they were made.'

In May 2003 Ian McAffer, chairman of the Manawatu Rugby Union, told the *Sunday Star-Times* that his board would consider foregoing its right to a promotion-relegation match should it win the second division.

'Just four years ago,' he said, 'you expected to run a reasonably successful first division campaign on $1–2 million. Now you need in excess of $4 million to buy players and retain players. For places like Manawatu, that's a big risk. It's putting ridiculous pressure on the smaller unions to keep pace. I can't see any resolution until the NZRU splits the professional competition and the amateur game completely.'

The player exodus is one of several direct consequences of professionalism towards which one can take a half-full or half-empty glass attitude. On the face of it, whenever current or former All Blacks or All Black contenders go overseas, New Zealand rugby, particularly the NPC, is the poorer for it.

'These days when you're dropped from the All Blacks, you're finished,' says John Graham. 'After I was dropped in 1965, I played one more season and I was a reserve. In those days you couldn't get on the field so I had a very good time socially. But then there was an obligation to put something back into the game; that no longer applies. They go overseas for the money. Errol Brain was a good thinker, had a good personality and captained sides with flair and ability. When guys like him go, you're losing intellectual property that may be lost for all time.'

'A number of older players may play on,' says Andrew Martin, 'but not at international level and perhaps we should be looking to get them back so that younger players can rub shoulders with them on and off the field, as was the case with [Liam] Barry, [Frano] Botica and [Glen] Osborne at North Harbour. It's a shame we can't hold onto them by giving them a contract to keep on playing club and NPC rugby.'

However, the impact of the outflow may be exaggerated. It is fair to say that the periodic outbursts of media panic — 'We can't afford to lose players like X and Y' — have not yet been vindicated by events.

While it would be nice to think that the experienced All Blacks who have gone offshore — the likes of Zinzan Brooke, Ian Jones, Craig Dowd, Mike Brewer and Todd Blackadder — would have carried on playing NPC and club rugby if juicy superannuation packages had not been dangled in front of them, how likely is it in this day and age? One suspects that most of them, having fulfilled their ambitions and/or no longer being in the All Black frame, would have simply retired.

A few players have turned their backs on the All Blacks: Bruce Reihana, Daryl Gibson, Andrew Blowers — rather more highly regarded in England than he was here — and Josh Kronfeld, although his case is instructive. Kronfeld's last test was the loss to South Africa in Pretoria in August 2000. Although he'd announced his intention to go overseas in 2001, he was keen to go on the end-of-year tour to France and Italy but Wayne Smith sensibly felt it was time to move on. Scott Robertson wore the number seven jersey on that tour and Taine Randell added another string to his bow in the 2001 Tri-Nations. Neither, it would be fair to say, was entirely convincing. When the All Blacks played Ireland in November 2001, Richard McCaw made his debut and open-side flanker has not been a selection issue since. Only 12 tests separated Kronfeld and McCaw, who will go to the World Cup with quite a lot of experience for a 22 year old — significantly more than if Kronfeld had decided to stick around for another year or so. If Kronfeld had set his sights on bowing out at the World Cup, the selectors would have faced a choice between a battle-hardened 32-year-old on his last lap and a prodigy barely over his first hurdle.

There are 140 Super 12 contracts awarded each year so if no one is going out at one end, how can anyone get in at the other? How do we regenerate our teams if there are no vacancies being created by players retiring or going offshore? Would Daniel Carter and Ma'a Nonu have been All Blacks in 2003 if Gibson, Alama Ieremia and Jason O'Halloran had stuck around? If we cannot offer the outstanding young talent being developed through the age-group and academy system a career path, then they will look elsewhere and better, surely, that 28-year-old ex-All Blacks go overseas than uncapped 19 year olds who in three years time could be playing for England or France.

Murray McCaw takes the pragmatic view: '[Former General Electric boss] Jack Welch said that an organisation should aim to drop off its 10 per cent worst-performed staff each year; others talk about planned redundancy. If people go offshore, it creates space — every NPC or Super 12 player or All Black who goes creates a vacancy for someone else. And why shouldn't people go offshore for their retirement money? It's better that someone else pays that money than we do.'

He cites the widely differing cases of Craig Newby and Blackadder as examples of players whose offshore stints should benefit both the individuals and New Zealand rugby. 'Newby went offshore when he failed to secure a Super 12 contract. He's a talented player who needs to change his body shape and ideally he'd go through a development programme in New Zealand, but seeing he's not playing rugby here, he's better off going overseas for a year or two. He could've carried on playing sevens but that wouldn't have done his physique any good in terms of playing fifteens, which is what he wants to do, so it's better he goes overseas and comes back a different shape. Not only was Blackadder going to Scotland to play but to develop his coaching career — that was part of the deal. He'll come back with significant coaching experience under his belt, which has to be good. We can't provide total career paths for all our good coaches so we've got to provide other options for them and there are global opportunities.'

The coaching exodus is more complicated: All Blacks who go to England cannot pop up in the England team but there are no such restrictions on coaches. Already Warren Gatland and John Kirwan have coached international teams against New Zealand and John Mitchell had five goes at beating the All Blacks when he was part of Team England.

'It's a real dilemma,' says Martin. 'I'm certain what happens is that very capable coaches enrich the local game with their knowledge and lift the standards of the competition around them.'

There are suggestions that Smith was asked — and declined — to join the England coaching set-up but it seems only a matter of time before a New Zealander ends up in charge of one of our major rivals. However, both Mitchell and Henry say they are better coaches for their overseas experiences so the knowledge transfer is working in both directions. The key would seem to be ensuring that when our coaches have been through their crash courses and finishing schools, they come home to coach rather than retire.

'Look at the impact Graham Henry's had,' says Auckland Rugby Union CEO David White. 'We have to keep the lines of communication open to our players and coaches overseas and welcome them back as part of the New Zealand rugby family.'

Last but certainly not least in this checklist of running sores is the race issue. Because people do not always say what they really mean or believe when talking about matters of race, the problem is ostensibly 'white flight' — Pakeha boys giving up rugby, usually for soccer, because they don't want to get knocked around by big Polynesians.

Is it for real? Murray Deaker thinks so: 'White flight is very real in Auckland. There's a minute number of Europeans playing senior club rugby and a drop off in the numbers coming in at the lower levels. There's a big growth in soccer on the North Shore and in the eastern suburbs. Kings College and St Kentigern College have first fifteens based on Polynesian scholarships. I'm not sure if there's an answer. It's like the US — kids come out of the ghettos of South Auckland and make a lot of money.'

Mourie believes the Polynesian factor 'is certainly an influence in the big cities but I think that, for the majority of kids, rugby is the same.'

'The way the game has changed,' says Murray McCaw, 'it's easier for bigger kids to succeed, which obviously suits Polynesians because they mature earlier. There are a lot of big white kids but they don't have the same physical or mental maturity. The [adult weight-restricted] 80/80 grade has been a real success in Wellington, going from four or five teams to 30 teams very quickly. You get a real mixture of ages and races. I understand the Wellington Rugby Union is introducing under-13 open and weight-restricted grades but weight restriction can work the other way. I know a Polynesian kid who's having to play against boys three years older than he is and is getting put under physical pressure. It's not an easy one, particularly in some provincial areas where there's not enough players to split them up on the basis of size. But when all's said and done, we want big rugby players in New Zealand.'

White takes the wide view: 'We're conscious that we must provide rugby for everyone. Whether we like it or not, Polynesian kids mature physically earlier, they're big and strong and we can't hide from that. But one in five Aucklanders is Asian and we've got to look at ways of bringing them into the game.'

Rutherford reckons the whole thing is 'crap'.

It is difficult to get a handle on white flight. Are those who see it as a real problem and a long-term threat to New Zealand rugby really saying that white, middle-class boys from Remuera, Khandallah and Fendalton, fifth-generation New Zealanders, should get preferential treatment or be quarantined from brown, working-class sons of more recent immigrants? Because when you get down to the nitty-gritty, what exactly is white flight? It is young New Zealanders deciding they do not want to play rugby because they are scared of getting hurt by other young New Zealanders. Well, that is their choice but why is it our problem? For generations New Zealanders have prided themselves on their physical approach to rugby. As we have often had to point out to gun-shy visiting teams, usually whinging Brits, it is 'a contact sport'. As that iconic Polynesian All Black Tana Umaga told referee Peter Marshall during the 2003 Hurricanes-Crusaders semi-final, 'We're not playing tiddly-winks here.'

Yes, we want rugby to remain the game for all New Zealanders, white, brown and in-between. No, we don't want rugby to become like so much of American professional sport, black athletes watched by white spectators. But if Pakeha kids are choosing not to play the game because it is too physical for them, then surely we should wish them luck with their soccer careers and move on to the next item on the agenda. Because one thing is for sure: we are not losing too many potential All Blacks in this exodus.

The best player in the junior club rugby team with which I've been involved for the past three seasons is usually one of the smaller forwards on the field but he is tough, committed and has a voracious appetite for the physical stuff. He doesn't care how big or what colour the opposition are; he just wants to get out there and get stuck into them. He is a first-generation New Zealander: his father is Welsh. Ali Williams, a soccer player until well into his teens and

Kings College's most recent All Black, has that attitude in spades. He too is a first-generation New Zealander: his father is English.

White flight is such a storm in a teacup that one suspects it is just a roundabout, mealy-mouthed way of expressing alarm over the browning of the game and specifically the All Blacks.

Romanos wondered 'if all New Zealanders still feel that the All Blacks are representative of New Zealand in general when half of them (sometimes more) are brown-skinned.' I wonder if Maori felt represented by the 1928, 1949 and 1960 All Black teams from which they were excluded in deference to the host country's racist ideology. In fact, the 2002 Tri-Nations All Blacks were white to a fault. Richard Harry, the former Wallaby prop, reckoned John Mitchell had picked a team of 'grumpy, white, South Island farmers' and Chris Laidlaw and one or two community leaders were moved to suggest that there was a bias against Polynesian players. (Mitchell emphatically denied it.)

One would like to believe that for the vast majority of New Zealanders the All Blacks are the All Blacks and skin colour does not enter into it. If that is not the case, we are in big trouble.

New Zealand rugby has benefited enormously from the Polynesian dimension. As David Kirk put it, 'International teams divide into two strands — the Latin temperament and the Anglo-Saxon. New Zealand is the only team that benefits from the Anglo-Saxon temperament enlivened and enriched by the Polynesian strand. The Polynesian strand in our national psyche lifts us — the more elusive running, the side step, the *joie de vivre*. You see it in Maori sportspeople, the cavalier attitude to failure, a devil-may-care certainty that fortune favours the bold.'

Rutherford recalls an IRB strategic plan that identified as a weakness the fact that the game was too Anglo-Saxon. New Zealand does not have that problem and that is to our advantage both on and off the field. It is undeniable that the All Blacks' international appeal is in large part due to their exotic appearance and flair and passion; it is equally undeniable that the contribution of Polynesian All Blacks to those aspects has outweighed their numerical representation. If we really want the All Blacks to be the Brazil of rugby, the last thing we should be doing is trying to water down the Polynesian influence. If you don't believe that, just ask yourself this question: would an international sportswear giant whose reported typical target consumer is a teenager in Detroit spend a fortune sponsoring a team of strong, silent, heads down, bums up white blokes?

7

Shaking the money tree

'The Life Cycle of a Sport' is an apocalyptic scenario that gets trotted out from time to time at international sporting conferences. Although much tweaked and modified, the basic version is a cautionary tale of rise and fall, the moral of which is that when a sport pushes its fans to the bottom of its list of priorities, it is in terminal decline.

This is how it unfolds.

Stage one: The sport begins as a casual recreational activity for the benefit of a few participants. More participants join in the fun and the sport attracts its first spectators. Those involved segment into organisers, players and spectators. As spectator numbers grow, the local media starts to take an interest.

Stage two: The sport's popularity among non-participants, including the media, increases. It attracts radio coverage and local sponsors. Running costs increase and a business structure is introduced. The players are accessible and interact with fans, who in turn identify with the players. Local and regional companies entertain at fixtures.

Stage three: Television and print coverage goes international. National and international sponsors invest in promotions that build the sport. The spectator base grows and national and international companies entertain at fixtures. The relationship between organisers and players becomes adversarial as the players demand a bigger slice of the pie. Organisers pay lip service to holding down costs and an elitist, gravy train mentality sets in. Organisers and players fail to communicate with their fans and communities.

Stage four: Organisers and players become contemptuous of the fans and their complaints; the public's emotional support erodes. Organisers come to realise that the balance sheet needs to be improved but sponsorship has been maximised and media rights sold at locked-in prices. The solution: raise ticket prices and squeeze the fans. Alienated fans seek more accessible and exciting entertainment, causing ticket sales and TV ratings to fall, which in turn makes the sport less attractive to sponsors and broadcasters. Impervious to this reality, organisers and players bicker over money. The players go on strike, the organisers take them to court, but nobody else cares.

Those who believe New Zealand rugby is in crisis would see this scenario as a grim vindication. They would argue that the good old days were stage two but, post-professionalism, rugby has sleepwalked into stage three, if not stage four. The elite's increasing remoteness from died-in-the-wool fans and rumblings of a player boycott of the World Cup over restraint and remuneration issues would be cited as proof that rugby has entered the decadent phase. Talkback hosts would add that by refusing to appear on their shows and dismissing their audiences as 'the lowest common denominator' and 'the flat earth society', leading figures in the game are, in effect, treating the fans with contempt. Ticket prices and availability are already a sore point, further evidence — if any were needed — that the NZRU is far too busy sucking up to sponsors and broadcasters to give a damn about the loyal, long-suffering fan base.

The NZRU is to rugby what the government is to the country as a whole. Both tend to be seen as ponderous, impersonal, inept, monolithic and convenient: the government/NZRU is responsible for everything/everything to do with rugby, therefore if anything goes wrong, it's their fault. Blame rolls easily off the tongue because it's directed at an organisation, a thing, a cast of anonymous thousands, rather than a specified individual who might bite back. And anyway, it's water off a duck's back because these monoliths are used to being criticised. They expect it: being the focus of generalised discontent is the price they pay for the power they wield.

Like the government, the NZRU is taken for granted. It gets no credit for its many unheralded, day-to-day achievements but its slip-ups and shortcomings, real and imagined, are greeted with weary scorn — 'here we go again' — and knowing shakes of the head. Over time this creates the perception that the government/NZRU can't do anything right, that mediocrity is as good as it gets. Just as the saying 'The cheque's in the mail' is code for glib unreliability and run-of-the-mill commercial dishonesty, so Americans use the line 'I'm from the government, I'm here to help' as code for a glaring contradiction in terms or a laughable gap between self-image and reality.

Size means bureaucracy; more means less. Just as government departments are supposedly full of arse-covering clock-watchers in grey cardigans, the new breed of professional administrators are seen as a bludge on the very people whose interests they're meant to be serving. One of the most frequently asked questions on talkback radio must be: 'What do all those people at the NZRU actually *do*?' Because as we know, in the good old days, Jack Sullivan and a secretary ran the whole show in their spare time . . .

Not many of us would presume to tell Telecom, say, or Fletcher Challenge how many staff they should employ, but there are no such inhibitions when it comes to the NZRU because its business is rugby and we're all experts on that subject. The fact is, however, that the NZRU is as much a business as it is a sports body and the imperatives of business are the same whether your product is rugby, refrigerators or rock 'n' roll. It's about making money.

John Graham: 'There are a lot of people employed in the game in the provinces and the NZRU — Ron Don would argue it's not necessary. I don't know enough about what they're doing to say one way or another. I would have thought 40 people could run the NZRU but I wouldn't really know so it's silly for me to pronounce on it. The criticism of the large number of administrators really comes from voluntarism — those who have spent all their lives in the game helping people and the game without being paid for it. The challenge is to marry paid employees with continued voluntarism and that's hard to do. The next group of volunteers will be different; they'll be parents brought in by their kids rather than the rabid rugby man whose life revolves around the club and who has no other interests.'

The NZRU is a significant operation. Its income in 2002 was $91.2 million while expenditure amounted to $81.4 million of which $16.9 million went on game development, $35.2 million on competitions, $22.1 million on representative teams and $7.2 million on governance and finances. If you're wondering what happened to the difference between income and expenditure, that $9.8 million went into reserves that now total $26 million. According to chairman Jock Hobbs, the NZRU is on track to achieve its 2005 target of reserves of $50 million, which it deems 'necessary for prudent governance'. The NZRU is financially responsible for the All Blacks, the Super 12 franchises, New Zealand A, New Zealand Maori, the Black Ferns and the national Under-21, Under-19, secondary school and university teams. Super 12 salaries for the five franchises account for around $6 million. By comparison each club in the NRL can spend up to $3.2 million on a squad of 26 players. All up, running the All Blacks eats up a third of total turnover but they are the cash cow, bringing in close to 90 per cent of the revenue.

The Rugby Union is organised into seven 'departments': Rugby, Commercial, Communications, Support Services, Finance, Legal and Human Resources.

Rugby covers outbound international tours, Super 12, NPC,

player and coach development, and relationships between provincial unions. There are three 'sub-departments' under the Rugby umbrella: Tournaments, Tours and Teams, which covers inbound tours, development competitions, sevens and age group rugby; Provincial Union/Community Support, which covers developing educational material and coaching resources, referee recruitment and development and liaising with the game at a community or grassroots level; and the All Blacks.

Commercial covers all sponsorship, marketing and broadcasting activities. Communications covers communications strategy and implementation, government relations, media liaison and content on intranet and internet websites. Support Services covers information technology and business operations, the adidas Institute of Rugby, and injury prevention and medical matters. Legal covers legal issues affecting the NZRU and player, coach and other management contracts while Human Resources and Finance perform the same broad functions as they do in any other business.

Money, of course, is the root of all evil. Those who are ill at ease with professional rugby's hype, razzamatazz, millionaire stars and the amazing expanding NZRU's spin doctors and brand managers believe that money has tainted the game. But money also makes the world go round. Great competitions featuring great players don't come cheap, nor does having the best international team in the world. If we want those things, we have to pay for them. The only way the NZRU can raise that sort of money is to go out and sell its product: our players, our teams, our competitions, our rugby.

'The rugby purist hasn't seen that money is vital to sustain and grow the game,' says Murray McCaw. 'He doesn't see the need for some of the things that are going on, for instance the NZRU having an employee with the title Brand Manager, NPC. The reality is that this and all the other branding exercises and promotional activity have to be undertaken if we're to come up with the $26 million a year we need to keep the game going. We can't have one without the other.'

'You've got to market the bloody game,' says John Graham. 'People expect to know what's on and why it's worth watching. When I was on the Auckland Rugby Union board and we were looking to cut costs, I suggested that we could save quite a lot of money by cutting out all the pre-game crap — entertainment — and just going back to having a curtain-raiser. I was told — correctly — that I was back in the dark ages.'

The new breed of professional administrators, promoters and marketers working for the NZRU and the provincial unions are sometimes dismissed as 'not real rugby people'. The same charge was levelled at some recent NZRU board members. Leaving aside the question of who, at the end of the day, is entitled to make the call on who is or isn't a real rugby person, this attitude derives from an inability to differentiate between the game of rugby and the business of rugby.

'People don't like the talk of brands to begin with,' says Graham, 'then they find a 25-year-old woman is doing the job. We now know that women can do things just as well if not better than men. You want the best person for the job so the question is: is she any good at marketing? It's a question of establishing that the job is necessary, then appointing the right person.'

McCaw, who was branded a corporate interloper rather than a real rugby person, argues the case for diversity at board level: 'You have some administrators who've put in 45 years in club rugby and some who haven't and why should they? They've done the miles in something else. You don't want a set of clones. What is important is to have a broad understanding of the fundamentals of the game and I think the board has been moving in the right direction since the introduction of professional rugby.'

While the provincial backlash over the loss of the Rugby World

Cup sub-hosting rights tipped McCaw and most of the other directors off the board and elevated a couple of former All Black captains, it didn't succeed in rolling back the corporate influence. David Rutherford's successor as CEO was investment banker Chris Moller, a former deputy chief executive of New Zealand's largest company Fonterra, a man with an impressive track record in business but next to no rugby background. The board may have changed; the world hasn't.

'No doubt there's an expectation that, with the new board, there will be greater consideration of what's loosely called grassroots rugby,' says Hobbs. 'There's certainly a view that we should simply concentrate on the grassroots and forget about the business but I don't agree with that. They're both important. The business and commercial imperatives have to be understood and met. We also have to understand the pressures and challenges facing club rugby. The NZRU board is no different from any other board — you need a balance and mix of skills and backgrounds.'

While the board upheaval was hailed as a robust exercise in accountability that tilted the balance back in favour of the traditional stakeholders, there are those who question whether this sort of ground-up democracy is desirable. They argue that the current system, under which the make-up of the board is primarily determined by the 27 provincial unions through the delegate method, is unlikely to consistently generate the skills and expertise needed to run the complex business of professional rugby.

David White: 'In 1996/97 Auckland changed its structure from a decision-making council elected by the clubs to a corporate model board comprising six independents and two board members appointed by the clubs. The independents are still appointed by the stakeholders in the form of an advisory group which conducts interviews, and the others are elected at the AGM. I don't believe the clubs have lost power in that sense. The irony is that while the provinces have adopted the corporate model, the NZRU only has two independents. It's very difficult to get the right mix with a politically appointed board.'

The fact of the matter is that the game hasn't been hijacked by people who see it as a business whose product just happens to be rugby. As was the case back in the amateur era with the likes of former NZRU chairman Eddie Tonks, successful businessmen who get involved in rugby do so first and foremost because they love the game. If money was their sole motivation, most of them could find much more profitable uses for their time. And if rugby is indeed too much of a game to be a business and too much of a business to be a game, then we could probably do with more of them.

The NZRU may get a rough ride on the airwaves and in print but it marks itself pretty hard too. In 2001 it introduced the balanced scoreboard, a system designed to bring some transparency to its performance and get away from the corporate world's conventional yardstick, the financial statement. In 2002 the NZRU awarded itself 47.5 per cent, not even a pass-mark. The irony is that the flunk was caused by the same unrealistic expectations that keep the rugby public in a semi-permanent state of dissatisfaction.

The performances of the various national teams under the NZRU umbrella count for 60 per cent and the vast majority of that — 50 per cent of the overall total — is riding on the All Blacks. So despite the fact that the All Blacks won eight and drew one of their 11 games (with one loss and the draw registered by an experimental team playing away against first-rank opposition), in the process winning the Tri-Nations championship, despite the fact that the sevens team won the Commonwealth gold medal and the World Series, despite the fact that the Black Ferns and the Under-19s were world champions, the NZRU scored a mere 21 out of 60 in this area. Just as on the field, it's a fine line between success and failure: if the All Blacks had hung on for a win in Sydney, for instance, the NZRU would have scored a respectable 67.5 per cent; if they'd also squeaked home in London and Paris, as they almost did, the NZRU would have scored 82.5 per cent and gone to the top of the class.

In the annual report, the then acting chief executive Steve Tew explained the rationale behind this weighting: 'This measure reflects a truth in modern sports that how the public and the marketplace judge an organisation's ability is linked to the performance of its top team in any given year.' However, elsewhere in the report, Hobbs revealed that the new board 'is of the opinion that some of the targets set for 2002 were too ambitious and has adjusted some of them accordingly for 2003.' Governance and financial is up to 20 per cent of the total, results down to 50 per cent. Winning the Bledisloe Cup is down from 20 per cent to 7.5 per cent while winning the World Cup counts for 25 per cent.

The biggest, juiciest plums on the NZRU's money tree are the Sanzar broadcasting rights deal with Rupert Murdoch's News Ltd and the adidas sponsorship. The deal with News — which brings in $US555 million over 10 years split between New Zealand, Australia and South Africa — expires in 2005 and some anxiety surrounds the upcoming renegotiation given that, globally, broadcasting rights to sports events is currently a buyer's market. During the recent negotiations for the rights to the Six Nations Championship, the rugby unions made the painful discovery that there was significantly less demand for the product than the previous time around, which was reflected in the eventual purchase price. With that in the background, the extension of the spectacular adidas deal through to 2011 was a strategic coup for the NZRU, all the more so given that, at one stage, it looked as if adidas was counting the days until it could pull the plug.

The original deal was driven, from the adidas end, by a French advertising man named Robert-Louis Dreyfus. Dreyfus and a group of his friends took over adidas when the company appeared to be on its last legs. They engineered a Lazarus-like recovery, making themselves fabulously rich in the process. Something of an eccentric, Dreyfus had a passion for rugby and the All Blacks in particular and when he heard that Nike was negotiating with the NZRU, he ambushed the American company with a jaw-dropping offer. Various figures are mentioned but it seems that Nike offered around $12 million a year and Dreyfus doubled that.

Then Dreyfus got cancer. He withdrew from adidas and the company was taken over by a group of hard-headed Germans who knew little about rugby and cared even less. By all accounts, their jaws also dropped when they discovered the company was lavishing more money on a team from the ends of the earth engaged in a minority sport with an insignificant following in most of Western Europe, than on the New York Yankees. When said team came a cropper at the 1999 World Cup, it began to look as if, come 2004, the NZRU would be queasily contemplating a big red hole in the balance sheet where adidas used to be.

(An off-field incident at the World Cup wouldn't have helped matters. John Hart recalls a senior adidas executive coming over from Germany to present the All·Blacks with thousand-dollar leather jackets. 'As Mike Banks introduced him and he began to speak, the players were yahooing. The jackets had a tiny embroidered adidas logo, which you could hardly see, but afterwards one player went up to the adidas man to ask how he could get rid of the logo when he got home.')

At this point, the Kiwi diaspora kicked in. Chief financial officer for adidas is Robin Stalker, an expatriate New Zealander whose great-grandfather Jack Stalker played for the 1903 All Blacks. Stalker, 45, grew up in Palmerston North. In 1982 he joined the Wellington branch of the accountancy firm Ernst & Young, where his duties included auditing the NZRU's books. He moved to London with the firm the following year and has lived and worked overseas ever since. Having no relationship with the new team at adidas, Stalker was the obvious first port of call for the NZRU who invited him out for the 2001 Springbok test at Eden Park. While apparently not a sentimentalist — one imagines not many CFOs of major multinational companies are — Stalker enjoyed the occasion, despite being forced to celebrate the All Black win until the sun came up.

Keen to build on this contact, the NZRU invited the adidas boss Herbert Hainer to the All Blacks game against Ireland in Dublin later that year. Hainer got his first surprise of the day when his taxi pulled up outside dowdy, down-at-heel Lansdowne Road, a far cry from the gleaming stadia where he watched Bayern Munich. The haka gave him his second inkling that this would be a bit different from a midtable clash in the Bundesliga: the crowd watched it in silence and erupted as it finished. The ferocious physical exchanges were the third eye-opener. Hainer was aware that the All Blacks had never lost to Ireland but they trailed at halftime and he'd barely settled back into his seat for the second half when the Irish scored again to lead 21–7. An epic cock-up loomed but the All Blacks came home with a wet sail, as they say in Australia, to win a thriller 40–29, six tries to three.

Hainer attended the traditional after-match dinner at which McCaw presented caps to the three debutants — Aaron Mauger, Dave Hewett and the 20-year-old Richard McCaw (no relation), the man of the match. As McCaw made his way forward, Syd Millar, one of the great figures in Irish and world rugby — Irish prop, Lions prop in New Zealand in 1959, Irish coach, victorious Lions coach in South Africa in 1974, deputy chairman of the IRB — stood to applaud him. Then the whole Irish team stood to applaud him. Then the remaining 600 people at the dinner stood to applaud him. In his speech, the Irish captain Keith Wood said his team couldn't believe that they'd got themselves into such a good position only to blow it. That was why the All Blacks were revered, he added: just when you thought you had them, they blew you out of the water.

Trevor McKewen, ex-Super League, ex-Warriors, now the NZRU's general manager, commercial: 'After the physicality of the game, Hainer couldn't believe that the players could shake hands and swap shirts, let alone address the opposition in the terms used by Keith Wood. He told us our sport had a soul and he wished he could have flown the entire UEFA committee to Dublin to see it. He told us the All Blacks were unique in world sport and a perfect fit for adidas: Nike is about being maverick and in your face; adidas is about passion and purity. That night was a turning point in getting an extension of the contract.

'One of my pet hates is the way New Zealanders dismiss adidas. They get blamed for things which are nothing to do with them, like taking the words "New Zealand" off the jersey. Of course it doesn't help when [Andrew] Mehrtens criticises the ball or [Justin] Marshall claims the only reason for that 2001 tour was that adidas wanted it. That was utter nonsense — it was part of the IRB schedule. Nike had the All Blacks playing exhibition matches in Europe with people like Michael Jordan taking part. Having paid the All Blacks an immense compliment by valuing them higher than the likes of the New York Yankees, these guys leave us alone. We should be proud of how this huge and successful multi-national views a team from the other end of the earth playing a code they're not interested in. This is their biggest sponsorship and it's because the All Blacks stand apart with a brand story that's unique.'

Apart from anything else, the adidas sponsorship means the All Blacks are now the only major international team without an advertising logo — as opposed to the outfitter's logo which the others have as well — on their jersey.

Some of the NZRU's critics believe that its heedless — as they see it — embrace of commercialism is eroding New Zealand's competitive edge by corrupting the culture of the game, thereby condemning us, in the long-run, to second-class status. It seems more likely that the reverse is true and that New Zealand's potential long-term vulnerability lies in the NZRU's incapacity to match the levels of revenue generated by our major rivals.

The report *Ensuring The Future Success Of New Zealand Rugby* concluded that while New Zealand was currently in a relatively strong competitive position, the long-term picture was clouded. Relative to our competitors, New Zealand rugby's capacity for growth is limited by its already high participation rate and its small population and market. Over the next five to 10 years, we can expect our rivals to utilise their greater ability to attract and generate funds to heavily promote the game to their large populations, improve the standards of their competitions, buy in talent and technology from offshore and implement coaching, talent identification, and development programmes on an ever-larger scale.

Describing England as 'a sleeping giant' — this was three years ago; the signs are that if the giant isn't yet wide awake, he's certainly rubbing the sleep out of his eyes — the report pointed out that English rugby has six times as many players and five times as many coaches as we do and would use the wealth flowing into the game there to extend this advantage and close the gap in areas where New Zealand is currently ahead, such as talent development. The report's authors added, 'France poses a similar threat.'

And we thought we only had to worry about the Aussies.

8

If it is broke . . .

Professional sport is about successful competitions. Successful competitions bring in the money that pays the players, funds development and generally keeps the game going. Successful competitions attract sponsors and broadcasters because they deliver a return on investment in terms of exposure, pay TV subscriptions, ratings and advertising revenue. When rugby went professional in 1995, the Sanzar partners — South Africa, Australia and New Zealand — had some leeway in framing their new competitions because the purchasing broadcaster, News Ltd, had signed on for 10 years. Given the administrators' lack of experience of professional sport and the abruptness of the transition, it would have been remarkable if they'd got everything dead right from the word go. As it was, they did pretty well but both the Super 12 and the Tri-Nations have inherent weaknesses that are becoming more evident with each passing year. If these are not addressed, New Zealand rugby runs the risk of being locked into less-than-optimum formats for what shapes up as a critical decade in the game's evolution.

Super 12's predecessors, the Super 6 and Super 10, didn't really work because they were embarked on half-heartedly. From the outset, Super 12 had the benefit of a clear-cut marketing strategy and a committed broadcaster and, for the most part, players and coaches responded to the opportunities of professionalism and the challenge of the new competition. Eight years on, Super 12 continues to deliver seven or eight hours of mostly satisfying rugby each weekend. Well, satisfying for New Zealanders anyway. By virtue of having five teams compared with South Africa's four and Australia's three and assuming people prefer to watch their own teams and players rather than those from other countries, New Zealand fans get more value from the competition than do Australians and South Africans. There are, for example, 10 all-New Zealand games compared with six all-South African and a mere three all-Australian. All told, two-thirds of the 66 round robin games involve a New Zealand team. Secondly, we pretty well own the tournament, having won it seven times out of eight and only once — in 2001 — not had a team in the play-offs. Every weekend from late February to late May, Friday night football kicks off a feel-good bonanza for Kiwi rugby fans.

Across the Indian Ocean, however, the feel-good factor is in desperately short supply. To South Africans, the Super 12 must seem like an Australasian conspiracy to sap their self-belief and undermine the Springboks. Writing before the 2003 semi-finals, another party at which no one asked the South Africans to dance, the experienced rugby writer Dan Retief declared, 'Whichever way you look at it, the Super 12 has been an unqualified success for New Zealand, a great innovation for Australia and an unmitigated disaster for South Africa.'

One can see what he means. No South African team has ever won the tournament. Only the Sharks have made the grand final, losing to the Blues by 24 points in 1996 and the Brumbies by 30 in 2001. And 2003 was the sixth year in a row that a South African team has finished bottom. In fact the South African teams have something of a stranglehold on the foot of the ladder, having occupied two of the three bottom rungs in four tournaments. In 2002 they went the whole hog and did the reverse trifecta.

For Retief the question that had to be asked was: 'Is the Super 12 good for South African rugby?' His answer: 'The record certainly indicates that it is possibly doing more damage than good.'

The juxtaposition of 'certainly' and 'possibly' indicates that Retief isn't quite ready to tuck his ball under his arm and go home but his negativity is entirely understandable. What must be so depressing for the South Africans is the double whammy effect: they never have the best teams and they usually have the worst. Over eight Super 12s, half the sides finishing in the bottom four — 16 out of 32 — have been South African, even though they provide only a third of the teams. The contrast with Australia is enlightening. If the yardstick is winning the competition, the Australians have only gone one better. The ACT Brumbies have obviously established themselves as one of the tournament's heavyweights but their success has arguably been at the expense of Australian rugby's traditional powerhouses, New South Wales and Queensland. However, in terms of avoiding the wretchedness and irrelevance of bumping along at the foot of the points table, the Australians have done remarkably well: they've never come last and despite having a quarter of the teams, they've provided only an eighth of the bottom four finishers — four out of 32. New Zealand's ratio of cellar-dwellers — 37 per cent — is about right seeing we provide 42 per cent of the participants.

While Retief admits that the South Africans haven't helped themselves by chopping and changing coaches and squads, he and many of his countrymen believe the odds are stacked against their teams: 'The tournament contains a seemingly unavoidable bogey for South African teams in a demanding overseas travel schedule that requires our teams to play four games away on the trot whereas the most any of the New Zealand or Australian teams can expect to play is three — and this is a rare occurrence.'

There are no easy pickings in Australia or New Zealand but if a Kiwi side gets cleaned out at Ballymore or Bruce Stadium,

IF IT IS BROKE . . .

they're nearly always back in their home town, tucked up in their own beds the following night. Pity a South African side after two weeks on the road and two losses under the belt with dates at Jade Stadium and Eden Park to look forward to. In that situation, it must be difficult for the players to resist the temptation to psychologically concede the remaining tour matches and count the days until they head home. South African sides in Australasia are often further handicapped by dizzyingly high injury tolls, which raises the perhaps unworthy suspicion that, like conscript soldiers in a far-flung hot zone, the players aren't exactly broken-hearted to be invalided out. In contrast the New Zealand teams seem to have come to terms with the demands and challenges of their two weeks in South Africa — except perhaps for those posed by the judiciary — and strive to turn a potential negative into a positive by using the time away from the distractions of home to build team spirit and togetherness.

It's hard to see a solution. Cost and travel fatigue would seem to rule out the South Africans making two two-week forays to Australasia. Perhaps the problem could be alleviated by having the Australian teams play one of their two home games against South African opponents in Perth, but this would have an adverse effect on revenue. The Australians would probably also argue that, given the large South African community in Perth, these would effectively become away games.

Retief suggests going back to a Super 10 format to shorten the trip. Unlike the South African Rugby Football Union (SARFU), which is pressing for another South African team in an expanded competition, he believes it may be time to concede that 'with the demands of development and affirmation, South Africa does not have a large enough core of competent players to be fielding four teams'.

Another, far more radical solution that is whispered about in rugby circles, and caused a stir when it leaked into the media in 2002, would be for South Africa to withdraw from Sanzar and become, for rugby purposes, part of Europe. The attractions from a South African point of view are obvious: they are in the Western European time zone so the travel, while still long-haul, would be less disruptive to the body clock. Secondly, they would be exposed to a huge viewer market with potentially far more lucrative sponsorship opportunities.

Although SARFU poured cold water on the reports and insisted that South Africa was joined at the hip to its Sanzar partners, there is more to this story than media speculation. 'South Africa would like to link with Europe,' says David Rutherford, 'but Europe don't want them.' It is worth noting that among a number of ambitious if not fanciful ideas in a discussion document prepared by the consulting group accenture for a Sanzar chief executives' workshop in 2001 was a blueprint for slicing the world into three time zone-based longitudinal conferences: a 12-team American conference with teams from Canada, USA, Argentina and Uruguay; a 16-team Continental conference with teams from Britain, France and South Africa; and a 16-team Pacific conference with teams from Japan, China, Hong Kong, Australia and New Zealand.

South Africa's defection wouldn't be universally mourned in this part of the world where some administrators question the long-term viability and desirability of a tournament with such a heavy and costly travel component operating across incompatible time zones. Others worry that issues of player security and social and political stability are going to loom ever larger in South Africa. These sceptics argue that, in the playing sense, the South Africans wouldn't be such a great loss and that Australia, New Zealand and perhaps the Pacific Islands could put on an equally good, cheaper, logistically more manageable tournament. Because of the sensitivity surrounding any discussion of South Africa's internal situation, the advocates of divorce prefer to remain anonymous.

There are even those who want to scrap the Super 12 altogether. Their argument is that we're trying to cram four competitions — Super 12, club, international and NPC — into a season that has only room for three. Something's got to give and at the moment it's club rugby, which is stripped of star players and therefore pulling power and profile and forced to share its traditional early season window with the Super 12. Their solution is to discontinue the Super 12, thereby restoring club rugby's place in the sun, and invite the three Australian teams and perhaps a Pacific Islands team or teams to take part in the NPC. Like many panaceas, this would solve one problem by creating another. It would certainly get the top players back into club rugby, assuming they were prepared to take a salary cut. Pulling out of the Super 12, though, would blow a hole in the NZRU's income, thus reducing its ability to retain the top players, which in turn would impact on the NPC. It seems pointless to clear a window for club rugby and internationalise the NPC if the stars won't stick around to take part in either.

Says David White, 'The fundamentals are that we have to fund the game, which means Super 12, and if we want a vibrant NPC, we must keep our top players.'

Of course, any move to whittle down the Super 12 will be resisted by the Australians who remain hell-bent on having a fourth team and, despite having extracted a terrible revenge, bitter towards New Zealand for blocking it. On the face of it, their logic is irresistible: they are the reigning world champions and the only country to have won the World Cup twice; they won the Tri-Nations in 2000 and 2001; they've held the Bledisloe Cup for five years. By what murky, convoluted reasoning do we arrive at the position that it's fair and reasonable for us to have five teams and them only three?

Actually, there's not a lot of reasoning — murky or otherwise —

involved. The NZRU wants less rugby, the ARU wants more. Besides, as we never tire of pointing out, Australia lacks the depth to sustain a fourth team.

What is the evidence for this contention? The 120 round robin matches between Australian and New Zealand teams over eight Super 12s have resulted in 60 wins apiece. Given that their talent is consolidated into three teams while ours is spread over five, this clearly suggests that we have greater depth. (On the subject of consolidation of talent, it's glaringly obvious that our playing talent is not evenly spread and the Crusaders' success has effectively come at the expense of the Chiefs and the Hurricanes.)

On the other hand, Australia's age group teams are highly competitive and every year the Brumbies, Reds and Waratahs unveil new players who make the step up as well as our rookies do, despite not having the grounding of an NPC. Club rugby in Brisbane and Sydney remains strong and well-supported, and benefits from some Wallaby involvement after the Tri-Nations. The ARU has invested heavily in talent identification and the academy system and selective recruitment from rugby league will no doubt continue.

But is their depth or lack of it really any of our business? There's an element of 'we know what's better for you than you do' paternalism in New Zealand's position. If the Aussies get it wrong, they'll suffer the consequences, not us. Ah yes, is the reply, but if their fourth team can't cut the mustard, the tournament will suffer. That's a strange tack to take seeing that the tournament is suffering now because the South Africans aren't competitive. If it's so important that the tournament is as competitive as possible, isn't that the place to start?

If depth is an issue then the New Zealand rugby 'industry' would probably benefit from a fourth Australian team. While a team with a smattering of Kiwis wouldn't strictly serve the ARU's purpose of building depth in their rugby, they may well feel that their overall

If it is broke . . .

strategy of spreading the code throughout Australia is better served in the short to medium term by ensuring the new team is competitive. From a New Zealand perspective, where's the downside in some of our players being paid by John O'Neill? While it's one thing to rule players plying their trade in Europe or Japan out of consideration for the All Blacks, why should the same apply to Kiwis playing for an Australian — or, for that matter, South African — Super 12 team? The Super 12 is now the official route to All Black selection so why should it make any difference which team a prospective All Black plays for? He will still be up against the best players in the Southern Hemisphere, he will still be appearing at a stadium near you, he will still go head to head with the other contenders and he can still come home to play in the NPC.

Part of Super 12's appeal is that it's a quasi-international tournament, although the local clashes often seem to have more of an edge. The Reds versus the Waratahs, for example, has a significance that transcends competition points and if the South Africans hoed into the Kiwis and Aussies the way they often hoe into each other, they'd probably do a lot better. However, soccer long ago came to the realisation that issues of nationalism and nationality are secondary, if not actually irrelevant, in club competitions. The accelerating internationalisation of the transfer market is now producing 'United Nations' clubs like Chelsea, which in recent seasons has fielded sides largely devoid of English players.

The problem with the Tri-Nations is more straightforward and, one feels, more easily rectified. The idea of the Southern Hemisphere giants tangling home and away every year has turned out to be better in theory than in practice. The moveable feast nature of Tri-Nations makes it difficult to generate momentum and excitement and, dare one say it, needle, and as a result it has the feel of a series of one-off games rather than a tournament. Adding weight to this perception is the fact that the Tri-Nations has never culminated in a de facto grand final with everything hanging on the last match. The fact that we've just spent three months watching the same players in the Super 12 probably doesn't help matters. One obvious casualty has been the mystique that used to surround the Springboks, although the Boks have contributed to this process through mediocre performances.

The most compelling rugby event of recent times in the Southern Hemisphere — and perhaps the world given the dross served up at the 1999 World Cup — was the 2001 British Lions tour of Australia. It was a case study in the tension, drama and controversy which builds up over the course of a tour culminating in a deciding test match and it left the Tri-Nations for dead. In view of the growing consensus that the tournament is wearing a bit thin and that tours should be reinstated, one option would be to stage the Tri-Nations every second or third year with the three countries either touring or hosting tours in the intervening years. The schedule might look something like this:

Year one: Tri-Nations championship
Year two: England tours New Zealand; Australia tours South Africa
Year three: New Zealand tours Australia; France tours South Africa
Year four: Tri-Nations championship
Year five: South Africa tours New Zealand; British Lions tour Australia
Year six: Australia tours New Zealand; England tours South Africa

A similar idea, but more radical in that it proposed doing away with the Tri-Nations altogether, was floated by the NZRU several years ago. Murray McCaw explains the 'Four Nations' concept: 'In year one Australia makes a three-test tour of South Africa with provincial games while England makes a three-test tour of New Zealand also with provincial games. At the end of the tours, the two series winners play off for a Four Nations trophy. The following year South Africa could tour New Zealand and France tour Australia; the year after that New Zealand tours Australia and the Lions tour South Africa. Every three years each country would host a tour from a Southern Hemisphere country and a Northern Hemisphere power and make a tour of a Southern Hemisphere country. You could still have Bledisloe Cup matches alongside it but it would promote the game outside the main centres and get the build up and excitement of tours, neither of which are happening now.'

So what happened to this concept? 'O'Neill ridiculed the idea — this was before the Lions tour — and they've been too absorbed with Rugby World Cup since,' says McCaw. 'South Africa loves the Tri-Nations; it's more important to them than the Super 12. Mainly there's a sense of "if it ain't broke, don't fix it". Sanzar members can't approach News with their own proposals — they have to be agreed Sanzar proposals — although all bets are off when the deal comes up for renegotiation. With the Four Nations, News would get seven games including two series with potential deciders, plus a grand final compared to what we've got at the moment, which is really a series of six one-off games that haven't ever thrown up a last-game final.'

The reinstatement of tours featuring provincial matches, some of them midweek, would also go a long way towards rectifying a failing of the Super 12/Tri-Nations format, which is that, in terms of quantity, the rugby season falls away after the Super 12 round robin. We go from six games a weekend to two to one to some fairly meaningless warm-up test matches (2003 being an exception) to the Tri-Nations that involves six matches spread over seven or eight weeks.

A WHOLE NEW BALL GAME

We hear a lot of vague talk about the desirability of a global season but little in the way of detail about what it would mean for the current competitions. It seems to be taken for granted that, come what may, international competition will remain the lifeblood, shop window and ultimate focus of player ambition and spectator interest but that assumption is based much more on the traditions of rugby's amateur past than the dynamics of its professional future.

Rugby may eventually have to choose between some variation on the status quo and the soccer model. In terms of meaningful competition, international soccer is about the World Cup and the European Cup and their respective qualifying processes. The primary emphasis is on the clubs participating in domestic league and cup competitions and, in the case of Europe where geography and infrastructure make it feasible, regional competitions.

'A big issue is whether rugby is going to remain an international game or become a club-based game on the soccer model,' says David Rutherford. 'Which model is going to dominate the season structure? Historically, international competition has been where the money is but the spectacular growth of the Super 12 and Heineken Cup may change that. Rugby isn't a true international sport. It may be played in 92 countries but there are probably 50 countries that can realistically aspire to winning the soccer World Cup. There are countries capable of winning — like Holland in 2002 — which don't even qualify.'

There are five countries that can realistically aspire to winning the Rugby World Cup. It was predicted that the introduction of the World Cup would galvanise the second and third-tier nations into lifting their standards but in fact little has changed since 1987. England's consolidation of its standing among the superpowers and the emergence of Samoa are balanced by the decline of Wales and Romania since their 1970s heydays. If the pattern is repeated at the 2003 and 2007 tournaments, sponsors and broadcasters may begin to

John Hart with the heart, soul, muscle and mind of the great 1995–97 All Black team: Frank Bunce (left), Sean Fitzpatrick (centre) and Zinzan Brooke.

Above: *'It could be worse, Sean — you could've lost.' Former NZRU board member Kevin Roberts fails to persuade Sean Fitzpatrick to look on the bright side.*

Left: *Plane daft — Taine Randell and friend walk away from one of the great aviation disasters of our time. Not everyone did.*

The buck stops here. The pressure of management shows on the faces of, clockwise from top left, All Black team doctor John 'Doc' Mayhew, former selector the late Gordon Hunter, former manager Andrew Martin and former coach Laurie Mains.

When we were kings: Sean Fitzpatrick holds aloft the Bledisloe Cup.

The changing shape of rugby is reflected in the 40 kg weight difference between these All Black left wings whose careers almost overlapped: Jonah Lomu and (above) Terry Wright.

We think it's super but then we've won it seven times out of eight. In 2003 it was the Blues captained by Xavier Rush who kept the Super 12 trophy in New Zealand.

If it is broke . . .

question the whole concept. What's the point in staging, sponsoring, and broadcasting all those games which have no bearing on the outcome of the tournament and are, at the end of the day, of little interest to anyone other than the participants? Why not just cut to the chase and have the top five or six countries contesting the world championship in an annual mini-tournament?

The Six Nations tournament has a similar problem. As things stand, it's hard to see any country other than England or France winning the thing and most of the matches between the other four countries, while generally not short of endeavour, lack the skill level and intensity of sport at the highest level. Those who insist otherwise were quick to cite Ireland's performance in 2003 but their wishful thinking was exposed when England went to Lansdowne Road on the final weekend and took Ireland apart. By staging the England-France game in the first round, the organisers effectively undermined the tournament. When France failed to win that crucial game, they predictably lost interest and thereafter went through the motions. However, the tournament's media cheer squad saw what they wanted to see and attached far too much importance to Ireland's narrow victory over the unmotivated French that set up the final round showdown. Unfortunately for Ireland, a highly motivated England team showed up. Given the vast disparity in resources between the big two and the rest, the likelihood is that Anglo-French dominance will become even more entrenched.

Recently former Australian cricket captain Greg Chappell, a take-no-prisoners competitor in his day, sounded the alarm over his country's unchallenged domination of international cricket: 'There are people within cricket who are very concerned about the state of the game worldwide,' he said. 'You can't play the game in a vacuum. Australian cricket can't run its business in a vacuum, and this must be of concern because it's going to affect the business in the long run.

'[The divide] is already showing up in television rights. There's a strong feeling within the sports community that the next round of television rights are not going to return the same income as the last round did, which is certainly going to have an impact from the game's point of view and the players' point of view.'

It's all about competition, successful formats that produce close contests. As McCaw put it, 'Ideally the All Blacks would win every game by two or three points. They need to win to maintain the aura, but one-sided games don't attract and hold an audience.'

If the IRB is incapable of creating compelling and meaningful competitions, then it will face the choice of presiding over the game's decline or switching to the soccer model, which could involve either a global competition or geographic conferences featuring the best clubs, provinces and franchises from around the world. Such a development could have grave implications for New Zealand rugby since, barring a seismic realignment of exchange rates, the clubs with the biggest chequebooks would be European. Taking the soccer comparison a stage further, the specific analogy here is with Brazil, which is somewhat ironic given the tentative attempts to position the All Blacks as the Brazil of rugby. Brazil produces the best soccer players in the world but few of them play for Brazilian clubs. One wonders if Brazil, the national team, would exist without the World Cup, but the soccer World Cup has a far greater tradition than the rugby version and retains its place in a club-based game because of its mesmerising uncertainty. It's such a huge event that the clubs have no choice but to take a back seat once every four years. If rugby goes down that path, will there actually be a world stage for the Brazil of rugby to perform on?

Rutherford believes that rugby can successfully pursue the international model providing more countries become genuinely competitive. 'In my time our view was that we needed to get to the point where any one of 10 to 12 countries could knock off anyone and long term I still think that's true.'

The biggest obstacle to that, he believes, is the narrow vision and inertia of the IRB, which is a by-product of the inappropriate level of influence wielded by the Celtic nations. 'We can't allow countries like Scotland and Ireland to maintain their incredibly privileged positions financially while the likes of Argentina, Samoa and Fiji, which would be equally competitive if given equal access to resources, are just cut out. Scotland's and Ireland's positions reflect their privileged position at the IRB — they both have two votes to Argentina's one and Samoa's none.'

(The accenture discussion document proposed a quadrennial 12 Nations tournament beginning in 2005. If rugby could get to the position where all 12 participants had a realistic chance of winning, this concept might make sense. If not, it would simply be the World Cup shorn of the real cannon fodder but still featuring games of lesser quality with little bearing on the ultimate outcome. This brings us back to the obvious question: why not just have the five or six of the best teams in the world fighting it out in an annual tournament?)

If reforming the IRB proves impossible — and it certainly won't be easy seeing it will entail persuading turkeys to vote for Thanksgiving — then New Zealand will have to think very carefully about where its long-term interests lie.

'If the IRB doesn't find a way to get the best nations playing each other, someone else will,' says Rutherford. 'We can grapple with it but the reality is it will be determined by external forces such as broadcasters or brewers. Heineken is an example of a brewer who could have massive interest in a globalised competition. Something I've reflected on since I left the job is that we have to be very clear on what view we have on the future shape of rugby and do whatever it takes to get it there. There's no room for sentimentality.'

In other words, it is no choice at all if the choice is between staying with the IRB — which continues to protect the privileged position of a few nations whose contribution doesn't warrant that status and run the game on a model that is inimical to New Zealand's long-term — or inking up with promoters, broadcasters and sponsors in an elite competition that ensures that the All Blacks remain the ultimate expression of New Zealand rugby and a leading world brand and which brings in revenue on a scale that enables us to keep our best players here.

The rebel schemes of the past, notably World Rugby Corporation (WRC), have foundered on the rock of establishment opposition, not surprisingly since what the promoters were essentially trying to do was steal the top tier of the game from the national unions. This scenario is different because it envisages the national unions of the major rugby powers becoming business partners of the promoters, sponsors and broadcasters who would promote, fund and showcase the new competition. The establishment opposition would come from the IRB, which would be in danger of losing its monopoly right to organise international rugby, to determine who plays who, when and where.

The second big difference is that, in the professional era, the primary responsibility of the NZRU is to manage the business side for the benefit of the playing side, which means, first and foremost, protecting and increasing the income stream. Remaining a member in good standing of the wider international rugby brotherhood comes a long way behind that.

'If it's going to come down to money,' says Rutherford, 'then New Zealand will be better off getting into the rich man's laager.'

9

Worthy of their hire?

> ***professional*** *n **6.** a person who engages for his livelihood in some activity also pursued by amateurs. **7.** a person who engages in an activity with great competence.*
>
> — Collins English Dictionary

Herewith the dichotomy of professionalism, the two sides of the central transaction: payment and performance.

In an article on retirement in the April 26, 2003 issue of *New Zealand Listener*, it was stated that 'close to 80 per cent of New Zealanders earn $40,000 a year or less before tax. More than half earn less than $20,000.' Meanwhile, our top rugby players earn hundreds of thousands of dollars a year for doing, as the refrain goes, what generations of New Zealanders readily did for the honour and glory, what Red Conway, in fact, cut off a finger to do.

As prime beneficiaries of the law of supply and demand, the players should be aware that there's no such thing as a free lunch so what do they think they're paid all that loot *for*? What is their side of the transaction?

The confusion that the dichotomy of professionalism has created in this country reached manic proportions when Team New Zealand lost the America's Cup to a Swiss syndicate heavily reliant on the expertise and experience of Russell Coutts, Brad Butterworth and other former members of Team New Zealand. After the hapless, haunted defenders had been buried at sea with the same cool and relentless precision with which Coutts and co had brought the cup to New Zealand in 1995 and kept it here in 2000, the victorious skipper was quoted in *The Dominion Post* thus: 'I am a New Zealander, make no bones about that, but I am immensely proud of what we have achieved at Alinghi and as a professional sailor, frankly, I am proud of what I've done.'

One suspects that, on reading these words, some New Zealanders struggled to keep down their Weet-Bix. To them, Coutts and co are and always will be turncoats who shafted their country for a swag of Swiss francs; professionalism Coutts-style means having no commitment, no loyalty, being permanently for sale to the highest bidder. Others would have shrugged and thought good luck to him. In their eyes, Coutts is just another Kiwi capitalising on his talent in the global marketplace, like hundreds of scientists, academics, businesspeople and big-name artists and entertainers like Kiri Te Kanawa and Russell Crowe who, whether he likes it or not, will always be a Kiwi as long as our media have anything to do with it. And for some readers, perhaps, Coutts' words would have evoked the dedication, organisation, discipline and flawless execution that reduced the event from a contest to an exhibition. Perhaps they would have compared the Alinghi campaign with the hubris and fallibility under pressure of Team New Zealand and decided that it was a mismatch from the word go, amateurs against pros.

True professionalism is about being worthy of your hire. The higher the reward, the greater the effort to do it right, to get the job done.

Andrew Martin, former commanding officer of the SAS and All Black manager: 'My observation is that the winning of test matches can be reduced to single-digit advantages, a one to two per cent edge on the day. In order to achieve that, you've got to do everything right — train right, analyse right, recover right, prepare right. You remove things that can go wrong. If you want something badly enough — in this case consistent victories for the All Blacks — then it's about going through hardships to get it. I'm not convinced our players can do that. Some of our competitors have embraced that approach and gone looking for it. My assessment is that some of them were more prepared to apply it and subordinate themselves to it than we were.'

One would have thought that if any country's players were going to take their professional obligations in their stride, it would be New Zealand's. Kiwis have always been renowned for their dedication and the intensity with which they approached and played the game. Professionalism levelled the playing field: now that they're being paid, players in other countries are prepared to take the game as seriously as we always have. It was inevitable that our competitive advantage would be eroded but it seems to have happened awfully quickly.

This raises the question: do our players understand how it works or are they overly focused on the reward side of the transaction at the expense of the performance side?

John Hart was All Black coach during the first four years of professionalism but goes back to the amateur era for his benchmark: 'The Auckland team of the 1980s was the most professional I've been associated with by a long way. They had one tracksuit that they had to hand back at the end of the season. The All Blacks now get a truly ridiculous amount of gear given to them. They don't appreciate it and it encourages a greedy, spoilt attitude.'

Dr John Mayhew, who began his long, ongoing association with the All Blacks in 1988, concurs: 'The 1988 All Blacks contained some of the most professional players I've come across. Grant Fox was meticulous in his preparation and the lengths he went to in order to ensure his goal-kicking was right. They were a quantum leap ahead of the rest of the world but the likes of the Whettons, Fox, Fitzpatrick and Kirwan prepared very well, analysed very well.

They looked at each opposition whereas today there seems to be a tendency to prepare the same way for all opponents. They weren't paid and I think there's a lot of truth in the view that we've gone from being unpaid professionals to paid amateurs. If you make the comparison with golf, a pro who's having problems with his swing will simply work on fixing the problem, whatever it takes. Some of our guys now need to be pushed to do the work to fix up their shortcomings or improve their game. If you want to achieve the best of which you're capable, you're willing to go to the nth degree. Doug Howlett prepares superbly, perhaps because of his track and field background that got him used to training on his own.

'The 1988 team were more professional than the current team. They certainly enjoyed their time and played to win within the constraints of their era that meant that video and computer analysis and the other tools weren't available to them. Cynics might say that Kirwan was professional in the sense of being paid but he was always looking outside the square as in getting a personal trainer to lift his speed and strength. Gary Whetton would have survived very well in the modern game; he mightn't have made many friends but he was a real athlete who knew how to win. To be fair to the current players, the 1988 team were on top of the world and had a unique bunch of talent.

'Most of the All Black management were professional before we got paid and I'd say the administration of the team has always been more professional than the players. Some of the players are still struggling to come up to that standard.'

Who is the best athlete on the planet? Who is the most professional athlete on the planet? The answer to both questions is probably Tiger Woods. Woods isn't driven by the desire to be the best golfer in the world; he achieved that status several years ago and has yet to be seriously challenged. The likelihood is that he could maintain his predominance for the foreseeable future without working any harder or doing anything differently. But Woods is driven by the desire to be as good as he can possibly be, which means he can never stop trying to improve.

Andy Haden played a round of golf with Steve Williams shortly after the New Zealander became Woods' caddie. 'I asked him what was the difference between the hugely talented Tiger Woods and the hugely talented Carlos Spencer. We played a hole and he didn't answer so I assumed he was thinking about it. The next hole was a par three and he still didn't answer so I assumed he didn't want to answer and was just ignoring the question.'

'Halfway down the twelfth fairway he came up alongside me and said there were three differences: when Tiger Woods practises, he looks for that centimetre of improvement. When Spencer practices, he doesn't give the impression that he's greatly concerned whether he gets one kick out of 20 or 20 out of 20. Spencer takes a penalty kick and just chips it into touch whereas Woods is always striving for that extra centimetre. Secondly, Woods has around him a small team of highly trained professionals — caddie, coach, manager, trainer — and blanks out everything and everyone else. Spencer reads what's written about him and listens to what's said and gets advice from amateur experts in every bar he goes into and he has coaches and advisors at club, NPC, Super 12 and All Black level, all of whom have suggestions, some of which are the same as those he gets from the amateurs in the bar. Third, Woods believes he's there for the long haul; Spencer isn't sure if he's there for the next month or next season.

Haden continues: 'Since then there's been a dramatic turnaround in Spencer's game, which has involved the disappearance of the yellow hair and the extraordinary antics on the field. He now appears to have minimised the excesses and be dealing more with basics and detail. Those are the trappings of professionalism. The more eccentric someone is, the less professional. [David] Beckham may be so skilled he can get away with it but if one's form varies, the fans start looking at the flamboyance as the reason for the decline.'

Woods' dedication is the ultimate acknowledgement of his obligation as a professional, of his side of the transaction. It would appear that some of our top rugby players have yet to make that acknowledgement.

'They have the time and income to dedicate themselves to be the best they can be,' says Mayhew, 'but it's not happening.'

Martin agrees: 'When I came into the All Blacks, I was surprised at both ends of the spectrum: how much had been done or attempted to be done in terms of educating the players about their professional responsibilities in the commercial sense — the inherent responsibility that comes from being bankrolled by sponsors and people looking for a return on their investment — and also the efforts that had been made to impress upon the whole industry — people don't like the term but it's appropriate — a strong vocational ethic: make sure they understood fitness targets, dietary regimes and so on. What surprised me at the other end of the spectrum was how little notice some of the players were taking of the information and advice that was given. We may not have communicated the knowledge we wanted the players to acquire particularly well. The other thing that surprised me was how vigorously, doggedly even, players at the most elite level were reluctant to surrender key elements of the amateur era while fully accepting that they were inhibiting us.'

One of those key elements of the amateur era that the players seem reluctant to surrender is alcohol.

Alcohol has traditionally been as much a part of the game as cauliflower ears and expletive-crammed pre-match team talks. Just as a round of golf can be seen as a good walk spoiled, the real point of a game of rugby, it sometimes seems, is to work up a thirst for a night on the piss. While traditionalists may decry attempts to break down the booze culture as yet another example of the prissy political correctness that has insinuated itself into the game in recent years, a more contemporary view might be that self-discipline goes with the territory and a professional athlete who compromises his performance through self-indulgence is welshing on his side of the deal.

'Hart took the team away from the booze culture,' says Mayhew, 'but now it's back in favour, which shows we still aren't professional enough. The issue isn't having a few drinks; it's getting totally pissed. Perhaps I did the same when I was 21 but I wasn't getting paid to play for my country and I didn't have another test match coming up the following weekend. We spend a lot of money on the whole recovery procedure — the ice baths and so on — but it's completely wasted if the players write themselves off and get hardly any sleep.'

Of course, the booze culture extends far beyond these shores as anyone who's spent time in an Australian, Welsh, French or even Italian rugby club can testify to. A few years ago an English reporter who accompanied the French team on their train journey to London on the Thursday before a crunch match at Twickenham was shocked and awed by the amount of red wine they put away at *lunch*. There were reports of heavy drinking by the Welsh squad at the 1995 World Cup and the existence of an embedded booze culture is often cited as a factor in Welsh rugby's ongoing wallow in a swamp of mediocrity. There are, however, indications that the All Blacks' major rivals have targeted alcohol in their quest for excellence. A couple of pints is apparently a big night out for the English team in the 'no excuses' environment created by Clive Woodward, while French coach Bernard Laporte is intent on reducing his team's red wine intake along with their penalty count.

'I think our major competitors are probably better than we are,' says Mayhew. 'The French have changed although not that much in terms of their wine and so on. The Australians are better, although they're no angels. Frankly, that's a matter of education and IQ and, with respect, the influx of leaguies might change that. It's not just confined to rugby, though — look at the Black Caps in Durban. Never mind the silliness of carrying on like that in a nightclub after they've just beaten South Africa, they've got another game in a couple of days and the tournament's barely got going.'

Like Mayhew, Martin worries that if the All Blacks don't jettison or at least tone down the booze culture, it will increasingly impact on their results, given that the opposition is moving in that direction: 'I don't care what anyone says, when you're involved in an industry in which the principle raw product is the fitness of the human body, there are some things you must do and some things you should not do. It requires a sensible management approach to the use of alcohol as a recreational drug — because that's what it is in that environment. There's no other industry anywhere in the world that would accept that level of alcohol consumption from its employees at the top end; no other sport. I continue to regard that as one of our great weaknesses. I was absolutely flabbergasted to see the state of some players, especially senior players.

'My observation is that the Australians are far smarter, more mature and disciplined. I'm not advocating a no-alcohol environment but we've got to get beyond spending the whole week recovering. A lot of the faults that I saw in the players came down to discipline. There's a social change issue here: previous generations of players drank beer but today, in common with a lot of young people, the players will drink spirits. Alcohol is readily available and it's very easy not to have to buy a drink night after night.'

When Hart became All Black coach, he had grave doubts, based on the 'frightening data' from professional sport in the United States, that our leading players would be able to cope with professionalism with its freedom and sudden, massive rewards.

WORTHY OF THEIR HIRE?

In his assessment, the vast majority of the 46 players who attended the seminar on professionalism in early 1996 'were totally ignorant on the subject. The exception were the likes of Sean Fitzpatrick and Olo Brown who understood that the issue was having a balance in one's life.'

It is an axiom of sport that one's strength can also be one's weakness. Hart's big-picture view alerted him to the problem and his attention to detail and organisational skills equipped him to deal with it, but in his zeal to protect the players from their own worst enemies — themselves — he might have gone too far.

'Hart was probably right in what he was trying to achieve but perhaps not always in the execution,' says Martin. 'Under him, the management did too much for the players. I had players coming to me and asking me to do things that you and I have to do to get through our lives. The other thing that grated with me is that they expect everything to be paid for. If the bus stops for a cup of tea or they hire a video, they expect it to be paid for. When we were at the adidas Institute of Rugby I selected a package that didn't include the beds being made. Ninety-nine per cent of New Zealanders have to make their own beds, why can't they?'

As Hart himself says, 'The degree of accountability required was not sheeted home to them and that was a mistake.'

A mistake for which he paid a far higher price than the players.

'In 1998 and 1999,' says Hart, 'we found out how few players would stand up and be accountable for what was happening on the field. After that crunch game in Christchurch [against Australia, 1998] when we played badly and it was obvious that a lot of changes had to be made, we heard a lot of shallow words in meetings — it was more about protecting themselves than offering more to the team. Ian Jones was an exception: he wrote to me addressing the issue of what he could do for the team rather than what we could do for him. Michael Jones also wanted to do the right thing but the point is if I'd told him to retire five years earlier, he would have done so. Instead he played on for another year for the money and was a shadow of his former self when he finished. We're talking about guys who stood to lose hundreds of thousands of dollars so it was natural they'd be concerned about the implications for their careers — going offshore wasn't so much of an option then. It was sad and a bit selfish.

'Perhaps the lack of player accountability was the reason we were a bit loose, a bit soft at the end of big matches in Sydney and the semi-final. We were complacent for that Sydney game. They were on the ropes and we had the chance to finish them off but we didn't and they took a lot of confidence from that game and came back. It's crucial that you get that player accountability for what happens on the field and I think that's what John Mitchell's about, which is positive. He's been really hard-nosed with guys; I don't agree with those methods but if it produces more hardness and self-reliance, there will be a benefit.'

One factor that may have contributed to this lack of player accountability is the reluctance of coaches to publicly call players on their sub-standard performances. That could be a long time coming given the firestorm Hart brought down on his head by publicly criticising Andrew Mehrtens after the loss in Melbourne in 1998. While it was certainly a high-risk thing to do in view of Mehrtens' favourite-son status in Canterbury and the fact that Hart was breaking one of his own cardinal rules, much of the outcry focused on the act of publicly criticising a player rather than the validity or otherwise of the criticism. Coaches in other countries are less inhibited, perhaps because the media and public are less protective of their stars. The former Springbok coach Nick Mallett often analysed individuals in blunt terms and after France lost to Ireland in the 2003 Six Nations, Laporte got personal, describing his players as 'liars', 'donkeys' and 'cheats'. 'Why does Serge Betsen make 15 mistakes a match now?' he asked the assembled media. 'Why does Jean-Jacques Crenca give away five penalties per match?'

Another factor may be the media's tendency to blame poor team performances on poor coaching. Many coaches, the most recent being former Queensland Reds coach John Connolly, have made the point that coaches get too much credit when their teams win and too much blame when they lose.

(I would add the rider that the degree of credit or blame can be a factor of their PR or lack of it. Peter Sloane, for instance, has put together a remarkable record in the Super 12, achieving success with three franchises — as assistant to Wayne Smith at the Crusaders and as head coach at the Highlanders and Blues. Yet when Laurie Mains took over the Highlanders in 2002 and coached them to the semifinals, leading rugby journalists credited him with having 'turned around' the franchise. Under Sloane the Highlanders finished third in 2000 and fifth — the highest placing achieved by a New Zealand side — in 2001. And when the Blues played vibrant, winning rugby in 2003, many pundits put it down to the Graham Henry factor even though defence was, ostensibly, his area of responsibility. Henry may have been the catalyst but this was never explicated or quantified, merely asserted as if the thing spoke for itself.)

This view of coaches as virtuoso or incompetent puppet-masters reduces the players to puppets who perform well or badly depending on who's pulling their strings. Surely a player who has played 25 tests and 50 Super 12 games and is paid several hundred thousand dollars a year knows what he has to do to get a good performance out of himself, knows what constitutes a good performance and knows when he hasn't delivered one? Is it the coach's fault if a player is yellow-carded for doing exactly what he's been exhorted not to do at countless team meetings? The fact that once the referee blows time-on, there's not a lot the coach can do cuts both ways: he can't lose games through his mistakes nor win them with his brilliance. To reverse Connolly's point, players are often given less credit than they deserve when they win and absolved of their fair share of responsibility when they lose.

Take the 1999 World Cup semi-final: 'I was there at halftime under the grandstand when Hart was strategising,' says Mike Banks, 'telling the players they couldn't afford to take their foot off the throat. But panic set in and we lost and that was Hart's fault. The whole thing sickens me. It was disappointing that the players said nothing. It really needed some of them to put their hands up and say, "We stuffed up." I guess it's a consequence of professionalism, a bit like being an employee and thinking you've got to take care of your own future.'

Hart admits he was 'surprised at how isolated I became and how quickly. Perhaps I hadn't established the right rapport.'

Should he have been surprised? He contemplated stepping down as Auckland coach at the end of the 1985 season but stayed on because he felt he owed it to his players despite being warned by his manager Alan Rear not to make decisions based on loyalty to the players. 'They'll be loyal to you only as long as it suits them,' Rear told him. Within a few months, many of those players had snuck off on the Cavaliers tour, leaving Hart and Auckland in the lurch.

Gordon Hunter wasn't surprised. Hart, after all, was yesterday's man and 'professional sportsmen are only interested in who's going to pick them'.

Graham Lowe certainly wouldn't have been surprised. 'Of the hundreds of players I've been involved with,' he says, 'I'd only regard three as being real friends: Darrell Williams, Tony Iro and Joe Lydon. Professional sportsmen just look after themselves — there's no place for loyalty or friendship in their world.'

Lowe adds, however, that Matthew Ridge, although not a nice person, was an example of 'a professional who put everything on the field'. Which is not a bad start: we don't necessarily want to have these guys around for dinner but we do want them to win and we do expect them to deliver on their side of the transaction without having to be pushed and prodded into it.

So what's the problem here? Not to put too fine a point on it, is it that our players are thick? That's certainly a claim that gets bandied around from time to time, although those making it don't seem to know where to go next. Is it a lack of maturity and worldliness that comes from knowing nothing of life outside rugby? Is it because all they care about is money?

John Plumtree believes that money is a red herring and today's All Blacks are cut from the same cloth as the heroes of the past: 'I don't think the players have changed. During my involvement with the All Blacks as an analyst in 2002, I found them very down to earth Kiwi guys who went about their business as professionals but still had their feet on the ground and took just as much pride in being All Blacks as their predecessors — perhaps even more so given the challenges they face, the opponents, the pressure, the analysis and the fact they're being paid.'

Mayhew sees the narrow focus of both players and coaches as a barrier to personal growth and maturity: 'The bar is being raised all the time. The players are fitter and stronger but whether they're rounded people is another matter. Fitting in another job or study is hard because they spend so much time training and playing. I suppose it's easy for a young guy earning hundreds of thousands of dollars not to see the need to prepare for life outside rugby and I don't think many coaches have an interest in structuring the training schedule to allow people to do very much outside rugby. When I went with Laurie Mains to look at the Brisbane Broncos set-up in the early nineties, Wayne Bennett wouldn't have a player on his books who wasn't doing some kind of part-time work. I don't know whether that's still the case and it's certainly easier for league teams because there's nothing like the amount of travel involved and they generally return to the same base each week. The question is, how do we convince these young players of the worth of going to work or study after he's spent the morning training?'

With great difficulty, if John Graham's experience with the Black Caps is anything to go by. He persuaded Lincoln College to tailor courses for the players but there were no takers. On tour in England, he encouraged the players to broaden their horizons by reading the quality newspapers but met similar resistance, not surprisingly perhaps given that one of the leading players had never actually read a book.

That 1988 Auckland team which set the benchmark for professionalism included a doctor, an MA student, an investment banker, two accountants, two owner/drivers, some marketing executives and two entrepreneurs, one of whom was already a millionaire. Graham has no doubt that by detaching athletes from the community, professional sport stunts their personal development.

'In the UK in 1962/63, Wilson Whineray had to make proper speeches to high-brow audiences but I don't know if many of today's captains could do that. In fact, it would be embarrassing. The fact that we had to work among the general public made us more mature and worldly. These guys fly around the world but I don't think they see much or learn much.'

Administrators at both national and provincial level recognise that players benefit from having a life outside rugby and need to prepare for a life after rugby; the issue is being addressed but it will be a long, slow, uncertain process.

'Just because they're professional players doesn't mean they're going to be perfect role models, robots who do everything perfectly,' says David White, the former cricketer who is now chief executive of the Auckland Rugby Union and the Blues. 'They're human beings, often from humble backgrounds, and some aren't going to handle it well. Our job is to give them tools but we can't hold their hands. Look at the problems in US sport and think how long they've been professional. We're dreaming if we think we're going to have a perfect world.'

We're also dreaming if we think the All Blacks are ever going to be a team of renaissance men. But then they never were and while one or two renaissance men might be an asset, you wouldn't want 15 of them going out to face the Springboks at Ellis Park. Besides, academic ability and refined sensibilities don't necessarily translate into rugby nous. Players like Zinzan Brooke and Frank Bunce might not have had bulging bookcases or letters after their names but they were as rugby-smart as they come and, according to Andrew Martin, the current crop of All Blacks are similarly endowed: 'Some are less intelligent but you get that anywhere. Generally the level of rugby intellect blew me away — Taine Randell has one of the finest rugby brains I've ever encountered but he wasn't the only one.'

Professional sportsmen are a tempting target and that's largely their fault: the preciousness, the ever-present sunglasses, the ever-changing hair styles, the lame post-match interviews, the ghosted autobiographies that reveal little other than the strength and sincerity of the subject's self-regard.

Perhaps, though, we expect too much of these young men with their unreal lives, distorted by overnight wealth, fame, physical drudgery, and the thrill and fear of entering the coliseum. There is a danger that if rugby becomes more gladiatorial, it will become a sport for ever younger, more limited, more physically freakish men and the combination of body worship and damage will leave them even less equipped for a life after rugby and the onset of middle age. Knowing only rugby and, like long-term convicts, uncertain of their capacity to function in the normal world, they will seek to postpone the evil day by extending their careers for as long as possible. English county cricket has suffered from this syndrome with players becoming time servers, hanging on for their benefit season or simply another dollop of income and occupying positions that would otherwise go to up-and-comers. County second elevens are full of 25 year olds who were once stars in the making but whose careers stalled because they weren't given the opportunity when they were young and hungry and needed advancement to sustain their ambition and self-belief.

While it's hard to imagine a more benign sporting scene than a county match somewhere in the shires in front of a handful of pensioners in deckchairs, the syndrome of professional sporting careers extended into impotent decline has provided some pitiful spectacles. Boxing, which represents professional sport gone terribly wrong or taken to its logical conclusion, depending on your point of view, today offers us Mike Tyson, ex-baddest man on the planet, now a deranged, self-destructive beast apparently unable to abide by the relaxed rules governing celebrity behaviour in the American fast lane. Tyson has become a professional loser: he derives his earnings from going in front of the cameras and losing his self-control, his freedom, his bouts, his wealth, his mind. Where will it end? And when it does, who will remember the phenomenon of a lisping delinquent from the ghetto who reduced the best heavyweights of the era to rabbits caught in his headlights and for a few short years came as close as any athlete has come to embodying the pure essence of his sport?

10

The shock of the new

Some things never change. 'A winning All Black team is important,' says Jock Hobbs. 'People will forgive a lot if the team is winning. There's always been enormous pressure to perform and win.'

But a lot has changed. Veteran French lock Fabien Pelous: 'In 1995 when I won my first cap, I only trained twice a week with my club. The professional era had not yet begun and rugby was a totally different game. In fact, it was so different that you cannot even compare it with today's game. On all levels, from the frequency of the training to the power of the impacts and the length of time the ball is in play, the game has changed immensely.'

Andy Haden describes new rugby as, 'fast, ferocious and not for the faint-hearted. We used to have Terry Wright, now we have Jonah.'

The comparison between the two left wings whose careers almost overlapped — Wright's All Black career finished in 1992; Lomu made his international debut in 1994 — provides a snapshot of rugby's on-field transformation.

John Hart described Wright as 'probably the best footballer, in terms of all round skills, with whom I've been associated. He had blinding speed, good hands, could kick well off either foot, counter-attacked well and was perhaps the most clinical finisher in the game. He read defensive situations well and tackled tenaciously. I often used to wonder how such an apparently frail figure could withstand the rigours of the game but he was superbly conditioned.' Wright weighed 79 kg.

A WHOLE NEW BALL GAME

When fully fit and switched on, Lomu has been the most potent ball-carrier the game has ever seen but even his staunchest advocates wouldn't base their case on his all-round skills or ability to read defensive situations. For most of his career, Lomu has weighed 40 kg more than Wright.

A striking example but also an extreme one: Lomu is still the heaviest back in the game while Wright cut a slender figure among his contemporaries. To get a more accurate picture of the All Blacks' physical evolution, we need to look at teams and individuals from different eras.

(A caveat: although players can no longer fudge their ages, weight measurement continues to be an inexact science, for whatever reason. In 1956, when the selectors became fixated with the bulk of the Springbok pack, aspiring All Black forwards gulped down gallons of water before being weighed at the trials. By the early 1960s, the thinking had changed: coach Neil McPhail weighed the players every Monday morning and a pattern of weight gain was a one-way ticket to the midweek team. Whether it's because the information isn't updated or players' weights fluctuate or no one's paying enough attention, listed weights should not be taken as gospel. In 1988, for instance, John Kirwan officially weighed 92 kg even though, according to his own careful monitoring, he played the 1987 World Cup at 104 kg. Even *The Rugby Almanack* isn't entirely free from discrepancies and if we can't trust the *Almanack*, who or what can we trust? Or perhaps the *Almanack* is onto something and the reason for Taine Randell's perplexing weight fluctuations is that there really are two Taine Randells. Far-fetched maybe, but it would explain a lot.)

For the all-important Welsh test on the 1962/63 tour, the All Black backline averaged 81 kg. However, this figure is seriously skewed by the presence of Don Clarke who was, in more ways than one, 'the Jonah Lomu of his day' as Colin Meads called him.

Clarke was 10 kg heavier than anyone else in the team and 30 kg heavier than the next heaviest back. If Clarke is replaced by Mac Herewini, who played fullback when The Boot had a game off, the backs' average weight drops to 76 kg. The pack weighed 760 kg, 95 kg a man. Number 8 John Graham and hooker Dennis Young weighed 84 kg and 86 kg respectively and both locks — Meads and Allan Stewart — were 100 kg, which is less than 16 stone in the old measurement.

Fast forward to the team that defeated Wales at Cardiff Arms Park a decade later. Not much had changed in the backs who averaged 78 kg but up front, the heavy brigade had arrived: the pack was 6 kg a man heavier despite including a 95 kg lock — Hamish Macdonald. The big difference, emphasised by coach Bob Duff's decision to do without a specialist open-side flanker, is in the loose forwards: Alan Sutherland, Alex Wyllie and Ian Kirkpatrick outweighed Graham, Waka Nathan and Kel Tremain by 14 kg a man. Noteworthy too are the dimensions of Peter Whiting, who, at 107 kg and a shade under 2 m tall, is pretty close to fitting the profile of the new model lock. The pack's increased size can't be put down to the phasing out of the raw-boned farmer since there were five farmers in the 1972/73 pack compared to three in the 1962/63 pack, which also contained three school teachers.

Fast forward again to the 1983 All Blacks who played the Wallabies: the backs were the same average weight — 78 kg — as a decade earlier while the pack was actually a kilo a man lighter, mainly due to the inclusion of specialist loose forwards. The most noticeable change was at hooker. Young and Tane Norton (85 kg) were old-fashioned rakes who struck for the ball on the opposition put-in. By 1983 the All Blacks had belatedly adopted one of Argentina's great contributions to the game (the other being Hugo Porta), the eight-man shove, the aim of which is to disrupt the opposition ball rather than steal tightheads. Andy Dalton's size —

92 kg — reflected the change in the hooker's role from rake to scrummager.

By 1988, when the All Blacks had stolen a march on the rest of the world, the forwards were up a couple of kilos, but there had been big changes behind the scrum: after a negligible increase from 1962 to 1983, the backs' average weight had jumped 4 kg in five years. The combined weights of the 1982 and 1988 inside backs are identical: the change has come out wide, most apparently in the shape of John Kirwan. In compensation terms, Kirwan was, of course, a shamateur and a pretty brazen one at that; in every other respect, he was ultra-professional. He pioneered the use of a personal trainer to take him to another level in terms of overall and position-specific fitness and physical capabilities, and directed his training programme towards what he wanted to be able to do on the field. His extraordinary try against Italy in the first match of the 1987 World Cup didn't just happen. He'd worked on his speed, strength, endurance and ability to change direction at speed with the specific goal of acquiring the capacity to score tries from deep positions, not through intercepts or being put into the clear by others, but by beating defenders, breaking tackles and going the length of the field without being run down in the last 20 m.

As he said in his autobiography *Running on Instinct*, 'The key to it all was doing everything I did at training, whether it was the first time or the tenth time, with absolute concentration and commitment so that whatever situation arose on the field, I could perform to the maximum.'

The 1992 test pack averaged 101 kg, so after a significant jump during the 1960s, All Black forwards had remained much the same size for the next two decades. The backs were up 2 kg a man since 1988, due to the presence of Inga Tuigamala and some bulking up on the part of Grant Fox. By 1996, the first year of professionalism, there is evidence of the dramatic change in players' physiques that has marked new rugby: if the Lomu factor is removed by replacing him with Glen Osborne, as happened for the South African series, the backs averaged 88 kg, up 4 kg in four years. The increase was mainly due to the introduction of a big halfback — Justin Marshall — and the spectacular bulking up of the midfielders Frank Bunce (up 9 kg) and Walter Little (up an extraordinary — and dubious — 14 kg). Even allowing for rubbery statistics, the age of the gym-built rugby player had dawned. The forwards were up to 104 kg a man with Michael Jones gaining 7 kg in the process of reinventing himself as a blindside flanker and Sean Fitzpatrick becoming the prototype modern hooker, barely distinguishable from his props.

After seven years of professionalism, the physical transformation of the All Blacks was there for all to see. Both the backs and the forwards had gained 6 kg a man since 1996 (comparing backlines with, respectively, Osborne and Caleb Ralph on the left wing). While the Polynesian influx had been a factor, especially in the backs, this was an international trend: our current crop of midfield and outside backs are smaller than their predominantly white Australian counterparts.

Between 1972 and 1996 the All Black forwards' average weight increased by a mere 3 kg. The 2002 pack averaged 110 kg, 17 stone 4 lb in the old measurement, which is heavier than all but two of the 18 forwards on the 1972/73 tour. Richie McCaw, a genuine openside flanker, is 5 kg heavier than 'Pinetree' Meads was.

Where will it end? One assumes, firstly, that weight training eventually begins to operate on the law of diminishing returns and, secondly, that the intensifying aerobic demands of rugby at the top level will impose a limit on the amount of muscle players can effectively carry. If not, if the pattern of the last seven years is repeated, the All Black backs at the 2011 World Cup will be as big as the forwards who won the tournament in 1987.

It's received wisdom in this country that our forwards are small by international standards. The English and French forwards are routinely described as 'giant' and, as we know, they breed them jumbo-sized up on the high veldt. While there are lies, damned lies and statistics, the stats on the respective national rugby unions' official web sites hardly bear this out. The English forward pack that just shaded the fresh-faced All Blacks at Twickenham in November 2002 outweighed them by less than 2 kg a man. That English pack's combined weight — 883 kg — is precisely the same as that of the All Black pack in the 2002 Tri-Nations. Perhaps more pertinently, the French forwards who bulldozed the All Blacks around Stade de France had a combined weight of just 819 kg, the same as the 1988 All Blacks.

The lesson here would seem to be that while a good big man will generally beat a good little man, the match-ups are seldom that straightforward. In Paris, a reasonably big but inexperienced and technically unsound All Black scrum was taken apart by a highly experienced, technically expert pack from a country where scrummaging is still regarded as the foundation of the structure and the key physical and psychological confrontation, and approached accordingly. We have been here before. In 1971 the 14 stone 7 lb (92 kg) Lions loosehead prop Ian 'Mighty Mouse' McLauchlan had the better of the 18 stone 7 lb (118 kg) All Black tighthead prop Jazz Muller. Speaking after the tour McLauchlan attributed it to Muller's predictability and lack of technique: '[Muller] planted his feet and set himself almost exactly the same way each time. His feet were in the same position and he did exactly the same thing in every scrum.' McLauchlan's team-mate and fellow loosehead prop Ray McLoughlin was more pointed: 'This business about Muller being so much stronger than everyone else was an illusion. There was a large quantity of unproductive weight in that 18 and a half stone.' McLoughlin, who reportedly possessed a genius-level IQ, used the example of the 13 stone (83 kg) Welsh wing John Bevan, who could lift heavier weights than almost all the Lions forwards to reinforce his argument that there isn't an automatic correlation between bulk and strength.

Similarly, the 100 kg Olo Brown's scrum battles with the 130 kg Os du Randt was arguably the most crucial one-on-one confrontation in the 1996 series in South Africa. The All Blacks' ascendancy at scrum-time was pivotal to the winning of the series, given that the Springboks had made no secret of their intention to target the All Black scrum and the fact that, as the series progressed, the All Blacks had their work cut out holding the Springboks physically in the other forward exchanges.

The emphasis on strength training and increasing muscularity has coincided with and contributed to rugby's evolution into what Hart calls 'a high velocity collision sport'. While out and out foul play has been largely eliminated, the 'hits' just keep getting bigger. 'Cleaning out' and 'blowing over' are often euphemisms for human missiles launching themselves shoulder-first at anyone unfortunate enough to be crouched over the tackled player in pursuit of a turnover. Who'd be an open-side flanker?

We hear a lot about player burn-out resulting from the administrators' apparent determination to leave no gaps in the calendar, but it's hard to believe that these frequent high-impact collisions won't also take their toll. An Australian study of elite players revealed an almost 50 per cent increase in injuries since the game went professional, from 47 per 1000 player-hours in 1995 to 69 per 1000 player-hours in 2002. All Black coach John Mitchell has expressed the view that rugby is becoming more and more a young man's game, presumably because of the ever-higher tempo and the increased time the ball is in play. One wonders how it works with regard to the high-impact collisions, whether battle-hardened veterans are better equipped to take the punishment or whether there's a mental element to it and, as a player gets older, youthful fearlessness gives way to calculating self-preservation. (On the subject of physical attrition, Hart believes the time has come to rethink the theory of 'train as you play' because of the wear and tear of highly physical training sessions. Rugby league, with its longer experience of the high-velocity collision game, seems to have come to this conclusion: if TV footage of league training sessions is anything to go by, physical contact is conspicuous by its absence.)

While some ex-players, pundits and a section of the public bristle whenever the subject of player fatigue and burn-out arises, John Mayhew believes they underestimate the extent to which the game has changed, both in terms of its increasingly physical nature and the imperative that drives a professional sport largely funded by broadcasters, which is to have the best playing the best, week in, week out, in cut-throat competitions. 'The Super 12 isn't that far below tests in terms of intensity,' he says, 'so when famous ex-All Blacks scoff at today's players being tired having only played 30 to 35 games in a year, the point is that far more of those games are high-intensity affairs compared to the ratio in the past. The 1988 team only played five tests, two of which were soft games against Wales.'

While professionalism tends to extend playing careers in non-contact sports like cricket, the opposite may be true of high-speed, high-impact new rugby. Alternatively, as Mitchell believes, the age profile may change. With talent being identified early and fast-tracked through the academy system into an elite game requiring athleticism, explosiveness and fearlessness, it may be that international careers will tend to start earlier and finish earlier, typically beginning at 19/20 and winding up at 26/27.

Says Mayhew, 'This view may be based on the belief that there's a finite number of games of this intensity that your body will let you play and the earlier you start, the earlier you'll reach that point.'

The World Cup is another factor driving down the exit age from international rugby. Unless the international programme is re-jigged and new competitions emerge to diminish the importance of the World Cup, thereby reversing the trend that has steadily gathered momentum since 1987, it seems likely that each tournament will be the trigger for a personnel shake-out as players who don't see themselves being in the frame four years' hence look offshore. Eighteen months out from the 2003 World Cup there was already talk of experienced Wallabies and All Blacks positioning themselves for profitable twilights in Europe and Japan. For their part, coaches are obviously going to apply the test 'Where will he be in four years' time?' during the inevitable rebuilding process the year after a World Cup. The newer the coach, the newer the broom, the bigger the shake-out.

By accident rather than design, New Zealand has broken the cycle of appointing coaches after a World Cup to take the team through to the next one. That may have benefits. Can coaches really be at their innovative and inspirational peak after four Tri-Nations championships, a few tours and 35-odd test matches or, as seems more likely, will familiarity breed contempt? The All Black coach is not in the position of Sir Alex Ferguson at Manchester United who, if he becomes disenchanted with a player, even a superstar, can simply put him up for sale and cherry-pick a suitable replacement from wherever in the world he happens to be. If the All Black coach falls out with, say, Andrew Mehrtens, he can't wash his hands of him and make Jonny Wilkinson an offer he can't refuse; he either has to drop Mehrtens and risk a public and media outcry if the replacement isn't up to it, or swallow his pride and soldier on. A coach coming in, like Mitchell, halfway through the cycle brings a new voice and new ideas and has less need of a crystal ball to determine who will and won't be in the frame come the World Cup.

Selection is another aspect of the game that has changed out of all recognition.

'Video and statistical analysis has made selection a much more exact process,' says John Plumtree. 'A science not an art. Selectors now have the information quickly and in detail and can measure one player against another. The public has no idea how much information and detailed analysis the selectors have, the players' strengths and weaknesses in attack and defence are pinpointed. The days of players who aren't up to it being picked are gone.'

Graham Mourie agrees: 'There's nowhere to hide now and therefore there are far fewer errors in selection — you don't get bolters who get in on the basis of one good performance and are never heard of again.'

The public gets an occasional glimpse of the black and white world of statistical analysis. When Marty Holah came in for criticism early in the 2003 Super 12, Chiefs coach Kevin Greene came to his defence armed with his trusty clipboard, revealing that Holah made 26 tackles and was among the first three players to nearly 50 rucks in the Chiefs-Blues match. Mourie passed on similar information when Jerry Collins copped some flak in 2002. In both instances the media had focused on a few highly visible handling errors without keeping track of what the players were doing during the other 79 minutes.

Obviously, the value of the output depends on the rigour of the input. Sceptics argue that tackle counts don't differentiate between the crushing hit that halts the opposition's momentum and perhaps forces a turnover, and the ineffectual scrag that doesn't prevent the ball carrier getting across the advantage-line and perhaps off-loading. It seems hard to believe that the All Black selectors' computer programme wouldn't make that distinction but it's certainly true that some of the statistics dished up by the broadcasters don't provide much enlightenment. Ruck and maul comparisons excite a lot of comment but the bald numbers really need supporting information on speed of recycling, continuous possession and metres gained between phases to be meaningful.

Given the amount of information available to the selectors and the fact that in Super 12 our top players are pitted against each other and the best in Australia and South Africa every weekend for almost three months, one can only wonder what lies behind the periodic calls for the reinstatement of All Black trials. What more could the selectors learn, especially since the previous year's NPC is, in effect, a series of trials from which the Super 12 squads are picked? While everyone loves a bolter — the bolter from the 1973 trials, incidentally, was a Kamo school teacher called Mel Hepple whose performance propelled him into the North Island team and then, presumably, back to the classroom — it seems unlikely that potential All Blacks are slipping through the net. One could cite the case of Royce Willis, who in 1998 initially missed out on a Super 12 contract, then went on to make the All Black starting XV before the season was out but Willis was very much in the system, having represented New Zealand at under 19 and under 21 level and been a member of the national Rugby Academy.

Some former All Blacks worry that after-match socialising and the camaraderie it generated among players who'd been belting the daylights out of each other a couple of hours earlier will be another casualty of professionalism. Meads, who gave wine a wide berth for nine years after a monumental after-match dinner with the 1961 French team, put it in his inimitable way: 'We had some fabulous dinners with the French. We formed great friendships. Those friendships don't exist between international players today. It's sad. The excuse for not meeting the Argentine side [in 2001] was that the All Blacks had a test next Saturday. So they were shipped away. Nowadays they are more worried about making sure they have a pool session, have their bananas and nuts and sandwiches and all that stuff in the dressing room, stuff that we never saw.'

Andrew Martin, a prime mover behind the change, believes after-match functions are quite simply an anachronism in the professional era: 'What was happening was that you'd have a roomful of 300 people not including the two teams. Forty per cent of them had been drinking since the early afternoon, some since well before the game and after. Very few of them were directly associated with the players. Quite a few of them were there because they were invited by someone who had access to the after-match, plus a small number of local officials. A group of people revelling in the fact that they're at a test match and making merry.

'Meanwhile under the grandstand you've got 44 players and the coaches who've just been through a very demanding physical activity and are often so physically drained that all they can do is lie down. They've no sooner gotten back to the changing room than they're being presented with the requirements to enter the recovery procedure, slipping in and out of ice baths, stretching, re-hydrating and eating. People don't realise the players eat a meal in the dressing room — it's part of the recovery process because it refuels the muscles, enabling them to recover better. Then you have the media hammering on the door saying we want to speak to the best player, the worst player, the coaches and the medical staff about injuries.

'The coaches and captain get whipped away to the media conference. You're trying to bring the guys together to celebrate as a team or sit in quiet reflection of what they haven't achieved. The manager's looking at his watch, which is telling him they have to be at the after-match an hour after the end of the game. Eventually you drag them along even though some of them are still sweating freely despite the ice baths and so on. They can't eat because it's not the food they're allowed to eat and they've eaten anyway. They don't drink because they're going to have a team drink back at the hotel and they struggle to find anyone to talk to. The sad fact is that the teams are at opposite ends of the room. It begs the question who are you going to the after-match for? In Australia the kick-off can be as late as 8 pm so by the time you get there it's nearly midnight.

The shock of the new

In France you can get there at 1 am and you've got to be up at the crack of dawn next day to catch a plane.

'Where it got confused was that everyone thought the players' liberty was being constrained and they were missing the chance to relax in each other's company, but the drive came from the players and coaches and it meant that we could do things much slower. What we did was arrange for the opposition to come up to our changing room at a time that suited them. An hour and a quarter after we'd beaten the Boks at Eden Park, I told them to come up. It was as close to a clubroom environment as you could get. People say the after-match is an integral part of rugby but no other sport does it. Super 12 doesn't generally have them and, if they do, they only send half a dozen players.'

Once again, tradition clashes with the new reality. Two questions arise: if the players are going to have a big night anyway, why can't they at least begin it in an organised environment with the opposition present? And while retired players enjoy reliving old rivalries when time has healed the wounds, how realistic is it to expect genuine fraternisation between teams who have to face each other again in a fortnight? It's certainly hard to see what's in it for the losers.

An interesting by-product of the new era is the frankness of players' books, whether biographies or ghosted autobiographies. Perhaps one should say 'apparent frankness'. Mayhew, who can speak with unique authority and perspective after 15 years with a foot in both camps, having been part of the All Black management and a confidant of the players, considers that much of the material isn't worth the paper it's written on.

It's hard to know whether this outspokenness is simply a reflection of the times and society we live in or whether, in a crowded marketplace, players and publishers are under pressure to be controversial and establish a point of difference. A bit of both, one suspects. Whatever is driving the trend, it would seem to spell the end for the old-style rugby book in which our hero traced his rise to fame, taking pains to give due credit to all those who helped him along the way, talked us through the highlights, told a few easy-going yarns to show what good jokers his team-mates were, picked a World XV containing at least 10 All Blacks and then sank into anonymous retirement without a ripple of controversy.

Apart from their willingness, if not determination, to hang out some dirty linen, what is striking about the new generation of player/authors is their lack of self-consciousness. False modesty is thin on the ground as is the real thing and there's little inclination to put the self-focus on hold for a chapter or two while we take in the big picture. As Norm Hewitt helpfully blurts out in *Gladiator*, perhaps the benchmark against which future books will be judged, 'Top sports people are very selfish. You don't get to the top unless you're self-centred.'

Take this from Josh Kronfeld's book *On the Loose*: 'We'd done it, the first All Black side to win a series in South Africa. But my pleasure was muted somewhat because I'd been asked to pull an injury in order to come off in the 72nd minute. I felt bummed out because I'd done all the hard work and to be pulled so near the end was frustrating . . . I felt short-changed, as if I'd missed out on some of the glory because I was not there on the field to experience the full flush of an historic victory.'

Then the grudging after-thought: 'I realise of course that a coach has to do what he thinks is best to ensure victory.'

Given the significance of that victory to generations of All Blacks who'd tried and failed to beat the Springboks on their own patch, not to mention to the wider New Zealand rugby community or the management or the rest of the team, it's a bit of an eye-opener to discover that Kronfeld's overriding emotion was this rather juvenile resentment at having been unofficially subbed off with eight minutes to go. Lomu, rugby's first global superstar, didn't even make the reserves bench for that game. How did he feel? Pretty damn good judging by the pictures of him performing a haka in the stand.

Kronfeld viewed his dropping for the 1997 Irish test as a product of Hart's predilection for mind games and inordinate admiration for the Auckland flanker Andrew Blowers. Even though he was immediately restored to the test starting line-up, Kronfeld gives the impression that he never forgave or forgot. Gordon Hunter saw it as a simple case of the coaching staff doing their job: 'We wanted to give Blowers a start with a view to the World Cup and Kronfeld could play better than he was performing so we used the Dublin game to put him in the reserves as a sign to everyone that even if you were the best player in your position, you weren't irreplaceable. It was the biggest shot in the arse he ever had and I think he even hated me, and I was his guide like I was Wilson's and Oliver's. The next game against England B, he and Jonah played outstanding rugby. It gave Kronfeld the biggest wind-up of his career. If you're going to accuse John Hart and Gordon Hunter of mind games, so be it. Our job was to use the resources at hand to win.'

The mantra that runs through Todd Blackadder's book *Loyal* is 'It's all about the team.' For instance, on the subject of Laurie Mains: 'You knew with him that the team always came first and whether he was right or wrong or you didn't like something he did, it didn't matter because the most important thing with Laurie was the team.'

This is hard to reconcile with what he had to say about being subbed off in his first starting test match: 'I thought it was pretty shitty; I still do. To have all my family up there too, Priscilla, my mum, Nana, and brother up there, I felt like I'd been short-changed a bit in what should have been a proud moment. You can say what you like but you give someone a fair go and to walk off there just after halftime wasn't nice. I felt bloody let down.'

Given that there is no mention of his performance or the situation in the game or the tactical implications of him being replaced by Isitolo Maka, it reads as if Blackadder believes Hart should have left him on the field because it was his first starting test and his family had come up from Canterbury for the occasion. Where does the team, the greater good, fit into that equation?

Norm Hewitt had numerous beefs with Hart but perhaps the biggest was over the bawling-out he received for his ungracious reaction to being subbed off for Sean Fitzpatrick at Wembley in 1997.

According to Hewitt, 'The guy shouldn't have even been on that tour and he'd never given me a look in at any time in my whole career. And I remembered all those sly elbows and the punches and the dirt he'd put in over the years . . .' No doubt the memory of the sly elbows and what-not contributed to Hewitt's sense of grievance but his complaint that Fitzpatrick had 'never given me a look in' is hard to square with his comment 70-odd pages later that, 'if it's between you and someone else to wear the silver fern, well . . . you don't give a snot about them.'

Blackadder's biographer Phil Gifford characterises Hart's reaction as 'a violent verbal attack' that reduced Hewitt to tears. We are given a precis of what was said that can be safely categorised as the Hewitt version. Blackadder regarded Hewitt's action as 'a nothing thing — I don't think Norm did anything wrong' — and was 'sickened' by Hart's reaction to it; Kronfeld also came down on Hewitt's side and Mayhew felt that Hart was 'out of order'. When *Gladiator* appeared, the media's treatment of the incident seemed to be based on the premise that Hart had done something self-evidently reprehensible.

Well, there are two sides to most stories and Hunter told the other side to this one: 'Bugger me, here's a player on a fantastic salary, the coach makes a decision regarding the All Black captain and he disrespected it. As for the severity of the dressing down, it was nothing compared to what I saw routinely in my police career. If it's too hot in the kitchen, stay out of it. Sure it was tough being Fitzy's understudy but that was the job, that's what he was being paid for. Let me tell you, when I'm the coach and someone upsets me, they know about it and they don't like it. If Hart lost his rag a bit and used strong words and body language, let's not forget what Hewitt did: on Wembley Stadium, in front of a worldwide TV audience, he'd humiliated the coach and his administration, insulted a great All Black and the captain, and undermined our mana and our preparation for the second game against England.'

It seems the players can rely on public sympathy when they reveal how they've suffered at the coach's hands. This reflects our egalitarian urge to cut authority figures down to size and, in Hart's case, his unpopularity. But isn't there something slightly feeble in labelling the coach a meanie because he had some run-ins with some players? Coaches have to win and they have to make a lot of hard decisions along the way. One player's joy at gaining selection is another player's deep disappointment: the coach can't please them both. I don't think it's an unduly cynical reading of *Loyal* and *Gladiator* to conclude that Hart's greatest sin was that he didn't rate the authors as the best players in their positions in New Zealand. As for the blow-ups and dressing-downs, top-level professional sport is a stressful environment populated by hard-nosed, aggressive people so isn't a certain amount of conflict inevitable? One would very much like to think that All Blacks are sufficiently tough-minded that they don't expect to be molly-coddled or let off the hook when they breach protocols or fail to perform. Equally, one would hope that the New Zealand rugby public are sufficiently tough-minded that they don't believe a coach's first and most important duty is to be liked. Consider too the nature of the player-coach relationship. As Mayhew says, 'Coaches and players are in a boss-employee relationship so why should it come as a sensation that a player doesn't like his coach? No one bothers to ask the coach what he thinks of the players.'

'If the players catch the coach telling one lie,' said Hunter, 'that's it. They don't apply that to themselves — they'll tell you whatever they think will make you feel good. These players are very quick to forget who gave them opportunity, compassion, love. They keep raising stuff in books but it's very selective.'

'Selective' may be putting it politely.

'I gave up reading players' books,' says Mayhew, 'because so much of what's in them is patently untrue.'

11

Matters of opinion

The mass media's stock response to criticism is that it merely 'reflects public opinion'. Leaving aside the question of how representative of public opinion are those individuals and groups who actively seek the media's attention, this statement surely only tells half the story. For just as what we see in the mirror might make us feel good about ourselves or want to slit our wrists, the media influences public opinion even as it reflects it.

The phenomenon of talkback radio is at the cutting edge of this two-way process, exemplifying key trends in the commercial mass media — the blurring of the line between news and entertainment and the rise of audience participation — and upholding one of the cornerstones underpinning democratic mass culture: that everyone's entitled to their opinion.

Everyone's entitled to their opinion. This is the mantra of our noisy, disputatious age. In its eagerness to engage with the market, the mass media is quietly extending this premise, via phone-ins and vox pops and on-line polls: now not only is everyone entitled to their opinion but all opinions are equally valid. Making this stick involves downgrading the value of knowledge for once knowledge is taken out of the equation, it just comes down to who shouts the loudest.

Rugby and talkback are made for each other. In lonely little New Zealand, there are only two running stories — rugby and national politics — and of the two, rugby is arguably taken more seriously.

Without this widespread enthusiasm for talking rugby, sports talkback wouldn't have got off the ground and talkback hosts wouldn't have become influential voices. (How influential is itself a matter of opinion: Radio Sport has only a small chunk of the national radio audience — around 5 per cent — and even Murray Deaker, its biggest star, lags well behind Paul Holmes in the ratings. On the other hand, anecdotal evidence suggests that Deaker has a following among the sort of people who sit on the boards of provincial unions and, as they demonstrated in 2002, these are the people who ultimately run New Zealand rugby. There is another, even less scientific, way of looking at it: if Deaker has little or no influence, why does he inspire so much antipathy in rugby circles?)

You won't hear many kind words for talkback in general and Deaker in particular from the movers and shakers. Former All Black selector Peter Thorburn labelled talkback listeners 'the flat earth society'. According to NZRU deputy chief executive Steve Tew, 'We now have an industry that survives on just being critical; they're issue raisers, not solution finders. You can't do this job with its profile and level of accountability to every person in the country if you listened to talkback. You'd go insane.' And NZRU board member Graham Mourie: 'People like Murray Deaker live and die by their ratings so they appeal to the lowest common denominator.'

Even in the most civilised of countries, the lowest common denominator in full cry is not a pretty sight or sound. In unruly, egalitarian Aotearoa, where the levelling impulse is alive and well and 'Accentuate the Negative' sometimes seems to be the national motto, it can be positively ugly.

Here Norm Hewitt, not someone you'd normally regard as an elitist, could be describing the typical caller, as seen by the anti-talkback brigade: 'The ugliest people in rugby — apart from the fishheads [administrators] — are the fans who live their life through their team. If you lose, it's as if you've personally let them down.

It doesn't matter how much effort you put in . . . whether the ball bounded wrong or the ref was a jerk . . . you still lost. So you let them down. And you're a jerk. And they let you know it.'

Jeff Wilson too, it seems, has been living through his own private Groundhog Day, courtesy of the obsessive negativity which — again, according to its critics — is talkback's lifeblood: 'I don't need any reminding that if I'd scored we would have won the game. I've been reminded about it almost every single week since and nothing in sport galls me more. Do people talk about how the All Blacks came back? No. Do people talk about how I beat three or four defenders to even get to the line? No. Do people ask how I scored this try or that try? No. All they can talk about, it seems, is how I was almost over the line when George Gregan pulled off the tackle of a lifetime and the ball shot forward out of my hands. That's the nature of sport. You win some; you lose some. The All Blacks win more than most. But what am I constantly, repetitively, boringly reminded about and asked about? That tackle.

'What irks me most is these people who like to dwell on the things that went wrong rather than all the other things that went right. Perhaps it tells me more about them. What dull, dissatisfying lives they must lead if they can only ever look for the negatives, always talk about losses rather than victories, always talk about mistakes rather than things that have been done well and successfully. What is it in the New Zealand psyche that finds it so difficult to praise, yet so quick to condemn?'

Take the mob and a predisposition to negativity, add rabble-rousers and a huge and unexpected disappointment, bring violently to the boil *et voila* — it's witch-hunt time! Says Wilson, 'Several All Blacks . . . stunned and disappointed by what we heard of the reaction to the semi-final loss to France, now refuse to speak to a particular broadcaster. The reason was that he took criticism way beyond the realms of objective and constructive to a personal level.'

That broadcaster, needless to say, is Murray Deaker.

Love him or loathe him, Deaker has always been hard to ignore. When I first met him 30-odd years ago, he was, to put it mildly, a handful — loud, irrepressible, hell on wheels with a few drinks under his belt. Warren Zevon's song *Mr Bad Example* — 'I like to have a good time and I don't care who gets hurt' — could almost have been his theme tune. When we met up again more than a decade later, he was off the booze and better behaved if not noticeably less combative. Kicking a habit takes willpower and strength of character, as does overcoming personal tragedy and being a successful single parent. Perhaps Deaker developed a certain steeliness during those dark days. Perhaps he also developed a touch of the impatient intolerance to which strong-minded individuals who have endured and survived can be susceptible.

What happened next was remarkable. Starting from scratch and without an apprenticeship, Deaker made himself a very big fish in the small pond of New Zealand broadcasting, our second-best broadcaster ever (trailing only Paul Holmes) in the opinion of one experienced industry figure. He was the right man in the right place at the right time: if you sat down and made a list of the attributes needed to be a successful sports talkback host, you'd pretty much end up with a profile of Deaker. He is passionate and knowledgeable about sport; he is an enthusiast; he has boundless self-confidence and loves the sound of his own voice; he has the common touch; he has a hide like a rhinoceros; he doesn't give a hoot in hell what anyone thinks of him.

When I began playing President's Grade cricket for the North Shore club, Deaker took me aside and explained the facts of life. Men like us, he said, on the cusp of middle age, didn't give up our Saturday afternoons for some fresh air and a bit of exercise; we did it because we wanted to have a decent bat. Rule one, therefore, was to make sure you batted in the top three of the order. Rule two was to forget about the run rate; if the blokes at the other end wanted to throw their wickets away, that was their look-out. Only after 30-odd overs, when your team-mates on the sideline had become too strident to ignore, did you even think about throwing caution to the wind. Deaker's self-focus was such that sometimes, after being dismissed, he took his pads off and simply disappeared. He is very definitely not one of nature's supporting acts.

Deaker doesn't accept the characterisation of his audience as whingeing ignoramuses. His listeners, he says, are rank and file Kiwis, ordinary blokes who love their footy: 'People have always talked rugby — often fiercely — in pubs. Whereas in the past, blokes got together to discuss the All Blacks, now they can do it on the radio, which they do for all sorts of reasons: ego, getting information that they couldn't get in a bar because the audience is so wide, being entertained in their own homes or cars. We get a lot of calls from people on their way home. The average caller is genuine and loves rugby. They ring when the All Blacks lose because they feel cheated but they ring out of love rather than hate. But because they ring when the team loses, they're dismissed as whingers and moaners.

'The most ill-informed talkback in this country is on cricket because if the current team gets beaten both the callers and the hosts say it didn't happen in the old days. In fact, the record of the current team is better than any except the Hadlee era. This team has won more test matches than any other. Most of these people have no background in the game and came into it when Lance Cairns whooshed the ball over the fence at the MCG. That was the most significant innings in our history because it introduced a whole lot of people to the game and they became overnight authorities who think that great team was the rule rather than the exception. The discussion about rugby is so much more accurate.'

It tickles Deaker's fancy to attribute much of his success to the outfit that gets a regular working-over on his shows — the NZRU.

His disdain for the national body is so volcanic it must just about register on the Richter scale.

'Talkback's been much more successful than anyone thought and it's been underestimated by the NZRU, who typically dismissed it and, in their arrogance, thought that because they'd dismissed it, it would go away. By doing that, they've contributed to its growth. Because everybody hates the NZRU, the fact that they detested talkback made talkback popular. They completely failed to realise that it's a safety valve — people can blow their fuse and get rid of it. They could turn that situation around overnight and use it positively by making the players and officials available and by using the opportunity instead of being fearful.'

To support this argument, he cites his regular spots with referee Paddy O'Brien and suggests players and administrators should take a leaf from his book. If they did, insists Deaker, his influence and that of his fellow hosts would rapidly diminish: 'It would push the host into insignificance because he'd be irrelevant to the discussion taking place between the personality and the public. But what's happened is that the hosts must lead the discussion and therefore they've become stars and the NZRU is seen as the enemy. The void between the NZRU and the public has been largely filled by talkback and I find that frightening. We're only opinions, not the authority, but since the authority is incapable of speaking, we've become it.'

John Hart is equally alarmed by the hosts' power and influence but believes that talkback created the vacuum in the first place: 'Talkback radio becomes a negative thing in a small country: the views of a vocal minority are espoused and everyone wants to criticise something. We cry out for leadership but where are the leaders? They're up against the tall poppy syndrome, our yen for kicking people to death. In the 1960s we had born leaders in our rugby teams and there were lots of them — any of 10 people could have captained the team. Now people don't want to lead because it's so tough and people are so critical. You've got to have a thick skin, be quick on your feet and perform pretty well. In the vacuum, some of these media people have become leaders and they haven't got the pedigree to lead.'

It is tempting to think that Deaker is being disingenuous here because he obviously enjoys being a star and revels in the influence that goes with that. However, he returns to the theme of rugby shooting itself in the foot through its lack of cooperation with the media too persistently to be entirely insincere.

'The media liaison person has been viewed as a media prevention person. Most of them have been worse than useless. I once contacted the NZRU to say that I was available day or night to do a five-minute piece with an All Black. They never even got back to me and I have a nationwide show on two networks. The comparison with the [New Zealand] Warriors is chalk and cheese. Their staff are available and bend over backwards for us. Any player within reason will be available on match day. When you stop to think about it, it's not going to put anyone off. Consequently, hours of radio we had allocated to rugby are allocated to rugby league because of the difficulties of dealing with the All Blacks.

'If I look at All Black coaches I've dealt with,' he says, '1996/97 stand out like a beacon. The players were encouraged to be available and the coach was skilled at handling the media. The tour of South Africa was the most complete exercise I've had anything to do with, both in terms of the performance on the field and the way the media were dealt with. It was a great tour to cover. What happened then was so sad. In 1998 Hart became ill. Because he was trying to control the media, the media turned on him. It was like a marriage break-up because the relationship had been so close before.

'It's hit a new low since [John] Mitchell became coach. He'd have to rank as our most uncooperative coach — you simply can't get hold of the man. It wasn't much better under [Wayne] Smith but now it's at its lowest point ever. Laurie Mains at his absolute worst was 500 per cent better than Mitchell because Mains would comment on the rugby if you pushed a microphone at him.'

It's impossible to believe that there isn't an element of disingenuousness in Deaker's complaints about the cone of silence surrounding Mitchell. Common sense suggests that Mitchell, like Smith before him, is media-averse largely because of what happened to Hart. Media relations were central to Hart's overall strategy for the All Blacks and he devoted a lot of time and effort to it. But when the All Blacks started losing, all that time and effort and those good intentions counted for naught and all the goodwill he'd supposedly stockpiled for a rainy day proved to be an illusion. Indeed, one of the criticisms levelled at him was that he'd overdone the media stuff at the expense of his coaching duties. The lessons were clear: every time the All Black coach opens his mouth, he gives a hostage to fortune or, as Gordon Hunter memorably put it, 'the ammunition you provide is the ammunition you get shot with'. If the media could crucify Hart, why waste time cultivating them and catering to their needs? The stark fact is that if the All Blacks are successful, the coach is untouchable no matter how much the media might detest him; conversely, if the All Blacks are unsuccessful, the coach is in the firing line, no matter how much the media might admire him.

All Black team doctor John Mayhew believes the media pressure on coaches is having dire consequences: 'Mitchell has deflected a lot of it by keeping his head down and not taking positions, but what happened to Hart was terrible and you see it happening at Super 12 level as well. I worry about the standard of coaching in this country. If Mitchell and Deans were to fall under a bus, where would we go? I'm not a big fan of Graham Henry but who else is there? Mains? He's back in the past, whatever the media may say. We drive away our thinkers and innovators like Smith and Thorburn and crank homogeneous coaches out of the Massey course.'

There are two striking aspects to talkback discussion about coaches and coaching. Firstly, it is largely results-driven: if the team is doing well, the coach is, by definition, good and vice versa. This would seem to assume that coaches are on an equal footing, particularly in terms of the resources and talent at their disposal, rather like sailors in regattas in which the contestants sail identical yachts. Secondly, much of the discussion concentrates on one aspect of coaching — selection. We are a nation of amateur selectors but how many of us have any real idea of how good a given coach is at planning and organisation, building a team culture, exercising discipline, running training sessions, honing individual and collective techniques, personnel management on an individual and team basis, creating an overall strategy and making tactical adjustments to the game plan for specific opposition? We can gain some sense of these things from the team's performances but even that assessment is coloured by what — if any — degree of responsibility for what happens on the field is placed on the players. If there is no evidence of a coherent game plan, for example, that doesn't necessarily mean that the players weren't given one. It's difficult for an outsider to gain an accurate picture of how well or poorly a coach is carrying out his various roles; you need to be inside or at least close to the camp to do that. Without that insight and in many cases, it must be said, with only a hazy idea of what a coach actually does, the talkback audience focuses on selection and results and passes judgement accordingly.

Wilson doubts that, 'any of the detractors of coaches such as John Hart or Laurie Mains had ever met either of them, had ever seen them coach a team at training or ever heard them speak to players. Yet their views, as personal and uninformed as they may be, get a nationwide audience.'

Graham Mourie took heavy flak when he coached the Hurricanes and the casual consensus seems to be that he made a mess of it.

A WHOLE NEW BALL GAME

One criticism — Norm Hewitt has been particularly vocal on this score — was that he over-complicated things and blinded his players with science. Mourie counters that his critics failed to recognise that the game has changed and that he, as coach, had no alternative but to try to equip his players for the new and more demanding environment: 'The game has changed in terms of skill and the technical base. Players have to be multi-skilled and there are a lot of mini-rucks and high continuity because the players are better at retaining the ball but the media reacted adversely, not recognising the change.'

Pressed on this point, he adds — and was that the ghost of a smile flitting across his lugubrious countenance? — that 'simple people prefer a simple game'.

Deaker's complaints about the difficulties of dealing with the All Blacks are upheld by former All Black manager Andrew Martin, whose efforts to make the players more media-friendly ran into a brick wall: 'My objective was to get the players to do interviews at 9.30 or 10 on the morning of a test. Why on earth not? There's something wrong if they have to be so mindlessly focused that they can't spare the time for a few pleasantries — because that's what they are — for the people who report on them. But they look at you as if you've sprouted a second head. It's another area where the Aussies make us look second rate.'

How many of us can honestly say that we haven't reached that invidious comparison? While the Australians' openness with the media may reflect the fact that, for all its recent success, the game there is not the national sport and therefore can't take media exposure for granted, Martin doesn't believe the reverse is true. He thinks it's more basic than that.

'It's not because the players think the media need us more than we need them, although that may be the case with the current coaches. The players are just dumb in the sense of not

'You know my phone number, Taine.' Will All Black coach John Mitchell's hard-nosed management style produce tougher-minded players?

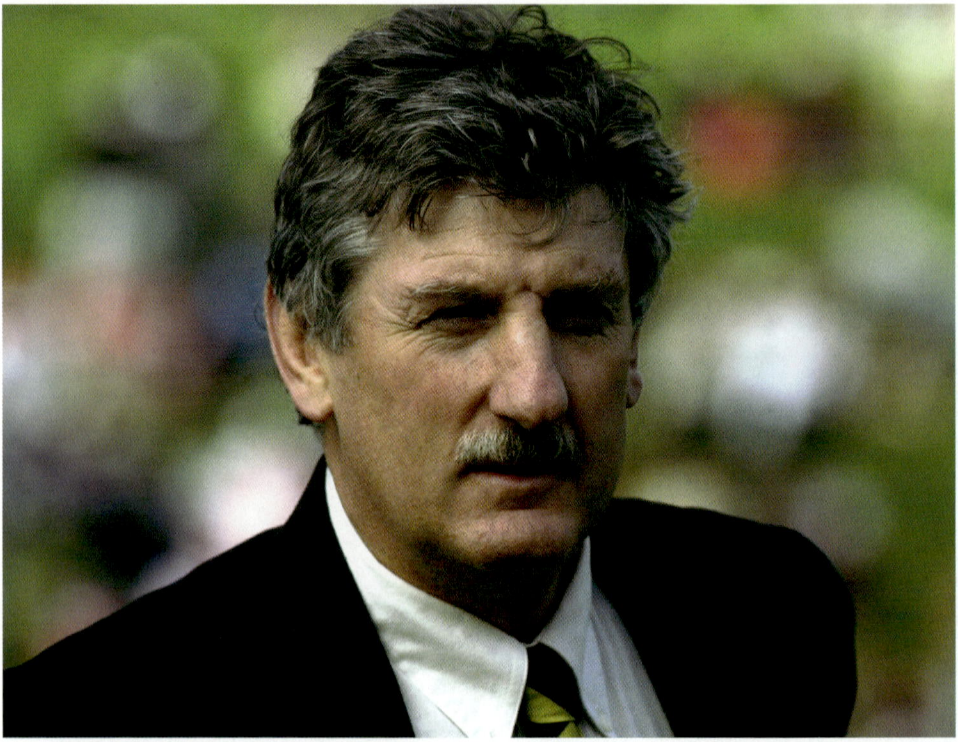

FOTOPRESS

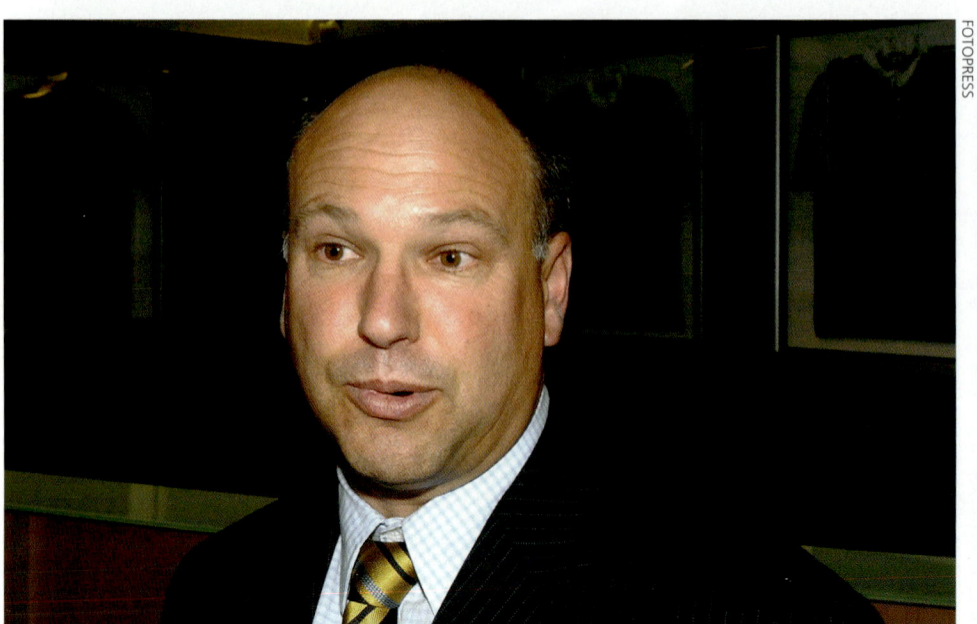

Right men in the right place at the right time? Former All Black captain now NZRU board member Graham Mourie (above) and Auckland Rugby Union and Blues chief executive David White.

FOTOPRESS

FOTOPRESS

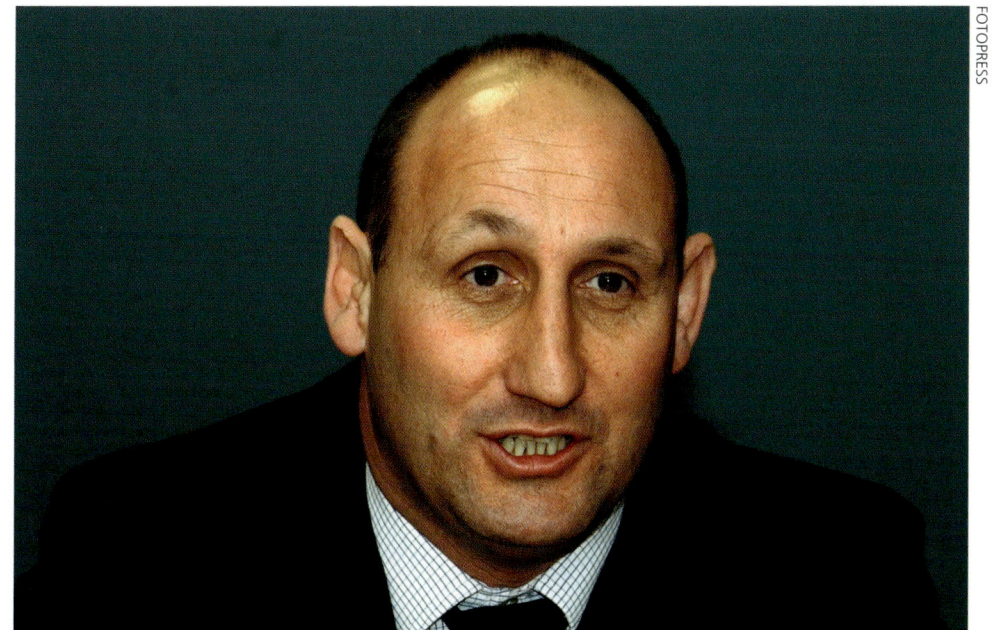

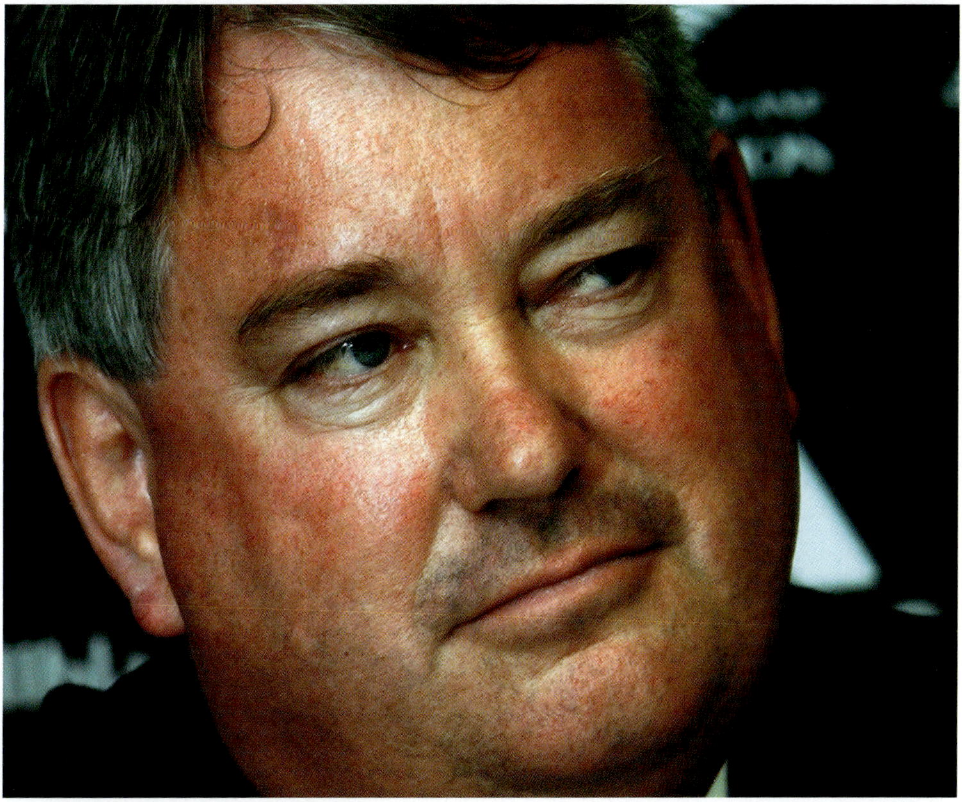

FOTOPRESS

Former All Black captain now NZRU chairman Jock Hobbs (top) and former business high-flyer now NZRU chief executive Chris Moller.

Say something even if it's only 'goodbye' — former NZRU chief executive David Rutherford (left) and chairman Murray McCaw.

understanding what the media can do and it's a combination of that and not wanting any distractions. Under Smith we managed to take a lot of the emotional and mental intensity out of the lead-up to a game because, frankly, that can be quite debilitating. Part of that is saying you don't have to be chewing broken glass on the morning of a game. I also had great difficulty in organising media training: if you're going to do it, you need to do it well, which means training but that was terribly low on the priority list.

'It's very much about how you manage the public's perception of how you're living. If the public see that you're accessible via the media then at least you're connecting with them. If they never hear from you or only hear glib one-liners, then you inevitably reinforce the view that here are some fairly privileged young men living lives that few of their supporters can aspire to. I made a pretty serious attempt to move away from five-star accommodation. I tried to implement a system that in test match week we stayed in motels and only moved into smart accommodation the night before the game. That became too hard, they didn't like moving — although it wasn't as if they had to do anything. I don't know if the players were behind that; maybe it was a couple of coaches.'

Deaker brushes aside most of the criticisms but he does concede that the dynamic of talkback is such that it thrives on failure and controversy and can be hard work and, let's face it, pretty boring when everything is going swimmingly.

'The best day for me as a talkback host is when the All Blacks lose and it's a wet day in Auckland,' he says. 'All I have to do is read the weather forecast. The worst thing is fine weather and a wonderful All Black victory. People will say it's negative but I would argue that some positive things come out of it because by voicing their opinions, people feel part of it. It's very difficult for the average Kiwi to feel part of the All Blacks. You can go along to practice, you and 5000 others, but they won't give interviews so talkback is the way.'

Talkback is about celebrating success and getting to the root cause of failure but it is the latter that really gets them going out in talkback land. The hosts get to do a lot of finger-pointing and make a lot of harsh judgements. Calling it as they see it is what they are paid to do.

'You have to choose between personal relationships and your audience,' says Deaker, 'and you make that choice when you accept your first pay cheque. It's a killer for personal relationships. This job has cost me friendships with John Hart and Jeff Wilson. I fell out with Laurie Mains, who I played club rugby with and for Otago with, for a long time and Martin Crowe didn't speak to me for years. That goes with the territory and that's why we're paid well — we know we're going to lose a lot of friends.

'The host gets the blame, not the caller. The number of times I've heard people say "Deaker said such and such" when in fact it was the caller telling me. You're inevitably misquoted. When I go into rugby environments, I'm very aware that I'm *persona non grata*, which doesn't worry me at all but I didn't like losing the friends. That's sad but not the other thing.'

Deaker has always been sure of himself and being a talkback host is not an occupation that is likely to generate self-doubt or second thoughts. Talkback is a self-contained, black and white world that has little room for doubt, equivocation or seeing both sides of the issue. Like coaching, it requires a healthy ego and, like coaches, talkback hosts have their sycophantic cheer squads. How often do callers praise Deaker and his colleagues for their wisdom, insight and even courage in shaping up to the issues of the day? The nature of their audience means that they are rarely challenged and, besides, they always have the option of cutting off stroppy callers.

There isn't a lot of humility in talkback. There is precious little recognition that the people they pass judgement on are actually out there doing it, trying as hard as they can in intensely competitive environments, as opposed to sitting in a studio running off at the mouth. Nor does there seem to be much recognition that their access to the airwaves and ability to influence public opinion carries with it some responsibility. The Canadian-English press baron Lord Beaverbrook told Rudyard Kipling that, 'What I want is power. Kiss 'em one day and kick 'em the next.' This, wrote Kipling, amounted to 'power without responsibility: the prerogative of the harlot throughout the ages.'

Although we have a number of good rugby writers, rugby coverage in our newspapers suffers from the restrictions on space that result when advertising rather than circulation drives revenue and from the amorphous nature of the readership. New Zealand newspapers have to be all things to all people; our population is too small to permit the sort of market segmentation that exists in Britain or even Australia. The rugby writers of *The Times* of London and *The Sydney Morning Herald* know that their readership is essentially the educated middle class and write accordingly, both in terms of content and length. *The New Zealand Herald*'s circulation depends on it being read beyond the eastern suburbs and the North Shore.

The same demographic imperative appears to drive Sky Television's rugby coverage. Although our commentators are as good as any in the world, it cannot be said that the analysis is particularly penetrating. Sky's experts, an assortment of former All Blacks, tend to keep it simple and seldom stray beyond the comfort zone of hackneyed terms and phrases — hard yards, backing himself, money man, fat man's alley, thanks for coming — and daggy humour.

Murray Mexted is the star turn. His persona — an original mix of macho man and ageing hippy — is, one feels, an acquired taste while his steadfast refusal to accept that there is such a document as

The Laws of Rugby Union is reminiscent of the Iraqi information minister who continued to insist that there were no live Americans in Baghdad even as one half-expected him to be tapped on the shoulder in mid-press conference by a US marine wanting to know the way to Saddam's bunker. Chris Laidlaw, the token pointy-head, sometimes resembles a bookworm who has gone to investigate what's cooking on the barbecue and found himself roped into a conversation with a bunch of yahoos. Ian Jones, encouragingly, strives for depth, but generally the level of analysis is significantly lower now than it was in the mid-1990s when Hart and Mains provided expert comment. There is an interesting comparison with the Channel 9 cricket commentary team which, for all its experience and familiarity and nice balance of voices and personalities, is stronger for the addition of Mark Taylor and, particularly, Ian Healy with their contemporary take and willingness to dwell on the technical and mental sides of the game.

All of which raises the question: is our media coverage worthy of New Zealand's standing in international rugby? Even given the handicaps imposed by the size of the market, does it reflect the expertise at the top of the game and the ingrained feel for rugby among its followers? Former NZRU chief executive David Rutherford thinks not: 'It's extremely frustrating what passes for debate. The interesting thing is the level of noise, which shouldn't be confused with the level of debate, although if you spend time in clubs and provinces, you come across plenty of people who understand the issues. New Zealand should be setting the standard with the level of analysis but we're not and that's one sad aspect of our game.'

Hart sees a decline in standards and a shift in focus resulting from blanket live TV coverage: 'Back in the seventies and eighties people like Terry McLean, Ron Palenski and Lindsay Knight were good writers who understood the game. Now, because of TV, there's no need to report. The emphasis is on sensationalism: everybody's looking for an angle and the media has tended to focus on negatives and personalities. I suppose that's a reflection of the exposure the game gets and the different sort of person now doing the job.'

The next decade will be critical for the future of New Zealand rugby. What happens over the next 10 years will probably determine whether, over the long term, rugby remains our national game and — and the two are obviously linked — whether the All Blacks can continue to realistically aspire, year in, year out, to being the best team in the world. The issues, both domestically and globally, are complex and immune to quick fixes. The battles will be numerous and difficult and there will be setbacks. The challenge for the media is to address these issues in all their complexity, to educate the public and to extend a little patience and tolerance towards those charged with guiding New Zealand rugby on and off the field. If they don't, if they go further down the populist route, insisting that the issues and challenges are clear-cut, easily surmountable and therefore that failure is inexcusable, if they settle for promoting controversy and making scapegoats, they will make this hard road much harder. And they will be guilty of the very failings they are so quick to charge others with — letting down true-blue rugby supporters and jeopardising a great heritage.

12

Survival of the fittest

Until recently, professional sport was foreign territory for most New Zealanders.

'If you were a full-time professional sportsperson before 1995,' says Andy Haden, 'you lived and worked overseas and were probably a golfer, a surfer, an endurance athlete or a rugby player who'd switched to league. People here have never had to deal with the implications of professional sport whereas in most other Western countries, professional sport had been a fact of life, a part of society, for decades. When I played rugby in Rome, we used to rub shoulders with the AC Roma footballers, who also included foreigners, and talk about what they did in their sporting lives. When I was spending time in London, I went to a lot of first-division matches because they were on just down the road. Now New Zealanders are going through the stage of discovering what people elsewhere have known for a long time.'

Change never suits everyone. There are always winners and losers and it is undeniable that some sectors of New Zealand rugby are less healthy than they used to be. The question is: is rugby in crisis or is it evolving into a new form that reflects social and economic reality? Is the game alienating its core supporters or making itself attractive and relevant to a more diverse and representative demographic?

John Graham recalls that in the 1950s Victoria University produced an entire All Black backline. 'That would be impossible today,' he says. 'It will never happen again.' He regrets that there is no place in professional rugby for academically minded young men who wish to pursue their studies full-time and believes that, in the long run, the game will be the poorer for it. However, this isn't a one-way process: these days the university system is also less accommodating of all-rounders.

Rugby's identity crisis is such that while professionalism and its trappings are accused of having spoilt the game, it is arguable that many of the recent failures and disappointments came about because New Zealand rugby, as an industry, wasn't professional enough. As an example, there's much resistance to what is invariably described as 'the army' of coaches and advisers surrounding the All Blacks that includes, among others, a kicking coach and a throwing-in coach. Ex-players scoff that in their day they didn't need specialist coaches to teach them basic skills. Don Clarke was the greatest goal-kicker of his era but his success rate, admittedly with less user-friendly balls, was not much over 50 per cent. Carlos Spencer had a 75 per cent success rate in the 2003 Super 12 without dispelling reservations about his goal-kicking. If Spencer has technical deficiencies, what better way to iron them out than one-on-one tuition from an expert? If it is good enough for Tiger Woods . . .

England, of course, are the leading exponents of micro-coaching. They seem to have a specialist coach for every bodily function performed on a rugby field, the latest being a South African lady whose mission is to improve the players' peripheral vision. While our reflex response is to find this degree of specialisation ridiculous, if not effete, it seems to have worked for them.

That doesn't mean we have to slavishly imitate: what suits the English temperament and style might not work for players who respond to being allowed some input at training and given the freedom to express themselves. 'Introducing too many people into the structure will impact on flair, innovation and creativity,' says John Hart. 'You do need the technical analysis which drives defence. England led the way with that but you can go too far and I think it erodes accountability.'

Nor, on the other hand, should we dismiss it because someone else thought of it first. Professionalism is about striving for continuous self-improvement, searching for the edge that might mean the difference between winning and losing, trying to be the best you can possibly be. If a throwing-in coach is the difference between hitting the target when the game hangs in the balance or mucking it up, then what is the problem?

'How can someone who was a club first-five coach a front row?' asks Graham. 'You can get the basic principles out of a manual but how do you tell a prop where he should put his outside arm, how deep his knee bend should be? Having a lot of advisers goes against my natural inclinations but you must have expertise.'

Competitive sport, by its very nature, is hierarchical. Professionalism accentuates that because of the rewards and profile that accrue to the leading performers. New Zealanders have been uncomfortable with the process whereby ever-greater rewards flow to an increasingly cocooned elite. It is a fine line between egalitarianism and envy and the players have had to learn to live with a greater degree of scrutiny and volume of criticism, some of which has a far sharper, more personal edge than would have been considered reasonable in the past. This raises the wider issue of the practicality and desirability of lumping the elite professional sport and the mass-participation amateur recreational game in together. Formal separation would be an anathema to those who believe that the NZRU's first and overriding priority is to ensure that the top level remains firmly connected to its grassroots and history, but sooner or later this evolution will have to be acknowledged.

'I'm a great advocate of developing amateur and professional streams,' says Andrew Martin. 'They've moved so far apart from a governance and administrative perspective and the demands of professionalism versus the wishes and desires of amateurism have almost become mutually exclusive. But we're not even close to that nettle let alone close to grasping it.'

A curious feature of the ongoing debate over the state of health of New Zealand rugby is that those who loudly extol its history, traditions and importance to the nation often seem to have a low regard for its resilience. There is a view, for example, that it is absolutely vital to the future of New Zealand rugby that the All Blacks win the 2003 World Cup. One hopes that that is not the case; one hopes that the game is not so fragile that its future rides on the outcome of one or two games that could be decided by a missed goal-kick or the bounce of the ball or a poor refereeing decision.

Says David Rutherford, 'A South African administrator once said to me that the World Cup was a strategic disaster for the big five nations because one of us will always be eliminated before the semi-finals and only one or perhaps two — like New Zealand in 1995 and France to a lesser extent in 1999 — can emerge in credit. It's a real problem, particularly for New Zealand and South Africa, that we emerge from World Cups in one of two states of being — euphoria or depression.'

When John Mitchell announced his first squad of 2003, he observed that, as a country, we tend to get carried away in the build-up to a World Cup. We should heed the lessons of the past, he suggested, and keep our feet on the ground. The higher the expectations, the greater the let-down. Countries that have bad World Cups relative to their expectations going into the tournament — like New Zealand in 1991 and 1999 and Australia in 1995 — can let disappointment cloud perspective and throw out the good with the bad. Perhaps the question is not whether we can afford not to win the World Cup but whether we can afford to over-react if we don't.

'Winning the World Cup is important,' says Jock Hobbs, 'but that can't be our sole focus as a board because there are a lot of other things to deal with. If we don't, will rugby still be our national sport and retain its place in the fabric of the community? It would be extremely disappointing but while there may be a reaction, given the enormous All Black history and heritage, I don't believe it's inevitable that it would be catastrophic for the game. I'd hope not. Winning the World Cup would assist dramatically in strengthening the game but I hope we can strengthen the game regardless of what happens at the World Cup.'

John Plumtree is in a position to make a detached, comparative assessment of New Zealand rugby. The former Taranaki and Hawke's Bay lock spent almost a decade in Natal, playing 80 games for the province and representing South Africa at sevens, before coaching Swansea for four largely successful years.

'I'm upbeat about New Zealand rugby,' he says, 'because I've come from a country with real problems. We have a lot of talent here despite the run-off to Japan and the UK and the elite players are well looked after. Since professional rugby came in, the entertainment has been superb. After work a guy goes along to a superb stadium and wants to be entertained and that's what happening. Things are organised towards producing quality rugby, which doesn't come about from practising on Tuesdays and Thursdays, it comes from planning and structures and quality competition. Compared to the UK and certainly Wales, the system here is geared towards producing high-quality, entertaining rugby. The majority of rugby people in the UK are pretty envious of what we've got and that's certainly also true of South Africa.'

Comparisons can be useful. 'Wales is really the only other country in which rugby is the national game,' says Graham Mourie.

'Rugby's the number one sport for the white community in South Africa and a "major minor" game in England, France and Australia.'

Wales is another small country where rugby is played and followed by all walks of life. Thirty years ago, the Welsh were riding so high that they had a serious claim to being the leading rugby nation. Through the 1970s Wales dominated European rugby to an even greater extent than England does now. Between 1969 and 1979 they won the Five Nations Championship outright six times (with three Grand Slams) and shared it once, plus they were unbeaten in their three games in 1972 when the tournament wasn't completed because of an outbreak of foot and mouth disease. They seemed to have an inexhaustible supply of high-quality players and their coaching programmes were admired and imitated by many countries, most notably Australia. In 1978, the year of the third Grand Slam, even the wildest nightmares of those who were aware that the history of Welsh rugby was one of peaks and troughs would not have pictured Wales slipping out of the international first division within a decade and becoming the game's basket case within two.

Consider this: by 1953 Wales had beaten the All Blacks three times in four meetings (all of them admittedly home games). They haven't done so since. The All Blacks have won the last eight clashes by the following scores: 55–3, 43–17, 42–7, 34–9, 34–9, 52–3, 54–9, 49–6. Only three of those games were in New Zealand. To have this rivalry, around which so many myths and legends had accumulated, reduced to a historical curiosity must be galling for the Welsh. Even more galling must be the decisive — and, one suspects, permanent — shift of British rugby's centre of power from Cardiff to London. The Welsh have always taken unbridled delight in beating England. Each victory was a small payback for centuries of political domination, economic exploitation and cultural vandalism. During the 1970s the three absolute certainties of

British life were strikes, soccer hooliganism and Wales beating England at Cardiff Arms Park. In 1990 England beat Wales at Twickenham by 34–6, an unheard of result in the context of the previous two decades. In hindsight, this signalled that the power shift was underway. The following year England won in Cardiff for the first time since 1963. Wales have only won one game against England in Cardiff since 1989. Some of the recent scorelines in England's favour — 50–10, 46–12, 60–26 — have been humiliations on the scale the Welsh have come to expect on their doomed ventures south of the equator.

'[Wales] was a country,' wrote David Kirk, 'that had gone through the huge emotional crisis of being one of the best teams in the world to being a shadow of their former selves . . . and it should cast a fear into rugby-playing nations how fast a demise can happen. The Welsh blame it, I believe, on teachers suddenly deciding not to coach rugby at school. And rugby league hasn't helped by taking the cream of their players. Their administration isn't that flash either, dominated by an old-boy network. The decline of Welsh rugby happened fast, within a decade, and it is an awful object lesson.'

In the six years since Kirk's book came out things have got even worse. The Welsh Rugby Union (WRU) has plunged into terrifying debt largely over the Millennium Stadium, coaches — including Graham Henry, prematurely hailed as a saviour — have come and gone and the clubs have continued to bicker over governance changes and playing structures, like barflies on the *Titanic* arguing over whose round it is. Early in 2003 Swansea, historically one of the four great Welsh clubs, effectively declared itself broke, despite private benefactors injecting £3 million in the past four years. Thirty-four players whose contracts extend into 2004 and beyond were asked to voluntarily sever them without compensation.

A perfect symbol of Welsh rugby's tragicomic penchant for stepping on banana skins was the team missing its flight to

Auckland in 2003 because they spent too long haggling over their tour match payments. With this farcical episode, Welsh rugby completed its 30-year journey from world leader to laughing-stock.

'The country most like New Zealand is Wales,' says Murray McCaw, 'but they didn't embrace professionalism. Yes, they lost the miners and steelworkers and the communities based on those industries declined and shrank but there's a direct parallel with farming here. There are 280-odd clubs in Wales and all of them have a vote on the WRU. Generally, you only get change when you have a crisis and the financial mess the WRU is in will drive the overdue changes to its governance structure.'

Speaking before agreement was reached on the consolidation of the leading clubs into five regional teams, Plumtree was cautiously optimistic: 'I think that if they get the structure right, they'll survive and succeed. The problem is the club men want their clubs to do well first and foremost when the big picture demands that the focus should be on Wales doing well. If they can come up with a quality structure that involves reducing the number of teams and which is supported by the public, I think they can once again be a force in the game — I know how good some of those players are. But it won't happen for three or four years — they've got some catching up to do and the other countries aren't standing still.'

The Welsh example should be heeded by every New Zealand rugby player and follower who thinks issues of governance and financial management are irrelevant and ongoing success is guaranteed providing we cling onto the past and remain passionate about the game. No rugby nation glorifies its past more than the Welsh and, according to Plumtree, passion is the least of their worries: 'They're almost mad about the game. During the Six Nations, they'll fill the Millennium Stadium to watch Wales lose but they'll be back for the next game a fortnight later.'

'I might be cynical,' says Haden, 'but you hear that restoring the old values and respect for tradition and those sorts of things are important to All Blacks these days but more important is knowing that the basics are being done right. It's nice to look back from time to time but it's nicer to do it right going forward.'

On the way down, Wales passed Australia and England coming up. New Zealanders have been forced to face up to the fact of Australia's emergence as a rugby superpower: the on-field evidence has been too compelling to ignore. The challenge now is to learn to love it, to recognise that we're actually lucky that our nearest neighbour is our greatest rival. As David Rutherford puts it, 'New Zealanders have to get away from the mindset that anything that works to Australia's advantage is, by definition, to our disadvantage.'

England is another matter altogether. New Zealanders have always had a problem with the English. The popular perception is of a bunch of Will Carling toffs — Oxbridge, the Guards, the City — who patronise us when they lose with 'It's only a game'-type comments (sub-text: 'No wonder you take it so seriously — you've got nothing else to do') and are insufferable when they win. Hence Andrew Mehrtens' comment that 'They're pricks to lose to', although, as was pointed out at the time, how did he know? We still get agitated over the fact that they call their rugby union The Rugby Football Union (RFU) even though that decision must have been made an awfully long time ago when it was, conceivably, *the* rugby union. We continue to wheel out the tired caricature of out-of-touch gin-swilling old farts even though their current administration includes great players of recent vintage like Bill Beaumont and Fran Cotton who look as if they've downed the odd pint in their time.

But now we have to accept that they're good. Really good. And rich, which means they're just going to get better.

'We wanted to be as good as we could be whereas they played the game for recreation,' says Andrew Martin. 'We played harder and were less forgiving but that's gone now. In the amateur era there was no one else like us but now we fund players to the tune of $2000 per player per year; in England that figure is £3000. The field has been tilted. It's about the resources you can bring to your system and the task of preparing national teams. England has far more players than we do. If you pour resources into that demographic, you're going to get bigger, faster, arguably more skilful individuals.'

Check out these numbers. The English Rugby Academy system, established in September 2002 with £8 million of lottery funding, involves a National Academy supported by 14 regional academies that will develop the 300 most talented players in the 16 to 21 age group. An elite squad of 60 players 19 to 21 years old will be selected for the National Academy where they will train alongside the senior England squad. According to Mourie, 'England has £20 million earmarked for player development. Sport England is funding 1100 fully paid coaches to work on player development which is more coaches than in the whole of New Zealand.'

How do we compete with that scale and financial muscle over the long term? Or as Mourie puts it, how do we 'maintain our ability to be competitive at the top end'?

A good start would be to accept the reality that the pendulum has swung and New Zealand has gone from having a competitive advantage over the other rugby nations — with the exception of South Africa — to being at a comparative disadvantage to our major competitors because of our small population and economy and geographic isolation. As a result New Zealand rugby will increasingly find itself in the same position as our other activities and enterprises that compete on the international stage and in the global market: having to work harder, be more innovative and make the money go further than the opposition in order to put itself on a competitive footing. If you can compete, you can win.

'What stands between us and world domination,' says Martin,

'is four or five other nations which can resource and fund their teams at as high if not higher a level than we can and have a greater demographic base. We have to do everything absolutely right to be able to compete, which is why it's so important we get the little things right. We've got to make maximum use of resources, maximise every little opportunity. We shouldn't be surprised by that — that's how life is for us as New Zealanders in every other sphere. Corporate New Zealand has always had to deal with that and has punched above its weight, being smarter and looking for every competitive advantage. New Zealand business is a good analogy for the way rugby must go to compete internationally. Any advantage you can take into a test match is only good for another two games, if that. If we expose something in the Tri-Nations, it will be analysed so that they know it backwards and know the circumstances in the game when it will be used and if it's any good they'll introduce their own variation of it. That's how tight it is.'

Our edge is our natural talent. In order to maximise that, we have to increase the efficiency and productivity of 'the factory' — the system that keeps producing All Blacks. As our player base relative to our competitors shrinks, there will need to be even greater focus on ensuring that special talents do not slip through the net. Once identified, they must be put in good environments and exposed to good coaches to bring out the absolute best in them.

'I think we've let the coaching and player development side slip and haven't brought it up to speed as far as where the game's going,' says Mourie. 'We're going to have to work harder at ground level and be a lot smarter at running the game at the top level if we want to retain our position in world rugby. If we don't continue to improve and work harder and smarter than we've done in the last few years, we'll have problems.'

John Graham, who, along with Brian Lochore, reviews the performances of Super 12 coaches and has been a member of the panel that reviews the All Black coach, believes we also have to ensure that we keep producing effective coaches who aren't carbon copies of each other:

'The first issue the NZRU and the provincial unions should concentrate on is the need to produce quality coaches. How you do that is an interesting challenge. Are you going to start paying them? What is the identification process for finding coaches? I've got a fear that we'll end up cloning coaches, which would be a mistake. We need good coaches who are challenging and innovative because if they're not, the youngsters will look at other options that don't demand the physical output and punishment. So much depends on the ability of the coach to make the game stimulating. You've got to have a passion for the game and an understanding of how it fits into our culture but you don't need to have been an outstanding player. The ability to manage young people then men is the hallmark of a good coach.

'Do you look at technical ability or human qualities? Fred Allen wasn't a good technical coach — he thought he was but he wasn't. You can't be a dummy on the game but if you combine the two things you have a proficient coach. Dealing with 26 young New Zealanders is a far, far more demanding task than it used to be because of social change. People won't do something just because you tell them to.'

The other thing that New Zealand has to maximise is money. A lot of rugby people are uncomfortable with this subject; they would rather not have to think about it. Some give the impression they would rather no one else thought about it either. But think about it we must. The money will not take care of itself. That might work for Bill Gates and the Sultan of Brunei but it won't work for New Zealand rugby.

So when people complain about rugby being on pay TV, they should understand that turning this particular clock back would seriously reduce the game's income. The free-to-air channels simply cannot match what the Murdoch organisation is prepared to pay for the broadcasting rights to New Zealand rugby nor can they provide it with international exposure that has a direct commercial value.

'At the end of the day,' says McCaw, 'the money comes from being tied up with a global broadcaster. The All Blacks and some of the Super 12 teams have an appeal and following far beyond these shores; we want our teams to be seen in the UK and elsewhere so they can sell merchandise offshore. Our revenue requirements are so big that we can't find it in New Zealand.

'When they complain about the downgrading of the NPC, they should understand that it is New Zealand's involvement in international competitions — Super 12 and Tri-Nations — that brings in the lion's share of the revenue. And when they complain about a glorious tradition being reduced to a brand, they should understand that the brand is New Zealand rugby's ace in the hole.'

'The All Black brand is built on the black uniform,' says Trevor McKewen, 'the haka, the iconic players, the fables — Dave Gallaher dying on the battlefield, Red Conway cutting off a finger to play for the All Blacks, Meads carrying a sheep under each arm. The Springboks were the nearest but they were tainted by apartheid. It doesn't depend on individuals. Take the black jersey off Lomu and his value diminishes by 95 per cent. They talked about the Chicago Bulls being a dynasty but as soon as Michael Jordan left they crumbled. The All Blacks are like Manchester United. I'm not a soccer fan but if Manchester United came to New Zealand, I'd go to see them. What attracts me is the aura, the legend of Busby's Babes and the Munich plane crash, the iconic players — George Best, Bobby Charlton.'

'The All Black brand is founded on the tradition of success but success with style,' says Murray McCaw. 'They need to win to maintain the aura but how you play is fundamental to the whole financial thing because if the players don't add vibrancy, the value of the brand suffers and therefore the revenue. Compare Brazil with Germany who'd be the second most successful soccer country. We want winning teams but teams that win with style, and in fact if the All Blacks lose playing good rugby, people don't denigrate the brand. The reaction to the loss to France at the last World Cup was extreme because they didn't compete and that was unworthy of the heritage.'

The All Black brand has brought in an extraordinary sponsorship deal and triggered the high-stakes poker game that ended with the 10-year Sanzar-News Ltd arrangement. It also draws the crowds, not that the NZRU or the players get a cent of the massive gate takings the All Blacks generate when they play in London, Paris and Sydney. Under the current system the home union takes all.

According to the NZRU, the RFU made £10 million in broadcasting rights, gate takings and hospitality when the All Blacks played at Twickenham in November 2002. The ARU, it's said, makes A$3 million when the All Blacks play at the Olympic Stadium. The Aussies pay for their accommodation and nothing else, not even the flight over.

The Boston Consulting Group's 2000 report, *Ensuring The Future Success Of New Zealand Rugby*, contained figures showing that the All Blacks are the biggest drawcard in the game, both in terms of live spectators and TV viewing audiences. The problem is at the moment they're making money for everybody else. The report's authors estimated that if receipts were shared between the participants, New Zealand would be making an extra $12 million a year under the current international calendar. The great challenge for the NZRU is to capitalise on the All Blacks' pulling power; that means persuading the IRB to accept revenue-sharing and reform the international calendar and playing programme to ensure that the best teams play each other more often and in a series or tournament format.

As Rutherford points out, the consequences of failure are unthinkable: 'New Zealand is at risk of becoming a King Country in world terms if we don't get things right. It can happen very quickly. We have to fight for the system that suits us best.'

Perhaps the most important thing that the wider rugby community can do to secure the game's future and the All Blacks' place among the international elite is to unite. We are small enough as it is. What chance of us being world-beaters if we're divided?

Unity requires tolerance, an acceptance of diversity and difference. This hasn't come easily because New Zealand rugby has traditionally been homogeneous and the myths that underpin that identity have proved resistant to social and economic change and continue to exert a hold on the imagination.

The most powerful of these myths is that of the Kiwi bloke. As historian James Belich has pointed out, the Kiwi bloke is a product of New Zealand populism and, as such, has been pressed into service in some pretty dubious causes over the years: 'New Zealand populism . . . vaguely imagined a community of the "common people", ultimately gendered, colloquialised and stereotyped into "the ordinary Kiwi bloke". Populism can be romanticised. It was in fact capable of such things as extreme racism and sexism. Typically, the enemies of populism were shadowy — absentee capital, absentee landlords, boardroom conspiracies, "money power".'

Ring a bell?

Even in its benign form, the Kiwi bloke is a fuzzy ideal rather than an accurate identikit of New Zealand manhood. Using Belich's figures, in 1881 40 per cent of non-Maori were urbanised, which was quite high by the standards of the time. Since then, the percentage of the population living in towns and cities has risen steadily to its current heights — 50 per cent by 1911, 69 per cent by 1926, 80 per cent by 1971, 85 per cent by 1996. As Belich observed, 'This of course makes the persistence of dominant rural stereotypes all the more striking. Farmer Backbone and the (rural) Kiwi bloke have not been anything like the average New Zealand man for almost a century, if they ever were.'

But the myth persists and like all collective self-images, it is a yardstick, a test as easily applied as a secret password or freemason's handshake to establish whether you are one of us or one of them. Consider the use of 'Kiwi' in this passage from Todd Blackadder's biography recalling some gracious living on the 1995 tour of France:

'We'd never seen anything like that, drinking vintage champagne, being served pheasant by people with white gloves. It was like things were 200 years ago. Then we retired to the smoking room and we all grabbed a cigar. We were given a huge bottle which we thought we'd save for after the test, plus a magnum each as well. On the bus, and we started having a wee drink. We probably had the best champagne in the world and we all just whacked the tops off them and were sculling them on the bus being good old Kiwis. We stopped the bus and Richard Fromont got out and did a nude down and up.'

There are a number of ways of looking at this: boys will be boys; a bit of harmless fun; a waste of good champagne. I imagine some Kiwis would prefer a little more class from their national team but the unconscious implication of this passage is that anyone whose idea of fun this is not cannot be a 'good old Kiwi'. When this mindset takes hold, either within the team or among the public, it becomes judgemental and exclusionary.

Thirty years ago Chris Laidlaw wrote that, 'New Zealanders have built around the concept of an All Black a stereotype, a standard figure who conforms to everyone's expectations of what a true New Zealander's character should be like. He is loyal, strong-willed, resilient, usually silent, and always modest. The 'ordinary bloke' image must always prevail. Unordinary or extraordinary blokes are, by definition, unreliable and are regarded with suspicion.'

Thirty years ago Austin Mitchell wrote that, 'Kiwis have a deep egalitarian drive, summed up in the law "Thou shalt not get up thyself". Anyone suspected of it faces severe retribution.'

In 2003 Brian Turner, New Zealand's Poet Laureate and Good Southern Man, remarked that, 'Where I come from, big-noters aren't greatly appreciated.'

That's probably a universal view. The problem comes in the definition: what exactly is a big-noter? Would the residents of, say, Gore, Te Kuiti and Ponsonby find common ground if they got together over a latte or a mug of tea or a Speight's to define big-noting? Is making regular changes to one's appearance, for instance tinkering with one's hair style and — God forbid — hair colouring, an automatic qualification? But that would make Justin Marshall a big-noter and that can't be right because he's a tough guy from Mataura. A southern man.

So let's play safe and nominate someone we can all agree on: Carlos Spencer. Does all sorts of fancy-dan stuff and does it with a cocky smile, what's more. And he plays for Auckland. And he's been Andrew Mehrtens' rival (nice sideburns, Mehrts, and I *love* the white boots) for the number 10 jersey.

The consensus in 2003 seemed to be that Spencer had matured and was finally worth taking seriously. I would suggest that he's been worth taking seriously for some time, certainly since 1997 when he produced a string of dazzling yet nicely controlled performances for the All Blacks as they slaughtered the Argentineans and won five straight against Australia and South Africa. It was transparently clear then that here was an exceptional talent; occasionally wayward perhaps but then most exceptional talents are. That's the nature of the beast. They see things that others don't see and they can do things that others cannot do, so they try things that others either wouldn't think of or don't have the nerve for. And sometimes they go wrong and then it starts: mercurial, erratic, unreliable, show pony, flake. Give a dog a bad name: when Mehrtens puts a kick-off out on the full or misses touch from a penalty, the commentators either let it pass in polite silence or remark on the rarity — 'Now that's something you don't see very often.' When Spencer does it, it's dwelt upon as if a fatal flaw, a character defect almost, has reared its ugly head again. Yet the fact is that Mehrtens is not as machine-like in his efficiency nor is Spencer as fallible as these divergent reactions would have us believe.

A couple of years ago Radio Sport's Martin Devlin, temporarily abandoning his knockabout persona, wrote a column in *New Zealand Rugby Monthly* denouncing Spencer and the NZRU for re-signing him. The gist of it was that he was not worth the money. The striking thing about it was that Spencer was given absolutely no credit for having signed on with New Zealand rugby for far less than he was being offered to go overseas (which he has done again since). Spencer doesn't wear his heart on his sleeve but he is still here while others, who wrapped themselves in the flag and waffled on about 'the jersey', are long gone.

Like Zinzan Brooke before him, Spencer has been devalued by sections of the public because he plays for Auckland and has been a rival of a popular figure in the heartland and doesn't fit the mould, either in the way he looks or the way he plays the game. Everyone has their favourites but we neglect the special ones at our peril. To neglect them out of prejudice is unforgivable.

'The Brumbies got far too structured in their game,' says Mourie, 'and Canterbury are very structured too and the reason we were able to beat those teams is that we could plan for what they were going to do. The hardest thing to combat is innovation and flair which Auckland usually have and Carlos Spencer in particular killed us on a couple of occasions.'

Talking of Jean-Pierre Rives, the great French flanker of the 1970s, Josh Kronfeld described him as 'a very unusual personality to find in rugby circles. He is extroverted, effervescent, intelligent, creative . . . in a word flamboyant. Rives is a well-known sculptor, an artist . . . in New Zealand we're still more likely to assume that people are either sports jocks or intellectuals. That doesn't necessarily follow. Generally, I'd say that flamboyance is not something that has been encouraged in New Zealand rugby.'

One senses that this state of affairs is changing as the country changes. We are a more extrovert, individualistic people than we used to be. Sometimes these expressions of individuality will seem irritatingly self-indulgent and banal but we are discussing professional rugby players here so it is not about their tattoos or what they do with their hair. Spencer looks like a finely tuned athlete. His team-mates praise his leadership and dedication. Grant Fox, as qualified a judge as there is, calls him a model professional. And we know the boy can play.

Parochialism is an essential part of the game and long may it remain so. But like all forms of collective emotion, parochialism can turn ugly. When pride inflates into triumphalism and being cheerfully one-eyed degenerates into warped judgement and a compulsion to demonise individuals who personify another tribe's difference or threaten to overshadow a local hero, parochialism becomes divisive.

Again, it's a fine line between being an intimidating crowd and a mob; what separates the two is probably a matter of how much of the crowd's energy and focus goes into supporting their team as opposed to abusing the opposition. It's a line that the Lancaster Park now Jade Stadium faithful have sometimes crossed. Graham Henry, himself a Cantabrian, complained about the reception his Auckland teams got there and Norm Hewitt let it all hang out:

'I never need any motivation when I play Canterbury or the

Crusaders because the crowd down there are so bad. They're on a par with the worst Afrikaners crowd. The kids swear at you with their parents looking on — the number of times I was told to 'fuck off home' or called a drunk when I was waiting to throw the ball in was amazing. If the Jerry Springer Show is ever looking for any foul-mouthed screamers, they should trawl the terraces down at Jade Stadium.'

Canterbury and the Crusaders have set the benchmark in recent years and there have been moments when, intentionally or otherwise, they, their media and their public have given the impression that they consider this to be the natural order of things: they are better at rugby and know more about it than the rest of the country, therefore it is only natural that they should win all the trophies and Cantabrians should coach, captain and form a majority of the All Blacks. The 2002 'Canter-blacks' caused a certain amount of grumbling around the country but it never got out of hand. (The fact that the team came through in the end obviously helped.) One cannot help wondering, however, what would have been the reaction in Canterbury to an All Black starting line-up containing 13 or 14 Aucklanders.

What ultimately matters is that parochialism does not become an agent of divisiveness and that for New Zealand rugby followers — wherever they hail from — the All Blacks always come first. One hopes never to hear an All Black utter the equivalent sentiment to that voiced by the former Wallaby and Queensland halfback Peter Slattery who proclaimed, 'It's great to be an Australian but it's even better to be a Queenslander.'

The most pernicious recent example of divisiveness has been the increasing use of the term 'real rugby person'. It positively bubbles with the implication that there are people in rugby who are unreal, fake, impostors. It was used against McCaw and Rutherford during the World Cup sub-hosting drama, the sub-text being why on earth are a businessman and a lawyer, neither of whom have significant playing pedigrees, running New Zealand rugby? Hobbs is a lawyer and a businessman, but of course he has the saving grace of having been an All Black captain.

'What makes a real rugby person?' asks Steve Tew. 'I have mates I grew up with in Lower Hutt who still drink at the Petone Working Men's Club who have very strong views on who should be in the All Blacks. I have mates I went to university with who became successful businesspeople who probably prefer a decent pinot noir to draught beer but have the same passion. One of them runs a French merchant bank in Hong Kong. He rings me in the middle of the night to find out scores. Are they less of a rugby person than the guys in the Petone Working Men's Club?'

While the term reflects the traditional fault line — southern, provincial suspicion of northern, urban influence — it has been pressed into service in the ongoing dispute over the direction of New Zealand rugby. The underlying accusation is that the game has been taken away from its true constituency and handed over to a bunch of carpetbaggers who don't have the background or the passion to warrant or discharge the responsibility. What those who throw this pejorative term around should realise is that rugby can only be the game for all New Zealanders if it is open to and welcoming of participants and supporters from every group and sub-group in our fragmented society.

John Graham suggests that our model should be Australian cricket, which reflects Australian society from the larrikin to the boardroom and the Prime Minister's Lodge. We could do a lot worse. Rugby certainly will not remain the national game for long if it is hijacked by one chunk of the demographic determined to preserve it in its own image.

Rugby is closer to being a game for all New Zealanders now than at many times in the past, if not ever. The passion might have dimmed slightly but that was inevitable because in the global village in the twenty-first century, it is impossible to regard a rugby match as a matter of life and death. No longer a male bastion, no longer confrontationally politicised through its South African connection, rugby has become a truly national game that gives New Zealand the credentials to cement its position as the definitive rugby nation. If we succeed in that, the rest will follow. The problems that loom worryingly large today will prove manageable if not solvable and the All Blacks will remain the most famous, most glamorous, most intriguing team in world rugby.

About the author

Paul Thomas has worked in journalism and public relations in Auckland, London, Toulouse and Sydney and is now a full-time writer based in Wellington. He has written a number of acclaimed sports books: *Christmas in Rarotonga* with cricketing great John Wright, *Running on Instinct* with All Black legend John Kirwan and *Straight from the Hart* and *Change of Hart* with former All Black coach John Hart.

He has also written five novels including the ground-breaking trilogy of New Zealand-based crime novels *Old School Tie*, *Inside Dope* and *Guerilla Season*, which were published by Hodder Moa Beckett. *Inside Dope* won the Crime Writers' Association of Australia's inaugural Ned Kelly Award for best crime novel of the year. His most recent novel *The Empty Bed* was published in 2002 and a collection of his short stories is appearing later this year. His fiction has been widely published and translated into several languages.